Exploring Intersectionality and Women in STEM

Luz Idalia Balderas
Tamaulipas Autonomous University, Mexico

Sanju Tiwari
Tamaulipas Autonomous University, Mexico

Elizabeth Verdugo
Pontifícia Universidade Católica do Rio de Janeiro, Brazil

Gina Paola Maestre-Gongora
Universidad de Antioquia, Colombia

Fernando Ortiz-Rodriguez
Tamaulipas Autonomous University, Mexico

A volume in the Advances
in Educational Marketing,
Administration, and Leadership
(AEMAL) Book Series

Published in the United States of America by
IGI Global
Information Science Reference (an imprint of IGI Global)
701 E. Chocolate Avenue
Hershey PA, USA 17033
Tel: 717-533-8845
Fax: 717-533-8661
E-mail: cust@igi-global.com
Web site: http://www.igi-global.com

Copyright © 2024 by IGI Global. All rights reserved. No part of this publication may be reproduced, stored or distributed in any form or by any means, electronic or mechanical, including photocopying, without written permission from the publisher.
Product or company names used in this set are for identification purposes only. Inclusion of the names of the products or companies does not indicate a claim of ownership by IGI Global of the trademark or registered trademark.

Library of Congress Cataloging-in-Publication Data

Names: Balderas Garcia, Luz Idalia, 1983- editor. | Tiwari, Sanju, 1979- editor. | Verdugo, Elizabeth, 1992- editor. | Maestre-Góngora, Gina, 1981- editor. | Ortiz-Rodriguez, Fernando, 1974- editor.
Title: Exploring intersectionality and women in STEM / edited by Luz Balderas Garcia, Sanju Tiwari, Elizabeth Verdugo, Gina Maestre-Góngora, Fernando Ortiz-Rodriguez.
Description: Hershey, PA : Information Science Reference, [2024] | Includes bibliographical references and index. | Summary: "Incorporating the gender perspective and its intersectionality in various areas of knowledge is necessary to determine inequalities, and social exclusions, among others; in addition to strengthening a transdisciplinary and diverse vision for incorporating more women in science"-- Provided by publisher.
Identifiers: LCCN 2024009390 (print) | LCCN 2024009391 (ebook) | ISBN 9798369311196 (hardcover) | ISBN 9798369311202 (ebook)
Subjects: LCSH: Sex discrimination in employment. | Intersectionality (Sociology) | Women in science.
Classification: LCC HD6060 .E975 2024 (print) | LCC HD6060 (ebook) | DDC 331.4/133--dc23/eng/20240422
LC record available at https://lccn.loc.gov/2024009390
LC ebook record available at https://lccn.loc.gov/2024009391

This book is published in the IGI Global book series Advances in Educational Marketing, Administration, and Leadership (AEMAL) (ISSN: 2326-9022; eISSN: 2326-9030)

British Cataloguing in Publication Data
A Cataloguing in Publication record for this book is available from the British Library.
All work contributed to this book is new, previously-unpublished material.
The views expressed in this book are those of the authors, but not necessarily of the publisher.
For electronic access to this publication, please contact: eresources@igi-global.com.

Advances in Educational Marketing, Administration, and Leadership (AEMAL) Book Series

ISSN:2326-9022
EISSN:2326-9030

Editor-in-Chief: Siran Mukerji, IGNOU, India, Purnendu Tripathi, IGNOU, India

MISSION

With more educational institutions entering into public, higher, and professional education, the educational environment has grown increasingly competitive. With this increase in competitiveness has come the need for a greater focus on leadership within the institutions, on administrative handling of educational matters, and on the marketing of the services offered.

The **Advances in Educational Marketing, Administration, & Leadership (AEMAL) Book Series** strives to provide publications that address all these areas and present trending, current research to assist professionals, administrators, and others involved in the education sector in making their decisions.

COVERAGE

- Educational Finance
- Students as Consumers
- Direct marketing of educational programs
- Educational Marketing Campaigns
- Faculty Administration and Management
- Advertising and Promotion of Academic Programs and Institutions
- Technologies and Educational Marketing
- Governance in P-12 and Higher Education
- Academic Administration
- Marketing Theories within Education

IGI Global is currently accepting manuscripts for publication within this series. To submit a proposal for a volume in this series, please contact our Acquisition Editors at Acquisitions@igi-global.com or visit: http://www.igi-global.com/publish/.

The Advances in Educational Marketing, Administration, and Leadership (AEMAL) Book Series (ISSN 2326-9022) is published by IGI Global, 701 E. Chocolate Avenue, Hershey, PA 17033-1240, USA, www.igi-global.com. This series is composed of titles available for purchase individually; each title is edited to be contextually exclusive from any other title within the series. For pricing and ordering information please visit http://www.igi-global.com/book-series/advances-educational-marketing-administration-leadership/73677. Postmaster: Send all address changes to above address. Copyright © 2024 IGI Global. All rights, including translation in other languages reserved by the publisher. No part of this series may be reproduced or used in any form or by any means – graphics, electronic, or mechanical, including photocopying, recording, taping, or information and retrieval systems – without written permission from the publisher, except for non commercial, educational use, including classroom teaching purposes. The views expressed in this series are those of the authors, but not necessarily of IGI Global.

Titles in this Series

For a list of additional titles in this series, please visit:
http://www.igi-global.com/book-series/advances-educational-marketing-administration-leadership/73677

Autoethnographic Tactics to Closing the Gap on Educational Attainment
Anika Chanell Thrower (Borough of Manhattan Community College, CUNY, USA) Alex Evangelista (Borough of Manhattan Community College, CUNY, USA) Ruth Baker-Gardner (University of the West Indies, Jamaica) and Hammed Mogaji (Federal University of Bahia, Brazil)
Information Science Reference • © 2024 • 258pp • H/C (ISBN: 9798369310748) • US $230.00

Pursuing Equity and Success for Marginalized Educational Leaders
LeAnne C. Salazar Montoya (University of Nevada, Las Vegas, USA) and Christopher Bonn (Bonn Fire Solutions and Consulting, USA)
Information Science Reference • © 2024 • 303pp • H/C (ISBN: 9798369310090) • US $230.00

Leading and Managing Change for School Improvement
Nadire Gülçin Yildiz (Istanbul Medipol University, Turkey)
Information Science Reference • © 2024 • 288pp • H/C (ISBN: 9781799839408) • US $215.00

Inquiries of Pedagogical Shifts and Critical Mindsets Among Educators
Aaron R. Gierhart (University of Wisconsin-Stevens Point, USA)
Information Science Reference • © 2024 • 229pp • H/C (ISBN: 9798369310786) • US $225.00

Handbook of Research on Inclusive and Accessible Education
Mbulaheni Obert Maguvhe (University of South Africa, South Africa) Nwacoye Gladness Mpya (University of South Africa, South Africa) and Marubini Christinah Sadiki (University of South Africa, South Africa)
Information Science Reference • © 2024 • 468pp • H/C (ISBN: 9798369311479) • US $310.00

For an entire list of titles in this series, please visit:
http://www.igi-global.com/book-series/advances-educational-marketing-administration-leadership/73677

701 East Chocolate Avenue, Hershey, PA 17033, USA
Tel: 717-533-8845 x100 • Fax: 717-533-8661
E-Mail: cust@igi-global.com • www.igi-global.com

Table of Contents

Preface xvi

Chapter 1
Technologies and the Circular Economy 1
    Jimena Sanchez, Tamaulipas Autonomous University, Mexico
    Daniel Avila-Guzman, Tamaulipas Autonomous University, Mexico
    Olegario Mendez, Tamaulipas Autonomous University, Mexico
    Juan Carlos Huerta, Tamaulipas Autonomous University, Mexico
    Vicente Villanueva, Tamaulipas Autonomous University, Mexico

Chapter 2
Is The Manager's Gender A Determining Factor in Tourism Companies' Commitment to Ict Training? A Study of The Destination of Extremadura (Spain) 12
    Marcelino Sánchez-Rivero, University of Extremadura, Spain
    Yakira Fernández-Torres, University of Extremadura, Spain
    Clara Gallego-Sosa, University of Extremadura, Spain
    Milagros Gutiérrez-Fernández, University of Extremadura, Spain

Chapter 3
Analysis of the Strategies of the Nibco Company From Reynosa to Compensate Intellectual Capital During the COVID-19 Pandemic 39
    María Blanca González Salazar, Tamaulipas Autonomous University, Mexico
    Jaime Gerardo Malacara, Tamaulipas Autonomous University, Mexico
    Olegario Méndez Cabrera, Tamaulipas Autonomous University, Mexico
    Daniel Avila-Guzman, Tamaulipas Autonomous University, Mexico

Chapter 4
Physical Sciences Teachers Integrating Information and Communication
Technologies in Education 4.0: Exploring Enablers and Constraints 56
    Colani Khoza, University of South Africa, South Africa
    Leila Goosen, University of South Africa, South Africa

Chapter 5
Optimization Model Applied to the Generation of Electrical Energy for a
Multi-Region Scenario 76
    *Marco A. Santibáñez-Díaz, Universidad Autónoma de Tamaulipas,
        Mexico*
    Esmeralda López-Garza, Universidad Autónoma de Tamaulipas, Mexico
    *René F. Domínguez-Cruz, Universidad Autónoma de Tamaulipas,
        Mexico*
    *Iván Salgado-Tránsito, Centro de Investigaciones en Óptica A.C.,
        Mexico*

Chapter 6
Honey Adulterant Detection System Using Fiber Optics Sensors 90
    *Mayeli Anais Pérez-Rosas, Unidad Académica Multidisciplinaria
        Reynosa-Rodhe, Mexico*
    *Leonardo Alvarez-Villarreal, Unidad Académica Multidisciplinaria
        Reynosa-Rodhe, Mexico*
    *Yadira Aracely Fuentes-Rubio, Unidad Académica Multidisciplinaria
        Reynosa-Rodhe, Mexico*
    *Rene Fernando Dominguez-Cruz, Unidad Académica Multidisciplinaria
        Reynosa-Rodhe, Mexico*
    *Luis A. Garcia-Garza, Unidad Académica Multidisciplinaria Reynosa-
        Rodhe, Mexico*
    *Oscar Baldovino-Pantaleón, Unidad Académica Multidisciplinaria
        Reynosa-Rodhe, Mexico*

Chapter 7
Design of Automated Locking Device for Geometry Test Equipment in Fiber
Optic Connectors Through Interferometry 120
    *Jesus Cruz Garza Moreno, Unidad Académica Multidisciplinaria
        Reynosa-Rodhe, Mexico*
    *Luz Idalia Balderas García, Unidad Académica Multidisciplinaria
        Reynosa-Rodhe, Mexico*
    *Lourdes Yajaira García Rivera, Unidad Académica Multidisciplinaria
        Reynosa-Rodhe, Mexico*
    Francisco Javier Reyes Mireles, Unidad Académica Multidisciplinaria

Reynosa-Rodhe, Mexico

Chapter 8
Vandalism Prevention and Trash Retention System Improvement on Hidalgo County Drainage District Pump Stations 151
    Jesus Cruz Garza Moreno, Unidad Académica Multidisciplinaria Reynosa-Rodhe, Mexico
    Luz Idalia Balderas García, Unidad Académica Multidisciplinaria Reynosa-Rodhe, Mexico
    Lourdes Yajaira García Rivera, Unidad Académica Multidisciplinaria Reynosa-Rodhe, Mexico

Chapter 9
Digital Inclusion, a Key Element Towards Digital Transformation: STEM Perspectives 169
    Constanza Alvarado, University ECCI, Colombia
    Philippe Aniorte, INDICATIC AIP, Panama
    Maria Catalina Ramirez, University of Andes, Colombia

Chapter 10
Languages With Artificial Intelligence Applications 192
    Sanjuanita C. Ortiz Valadez, Unidad Académica Multidisciplinaria Reynosa-Rodhe, Mexico
    Juan Carlos Huerta Mendoza, Unidad Académica Multidisciplinaria Reynosa-Rodhe, Mexico
    Vicente Villanueva-Hernandez, Unidad Académica Multidisciplinaria Reynosa-Rodhe, Mexico
    Gerardo Tijerina, Unidad Académica Multidisciplinaria Reynosa-Rodhe, Mexico
    Daniel Avila-Guzman, Unidad Académica Multidisciplinaria Reynosa-Rodhe, Mexico

Chapter 11
Understanding Sensory Marketing and Women Consumers' Behavior 202
    Anabel Sofia Villegas-Garza, Tamaulipas Autonomous University, Mexico
    Melchor Medina-Quintero, Tamaulipas Autonomous University, Mexico
    Fernando Ortiz-Rodriguez, Tamaulipas Autonomous University, Mexico

Compilation of References 220

Related References 241

About the Contributors 263

Index 267

Detailed Table of Contents

Preface xvi

Chapter 1
Technologies and the Circular Economy 1
    Jimena Sanchez, Tamaulipas Autonomous University, Mexico
    Daniel Avila-Guzman, Tamaulipas Autonomous University, Mexico
    Olegario Mendez, Tamaulipas Autonomous University, Mexico
    Juan Carlos Huerta, Tamaulipas Autonomous University, Mexico
    Vicente Villanueva, Tamaulipas Autonomous University, Mexico

The word economy comes from the Greek "oikonomos," meaning "household management": Oikos means home and nemein, means administration. Hence, economics is concerned with how available resources are managed to produce a variety of goods and distribute them for consumption among the members of a society. In the opinion of Gregory Mankiw one of the principles of economics that have to do with "People face trade-offs," is important for modern society, since currently, companies face the dilemma between a clean environment and a high level of income, Mankiw believes, faced with this dilemma.

Chapter 2
Is The Manager's Gender A Determining Factor in Tourism Companies' Commitment to Ict Training? A Study of The Destination of Extremadura (Spain) 12
    Marcelino Sánchez-Rivero, University of Extremadura, Spain
    Yakira Fernández-Torres, University of Extremadura, Spain
    Clara Gallego-Sosa, University of Extremadura, Spain
    Milagros Gutiérrez-Fernández, University of Extremadura, Spain

An organisation's ability to exploit information and communication technologies (ICTs) depends on the ICT training of its employees, which is conditioned by the strategies implemented by managers. These business strategies may be influenced by the manager's gender. In this study, the manager's gender is used as a factor to determine the level of commitment to ICT training of tourism managers in the Spanish region of Extremadura. The study also examines their satisfaction with the ICT training they have received, their preferences regarding training providers, and their perceptions regarding how well ICT knowledge supply meets demand in this region. Online questionnaire data from a sample of 238 tourist lodgings were collected. Inferential statistical analysis was applied. The results suggest that the values for the majority of the ICT training variables considered in this study do not differ between companies managed by men and women.

Chapter 3
Analysis of the Strategies of the Nibco Company From Reynosa to
Compensate Intellectual Capital During the COVID-19 Pandemic 39
 María Blanca González Salazar, Tamaulipas Autonomous University,
  Mexico
 Jaime Gerardo Malacara, Tamaulipas Autonomous University, Mexico
 Olegario Méndez Cabrera, Tamaulipas Autonomous University, Mexico
 Daniel Avila-Guzman, Tamaulipas Autonomous University, Mexico

An analysis of the strategies of the NIBCO Company of Reynosa to compensate intellectual capital during the Covid-19 pandemic is presented. The objective is to know what are the reasonings that led the company to implement compensation strategies in favor of its intellectual capital in response to the COVID-19 pandemic and its possible impacts on its productivity. A non-experimental, descriptive, and cross-sectional methodological design is used. Information collected through the method of interviews with managers and administrators of the same is analyzed. It is concluded that the company reacted favorably towards its intellectual capital, strengthening it through a scheme of additional compensation so that the staff can face greater financial and social security capacity, the effects of this new disease on health, and the disruption of daily forms and lifestyles.

Chapter 4
Physical Sciences Teachers Integrating Information and Communication
Technologies in Education 4.0: Exploring Enablers and Constraints 56
 Colani Khoza, University of South Africa, South Africa
 Leila Goosen, University of South Africa, South Africa

The purpose of the study reported on in this chapter is to evaluate how effectively physical sciences secondary school teachers are integrating information and communication technologies (ICTs) in the context of Education 4.0 and one of the northern districts in the city of Tshwane, Gauteng province, South Africa. Against the background of exploring intersectionality and women in science, technology, engineering and mathematics (STEM), the chapter will be exploring enablers and constraints in this regard.

Chapter 5
Optimization Model Applied to the Generation of Electrical Energy for a
Multi-Region Scenario 76
    Marco A. Santibáñez-Díaz, Universidad Autónoma de Tamaulipas,
        Mexico
    Esmeralda López-Garza, Universidad Autónoma de Tamaulipas, Mexico
    René F. Domínguez-Cruz, Universidad Autónoma de Tamaulipas,
        Mexico
    Iván Salgado-Tránsito, Centro de Investigaciones en Óptica A.C.,
        Mexico

In this work, an optimization model based on linear programming is proposed applied to the eastern energy generation zone in Mexico. This model is formulated from the division into different regions that make up the study area and allows for scheduling the production of the plants in various time periods, minimizing operating costs. The division of the area consists of four regions where each one has various generation technologies, described with their parameters. The model establishes linear operating restrictions for the operation of the plants and restrictions that guarantee satisfying the demand for each region in each established period, through an analysis of the demand of the area, taking into account different costs at the time of generation and allocation of power. The results of the model show the transfers of electrical energy between the regions for an efficient economic dispatch of the area, this being a useful instrument for making decisions with a sustainable perspective in the efficient allocation of energy resources.

Chapter 6
Honey Adulterant Detection System Using Fiber Optics Sensors 90
    Mayeli Anais Pérez-Rosas, Unidad Académica Multidisciplinaria
        Reynosa-Rodhe, Mexico
    Leonardo Alvarez-Villarreal, Unidad Académica Multidisciplinaria
        Reynosa-Rodhe, Mexico
    Yadira Aracely Fuentes-Rubio, Unidad Académica Multidisciplinaria
        Reynosa-Rodhe, Mexico
    Rene Fernando Dominguez-Cruz, Unidad Académica Multidisciplinaria
        Reynosa-Rodhe, Mexico
    Luis A. Garcia-Garza, Unidad Académica Multidisciplinaria Reynosa-
        Rodhe, Mexico
    Oscar Baldovino-Pantaleón, Unidad Académica Multidisciplinaria
        Reynosa-Rodhe, Mexico

Honey's valued for nutrition and antioxidants, but adulteration, mainly sugar addition, reduces quality and nutritional value. In this chapter, a detection system for honey adulterated with sucrose syrup is reported using a sensor built with fiber optics. The sensor consists of the union of a segment of non-core multimode fiber (NC-MMF) joined at its ends to two segments of single-mode fiber (SMF). The principle of operation is that, when propagating an optical field in the device, a transmission peak appears at its output due to its filter-like response, the position of which depends on the effective refractive index of the medium surrounding the NC-MMF. Therefore, when different mixtures of adulterated honey are coated on the NC-MMF section, the peak wavelength changes according to the refractive index of the mixture. In this way, adulterated honey can be detected from the shift in wavelength of the transmission peak. The device was tested on a compliant commercial honey brand, exhibiting a linear response with a sensitivity of -0.5417 nm/% in the 1%-5% adulteration range.

Chapter 7
Design of Automated Locking Device for Geometry Test Equipment in Fiber
Optic Connectors Through Interferometry 120
    Jesus Cruz Garza Moreno, Unidad Académica Multidisciplinaria
        Reynosa-Rodhe, Mexico
    Luz Idalia Balderas García, Unidad Académica Multidisciplinaria
        Reynosa-Rodhe, Mexico
    Lourdes Yajaira García Rivera, Unidad Académica Multidisciplinaria
        Reynosa-Rodhe, Mexico
    Francisco Javier Reyes Mireles, Unidad Académica Multidisciplinaria
        Reynosa-Rodhe, Mexico

In this project, an improvement will be made to reduce the costs for the purchase and repair of measurement fixtures that are used in the equipment that performs the geometry test. This improvement was decided to be implemented since there are constant replacements of measurement fixtures in a brief period, which causes them to have to buy more fixtures because the stock in the warehouse runs out quickly. The stock in the warehouse runs out quickly because the fixtures that are damaged are sent to be repaired by the supplier, therefore, they have an estimated return time. When a measurement fixture is damaged very quickly, it causes it to have to be replaced immediately; that means that the stock is running out because the fixtures that were sent for repair have not yet arrived, causing more to be purchased urgently.

Chapter 8
Vandalism Prevention and Trash Retention System Improvement on Hidalgo
County Drainage District Pump Stations 151
    Jesus Cruz Garza Moreno, Unidad Académica Multidisciplinaria
        Reynosa-Rodhe, Mexico
    Luz Idalia Balderas García, Unidad Académica Multidisciplinaria
        Reynosa-Rodhe, Mexico
    Lourdes Yajaira García Rivera, Unidad Académica Multidisciplinaria
        Reynosa-Rodhe, Mexico

The project of redesign and improvement of the trash collection system and vandalism prevention on stationary and portable pumps was implemented by the Welding Department of the Hidalgo County Drainage District No. 1. The purpose of this project is to minimize downtime caused by trash and debris entering the pump stations and the damage caused by vandalism. All this is to reduce flooding risk to the Hidalgo County residents. The Hidalgo County Drainage District No.1 is a government entity dedicated to the cleaning and maintenance of the pluvial drainage system along Hidalgo County—it is located at 902 N Doolittle Rd. in Edinburg Texas.

Chapter 9
Digital Inclusion, a Key Element Towards Digital Transformation: STEM
Perspectives 169
    Constanza Alvarado, University ECCI, Colombia
    Philippe Aniorte, INDICATIC AIP, Panama
    Maria Catalina Ramirez, University of Andes, Colombia

New digital economies, globalization of information and knowledge, technological infrastructures (emerging computer and internet revolution) that impose transformation of business models for value creation, suggest challenges in education for innovation, sustainability, and open knowledge, demanding the mastery and development of 21st-century competencies for problem-solving in context, with capacities and skills. As well as new workforce dynamics, disruptive jobs, management of legal aspects (intellectual property), and operations resolved through services and/or "digital transactions" increased in number and intensity, serving users as employees, organizations, government, and digital citizens in general. Such a response does not ensure the integration and social appropriation of ICT, generating a distance, divide, and digital gap (DG), exacerbated in the race for transition on the way to digital transformation (DxTx).

Chapter 10
Languages With Artificial Intelligence Applications 192
    Sanjuanita C. Ortiz Valadez, Unidad Académica Multidisciplinaria
        Reynosa-Rodhe, Mexico
    Juan Carlos Huerta Mendoza, Unidad Académica Multidisciplinaria
        Reynosa-Rodhe, Mexico
    Vicente Villanueva-Hernandez, Unidad Académica Multidisciplinaria
        Reynosa-Rodhe, Mexico
    Gerardo Tijerina, Unidad Académica Multidisciplinaria Reynosa-
        Rodhe, Mexico
    Daniel Avila-Guzman, Unidad Académica Multidisciplinaria Reynosa-
        Rodhe, Mexico

Artificial intelligence (AI) refers to the simulation of human intelligence in machines programmed to think like humans and imitate their actions. The term can also be applied to any machine that exhibits traits associated with a human mind, such as learning and problem-solving. The ideal characteristic of artificial intelligence is its ability to rationalize and take actions that have the best chance of achieving a specific goal. A subset of artificial intelligence is machine learning (ML), which refers to the concept that computer programs can automatically learn from and adapt to new data without the help of humans. Deep learning techniques enable this machine learning by absorbing vast amounts of unstructured data, such as text, images, or video.

Chapter 11
Understanding Sensory Marketing and Women Consumers' Behavior............202
    Anabel Sofia Villegas-Garza, Tamaulipas Autonomous University, Mexico
    Melchor Medina-Quintero, Tamaulipas Autonomous University, Mexico
    Fernando Ortiz-Rodriguez, Tamaulipas Autonomous University, Mexico

Sensory marketing has been evolving in tandem with consumer preferences, adapting new techniques to enhance the consumer experience. However, there is a need for gender-based research in sensory marketing, particularly about women. This study aims to analyze the impact of stimuli received through the five senses on consumer satisfaction and subsequent purchase intention among women. For this purpose, 208 questionnaires were distributed to women in Tamaulipas, Mexico, and structural equation modeling using SmartPLS 4 was employed for analysis. The study found that the sense of sight has the greatest influence on consumer satisfaction, while the senses of smell and hearing do not significantly impact this variable. Additionally, the study identified that consumer satisfaction is a significant factor influencing women's purchase intention.

Compilation of References 220

Related References 241

About the Contributors 263

Index 267

Preface

This work shares information about the positive impact that technology can generate in society, and on this occasion, we will explore a fundamental and constantly evolving topic: the intersection of gender, technology, and science. Intersectionality allows us to recognize that individual identities are interconnected, and that people experience oppression and discrimination differently based on their gender, race, sexual orientation, disability, and other identities. Technology and science are not neutral; They may reflect and amplify these inequalities, but they also offer opportunities. Our mission is to explore how technology and science can serve to overcome these barriers, providing opportunities for diversity and equality in an ever-evolving society.

The incorporation of women into the world of work has been the result of multiple social transformations, motivated by the need to recognize our right to participate in all areas of the public life of societies. In the specific case of working life, female participation in professions related to science, technology, engineering, and mathematics has been marginal, as they are considered non-traditional professions. Social struggles have sought to guarantee equal opportunities between people, regardless of social, economic, racial, religious, and, of course, gender origin.

This book collects works that are the result of research carried out in the various branches of knowledge where the advances carried out in the field of Science and Engineering are presented. These are works with an impact on the industrial sector, a multidisciplinary approach, and the participation of teams made up of researchers at different levels.

The authors hope to disseminate the research carried out, as well as possible synergies that may occur between the different research groups present in the same current context of women in STEM and discuss the main factors that generate and sustain the gender gap. and explore its effects on female students. Motivated by the recent experience of established scientists, including the authors of this document, who have accompanied STEM women in training from various institutions. Finally, we highlight that mentoring with a gender perspective can be beneficial for the comprehensive training of students.

Chapter 1
Technologies and the Circular Economy

Jimena Sanchez
https://orcid.org/0000-0003-1607-8833
Tamaulipas Autonomous University, Mexico

Daniel Avila-Guzman
https://orcid.org/0009-0008-9547-7544
Tamaulipas Autonomous University, Mexico

Olegario Mendez
https://orcid.org/0000-0002-0126-4775
Tamaulipas Autonomous University, Mexico

Juan Carlos Huerta
https://orcid.org/0009-0005-4713-5759
Tamaulipas Autonomous University, Mexico

Vicente Villanueva
Tamaulipas Autonomous University, Mexico

ABSTRACT

The word economy comes from the Greek "oikonomos," meaning "household management": Oikos means home and nemein, means administration. Hence, economics is concerned with how available resources are managed to produce a variety of goods and distribute them for consumption among the members of a society. In the opinion of Gregory Mankiw one of the principles of economics that have to do with "People face trade-offs," is important for modern society, since currently, companies face the dilemma between a clean environment and a high level of income, Mankiw believes, faced with this dilemma.

DOI: 10.4018/979-8-3693-1119-6.ch001

INTRODUCTION

Economics, as a social science, analyzes in practical terms the production, distribution, and consumption of goods and services, identifying the effect of well-being on society ((Parkin, 2018)Recently the circular approach has been mentioned as an important topic, that is, it considers the economy while continuing to comply with the above, but now from the perspective of renting, reusing, repairing, renovating and recycling materials creating additional value as many times as possible, thus increasing the life cycle of products ((Da Costa, 2022)According to this same author, this conception is based on a series of principles and pointing out what Dangond (Oblitas, Sangay, Rojas, & Castro, 2019)) synthesizes, namely, that it is to preserve and improve human capital; optimize the use of resources and promote the efficiency of the system. For this reason, here we analyze the importance of identifying the effect that this process would have on the use and consumption of goods associated with information technologies, which some authors such as (Oblitas, Sangay, Rojas, & Castro, 2019)mention as electronic waste, determine that their study is gaining importance, given that in waste management and that technological advances, are increasing. This constant evolution has allowed many industries to use them for their transformation processes in production. Therefore, through a qualitative case study it is intended to relate the circular economy in the use of technological resources and the effect they have on the environment considering the framework of the United Nations Environment Programme (UNEP) and the Sustainable Development Goals (SDGs) of the UN. to raise awareness and align them with circular economy indicators.

THE ECONOMIC CONTEXT

In the opinion of Gregory Mankiw (2021) one of the principles of economics that has to do with "People face trade-offs", is important for modern society, since currently companies face the dilemma between a clean environment and a high level of income, Mankiw believes, faced with this dilemma, that the laws necessary to make companies pollute less cause the costs of production of goods and services to be lower Because of these higher costs, firms earn less, or pay low wages, or sell at higher prices, or create a combination of these variables. Thus, although laws to pollute less result in a cleaner environment and improve health, their cost is the reduction of the income of business owners, employees, and consumers.

Another principal Mankiw emphasizes is that "markets are usually a good mechanism for organizing economic activity." Companies and families interact in the market, where prices and personal interest focus their decisions, in a Market Economy, which were previously made in a centralized way are replaced by the decisions of millions of companies and families. Companies are responsible for deciding who to hire and what to manufacture, families decide where to work and what they want to buy with their income. Market economies have shown that they are capable of successfully organizing economic activity to promote the general welfare.

Within this context, the linear production systems that currently prevail in the world's economy have proven to have limits when it comes to the use of resources and with consequences with a great environmental and social impact; This is where the role of the circular economy plays an important role for a planet in urgent need of change.

According to the editorial staff of National Geographic (2023), the Latin American Circular Economy Forum reveals that linear production models are exposed to constant changes in prices and access to raw materials, which in some way contribute to the degeneration of the environment, affecting ecosystem services essential for development, but, Conversely, the circular model is restored and regenerated by design, aiming to keep products, components, and materials at their highest utility and value at all times. And when it comes to returning materials to the production cycle, it could be an option to reduce the amount of raw material that is obtained from nature, which would reduce waste along the chain.

In the opinion of specialist Edson Grandisoli (Geographic, 2023), the fact of using fewer resources causes a decrease in the need to transport the materials involved, which would contribute to the reduction of the carbon footprint of production, since as is well known, today we still depend mostly on petroleum-based fuels.

In addition to helping to reduce waste production, the circular economy model contributes to using waste as a source that creates wealth. For example, in the agricultural sector, the use of chemicals in plantations can be reduced by making use of compost that is made from organic waste.

DIMENSIONS OF SUSTAINABLE DEVELOPMENT

The decision-making of companies in any functional area is based on the generation of value, that is, generating profits, wealth and profitability, however it must not be forgotten that although it seeks to generate value as a company, it must be generated considering not only the economic aspect, but also the environmental and social aspect; As is well known in the economic field, it is about creating financial value for shareholders or owners; In environmental terms, creating sustainable value implies considering sustainable, green, and climate finance; and socially, to create shared value.

Given the above, and to highlight the importance of the circular economy, it is first necessary to clarify the role of sustainability in this issue.

According to Díaz Coutiño (2015) in ecological terms, it is increasingly evident that many industries, some sectors of agriculture and the use of renewable and non-renewable natural resources are unsustainable. The problem of the unsustainability of industrial society lies in the fact that, unlike the biosphere, it has not been able to close material cycles by reconverting waste into resources with the help of the sun and its derivatives. According to Naredo (2002), this is because the system faces problems of resource scarcity and excess waste, while it is more difficult and expensive to maintain its internal quality. Given this circumstance, it can be said that an economic system reduces its global sustainability to the extent that, directly or indirectly, it uses and degrades large amounts of energy and materials that it extracts from the earth's crust or from those obtained from the overexploitation of ecosystems, species or resources considered renewable. These uses leave a trail of evident ecological loss in the territory that is required to obtain resources, deposit, or digest waste. In addition, the deterioration of the internal quality of this system can lead to its unsustainability not only globally, but also locally (Naredo, 2002).

Sustainability is related to the quality of life of a community, to the extent that the economic, social, and environmental systems that compose it also favor maintaining an important level of health and productive capacity for the inhabitants of the present, as well as for future generations (Maureen, 1998).

In the opinion of Díaz (2015), when society, the economy and the environment are perceived as separate entities, as unrelated parts of the community, the problems generated are also seen as separate issues. Based on this paradigm, each public entity goes its own way: economic development councils try to create jobs, social security focuses on health care and housing services, environmental offices try to prevent and correct pollution problems. This piecemeal approach can generate a significant number of negative side effects.

Rather than continuing with a non-systematic approach, a community-based approach is required to consider the relationships between the economy, the environment, and society as shown in the figure below:

Figure 1. Own elaboration

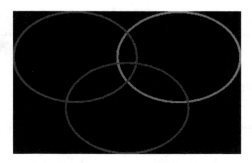

In the opinion of Díaz (2015), actions to improve the conditions of a community that is moving towards sustainability must consider these relationships that can be illustrated in a circular way, where each circle, which represents one category, comprises another, as shown in the following image:

Figure 2. Own elaboration

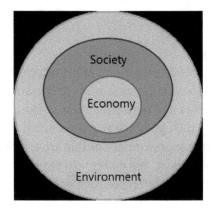

According to the illustration above, the economy develops within a society since all parts of the human economy require the interaction of all people. However, society is more than just an economy, it also includes friends, families, music, art, religion, and values, all of which are very important elements. Today's society exists entirely within the environment. Our basic requirements (air, food, water) come from the environment, as well as energy and raw materials for households, transportation, and the products we depend on (Díaz Coutiño, 2015).

Given Figure 2, the environment envelops society. From the earliest times of human history, the environment has determined the type of society. Today, the opposite is true: human activity redesigns the environment at ever-incremental rates. The parts that have not been affected are getting smaller and smaller. Since people need food, water, and air to survive, society should never be greater than the environment (Sanju et al, 2023).

Economic Dimension

The economic dimension of sustainable development focuses on maintaining the process of economic development on optimal paths towards the maximization of human well-being, but the constraints imposed by the availability of natural capital must always be considered (Priego, 2003). This economic perspective views factors as complementary, rather than surrogate, aspects. Appealing to complementarity is done in the sense of a limiting factor. A factor acquires a limiting character when an increase in the other factor(s) does not increase output, but an increase in the factor in question (the limiting) does. The complementary nature of natural capital and human-made capital is understood when the answer is the following: what good is a good sawmill if there are no forests, or a refinery if there is no oil, or a fishing boat without fish.

Social Dimension

This dimension of sustainable development implies recognizing all human beings with their right to equal access to the commons, in intragenerational and intergenerational terms, both between genders and between cultures. This dimension not only refers to the spatial distribution and age of the population, but also considers in a special way, the set of social and economic relations that are established in any society and that are based on religion, ethics, and culture. In the same way, this dimension has the population as an obligatory reference, and pays special attention to their ways of organizing and participating in decision-making. It also includes the relations between civil society and the public sector (Díaz Coutiño, 2015).

Environmental Dimension

This dimension arises from the premise that the future of development depends on the capacity of institutional and economic actors to know and manage, according to a long-term perspective, their reserves of renewable natural resources and their environment. Here, special attention is paid to biodiversity and especially to resources such as soil, water, and forests, which are the factors that determine the productive capacity of certain areas in the shortest period (Sepulveda, Castro, & Rojas, 1998).

In ecological terms, sustainable development proposes that the economy be circular, that there be a closing of cycles to imitate nature. In other words, production systems are designed to use only renewable resources and energies, so as not to produce waste, as these return to nature or become the input for another manufactured product. During its operation, this model considers the entire life cycle of the product, from its extraction to the final disposal of the waste when its useful life ends. This interval is divided into three stages: the first is to apply the "polluter pays" principle when setting prices; the second is informed consumer choice through labelling; the third refers to the ecological design of the product, for which certain tools called Life Cycle Inventories (LCI) and Life Cycle Assessment (LCA) are applied (Artaraz, 2002).

CONCEPTUALIZING THE CIRCULAR ECONOMY

According to Lambarry, Cardoso and Cortés (2022), the Circular Economy (CE) arises from the need to have a functional strategy that promotes the application of a different way in the production and consumption of goods that incorporate materials for single use, and even more so, if these manufactured products are for mass consumption.

Given the above, the concept of circular economy has been defined in various ways by organizations, institutions and even authors. Such is the case of the European Environment Agency (2023), which believes that the circular economy is "where the value of products, materials and resources is maintained in the economy for as long as possible, from minimized waste generation".

For its part, the Ellen MacArthur Foundation (2015) conceptualizes the circular economy as a restorative model whose primary objective is to maintain the usefulness of products, components, and materials to retain their value. Thus, it is characterized by minimizing the need for new inputs and energy, thus reducing environmental pressures linked to resource extraction, emissions, and waste.

Similarly, Kirchherr et al. (2017) conceptualize it as an economic system in which the term end-of-life of a product or resource is replaced by actions that reduce waste generation, as well as facilitate the recovery, reuse, recycling, and reconditioning of material, energy, and water flows to incorporate them into new cycles and processes of distribution and consumption.

While Kowszyk et al. (2022) establish that the circular economy model consists of a strategy that minimizes the negative impact on the environment, aimed at the final product being considered as a source of value creation. Thus, the objectives of circularity are to increase the useful life of the product, to produce goods with long life cycles, and to focus on services rather than products. Through a systemic vision focused on the analysis of the permanent flow of technical, technological, biological, and human materials that participate in the creation of value of goods and services based on a redefinition of the management of financial, human, social and natural capital.

Technological Tools in the Circular Economy

It is for them that information and communications technologies (ICT) are constantly evolving (Quintero et al. 2020) and (Quintero et al 2022) may affect their dynamic and evolutionary form leading the continuous emergence of new technologies and business. Advances in different areas such as computing, software and communication networks have allowed companies to benefit from their implementation. A technological (Ortiz et al., 2006 and Villazon et al, 2020) and social ecosystem that has been emerging in organizations and companies for years is the Internet of Things (IoT), which is supporting their digital transformation with the integration of new disruptive technologies such as Big data, the cloud, cybersecurity, 3D printing, virtual and augmented reality. As the years have passed, new technologies have emerged such as applied artificial intelligence, drones, virtual voice assistants, implementation of embedded systems, communications systems, web systems, mobile devices and applications, all of which contribute and are part of the Industry. 4.0.

(Luis., 2021)Most of these technologies are already being used in the industry which are transforming production, isolated and optimized cells will be joined together forming fully integrated, automated and optimized production flows, producing greater efficiency by changing traditional forms of production between producers, distributors and clients. On the other hand, the communication between the machine and the human has undergone a transformation.

The implementation of these technologies in companies, besides optimizing their processes, also allows the optimization of resources and contributes to the circular economy, on the one hand, the IoT as a generator of application information in waste, the manufacturing of reusable parts in 3D printers and simulation. Artificial intelligence allows us to reduce production costs thanks to the development and implementation of intelligent applications. Robotics with the use of robots for any production chain, favoring optimization in waste management. Below are some examples that allow the implementation of circular economies.

(Veronica, 2021) (Ortiz-Rodriguez et al, 2006) Internet of Things: Allows digital interconnection and cooperation between people and devices or objects through wireless networks or sensors, which allows processing vast amounts of data which must be stored and managed for later use. As in the management of urban solid waste, allowing the reduction of raw materials and waste reduction. Enabling supply chain improvement and remanufacturing.

In the opinion of Veronica, 2021 additive Manufacturing: It has caused an assumption in product manufacturing methods by making use of 3D printing by using new products with recycled materials and biomaterials as their raw materials. This allows the reduction of energy consumption compared to traditional systems, benefiting the eco-design of products, improving the manufacturing of components of different geometries allowing better repair.

Simulation: They allow errors to be anticipated and thus improve decision making. Furthermore, it benefits the development of remanufacturing and the development of closed-loop processes within the supply chain.

Big Data: It is used for the centralization of data from different sources of information such as sensors, web applications, mobile applications and satellites to convert them into valuable data that allow greater efficiency in the recycling of plastic waste (Villazon et al 2020).

(Canu, 2017) Artificial intelligence (AI): It provides many important benefits in optimizing processes that cause cost reduction and better use of resources. Its benefits are also reflected in the reduction of production errors, generating greater quality and efficiency.

Robotics: The use of robots in factories allows the automation of waste management. As well as the implementation of the circular economy in the robotics sector allows the generation of reconditioned robots and robots manufactured with technologies such as 3D printing. (circular, 2024)

These technologies allow companies to facilitate the conversion of their traditional, mechanized production systems into optimized, ICT-enabled, environmentally conscious systems. Companies that have a vision committed to the planet and society will be the leading companies accepting the new models supported by industry 4.0.

CONCLUSION

The digital technologies can benefit society by making the processes more efficient. A broad field of digital technologies are available and continuously scaling, including artificial intelligence, big data, cloud computing, cyber physical systems, blockchain and virtual and augmented reality. However, the society has just begun to adopt these emerging technologies. Integrating these technologies into daily work processes would significantly add value to the companies and help the environment.

REFERENCES

Aguilar Luis, J. (2021). *Internet de las cosas, Un futuro hiperconectado: 5G.* Inteligencia Artificial, Big Data, Cloud, Blockchain, Ciberseguridad.

Artaraz, M. (2002). *Teoria de las tres dimensiones de desarrollo sostenible.* Ecosistemas. https://www.aeet.org/ecosistemas/022/informe1.htm

Canu, M. E. (2017). *Economia Circular y Sostenibilidad.*

Da Costa, C. (2022). La economia circular, como eje de desarrollo de los países latinoamericanos. *Revista de Economia Política*, 11.

Díaz Coutiño, R. (2015). *Desarrollo Sustentable, una oportunidad para la vida.* Mc Graw Hill.

EEA. (2023). *European Enviroment Agency*. EEA. https://www.eea.europa.eu/en

EMF. (2015). Obtenido de Towards the circular economy - Economic and business rationale for an accelerated transition. *Circular economy overview*. https://www.ellenmacarthurfoundation.org/circular-economy/overview/concept>

Geographic, R. N. (2023). Economica circular que es y por que benefica al medio ambiente. *National Geographic*. https://www.nationalgeographicla.com/medio-ambiente/2022/05/economia-circular-que-es-y-por-que-beneficia-al-medio-ambiente

Kirchherr, J., Reike, D., & Hekkert, M. (2017). Conceptualizing the circular economy: An analysis of 114 definitions. *Elsevier, Resources, Conservation & Recycling, 127*, 221-232. doi:10.1016/j.resconrec.2017.09.005

Kowszyk, Y., Vanclay, F., & Maher, R. (2022). Conflict management in the extractive industries: A comparison of four mining projects in Latin America. *Elsevier. The Extractive Industries and Society*, 2–9. doi:10.1016/j.exis.2022.101161

Lambarry, F., Cardoso, E. O., & Cortés, J. (2022). *Economía Circular. Indicadores de gestión empresarial*. Fontamara.

Luis., J. A. (2021). *Internet de las cosas, Un futuro hiperconectado: 5G, Inteligencia Artificial, Big Data, Cloud, Blockchain, Ciberseguridad.*

Mankiw, G. (2021). *Principles of Economics* (9th ed.). Cengage.

Maureen, H. (1998). *Sustainable community indicators trainer's workshop*. Sustainable Measures. http://www.sustainablemeasures.com/indicators/WhatIs.html

Medina-Quintero, J. M., Abrego-Almazán, D., & Ortiz-Rodríguez, F. (2018). Use and usefulness of the information systems measurement. a quality approach at the mexican northeastern region. *Cuadernos Americanos, 31*(56), 7–30. doi:10.11144/Javeriana.cao.31-56.ubwm

Naredo, J. M. (Marzo de 2002). *Instrumentos para paliar la insostenibilidad de los sistema urbanos, Ciudades para un futuro más sostenible"*. Habitat. http://habitat.aq.upm.es/boletin/n24/ajnar.html#fntext-1

Oblitas, J., Sangay, M., Rojas, E., & Castro, W. (2019). EconomíaCircular en residuos de aparatos eléctricos y electrónicos. *Revista de Ciencias Sociales*, 195–205.

Ortiz-Rodríguez, F., Palma, R., & Villazón-Terrazas, B. (2006). Semantic based P2P System for local e-Government. In Proceedings of Informatik 2006. GI-Edition-Lecture Notes in Informatics (LNI).

Parkin, M. (2018). *Economía*. Pearson.

Parkin, M. (2018). *Economía*. Pearson.

Priego, C. (2003). *La institucionalidad ambiental nacional e internacional. Conceptos básicos sobre medio ambiente y desarrollo sustentable.* INET, GTZ.

Quintero, J. M. M., Echeverría, O. R., & Rodríguez, F. O. (2022). Trust and information quality for the customer satisfaction and loyalty in e-Banking with the use of the mobile phone. *Contaduría y Administración, 67*(1), 283–304.

Sepulveda, S., Castro, A., & Rojas, P. (1998). *Metodología para estimar el nivel de desarrollo sostenible en espacios territoriales.* IICA.

Tiwari, S., Ortiz-Rodríguez, F., Mishra, S., Vakaj, E., & Kotecha, K. (2023). *Artificial Intelligence: Towards Sustainable Intelligence.* First International Conference, AI4S 2023, Pune, India. . Springer Cham10.1007/978-3-031-47997-7

Veronica, B. (2021). *Oportunidades tecnológicas de la industria 4.0 en el sector empresarial de economía circular.*

Villazón-Terrazas, B., Ortiz-Rodríguez, F., Tiwari, S. M., & Shandilya, S. K. (2020). Knowledge graphs and semantic web. *Communications in Computer and Information Science, 1232*, 1–225. doi:10.1007/978-3-030-65384-2

Chapter 2
Is The Manager's Gender A Determining Factor in Tourism Companies' Commitment to Ict Training?
A Study of The Destination of Extremadura (Spain)

Marcelino Sánchez-Rivero
https://orcid.org/0000-0003-3988-6278
University of Extremadura, Spain

Clara Gallego-Sosa
https://orcid.org/0000-0002-7267-0842
University of Extremadura, Spain

Yakira Fernández-Torres
https://orcid.org/0000-0001-5672-3185
University of Extremadura, Spain

Milagros Gutiérrez-Fernández
https://orcid.org/0000-0003-4819-2956
University of Extremadura, Spain

ABSTRACT

An organisation's ability to exploit information and communication technologies (ICTs) depends on the ICT training of its employees, which is conditioned by the strategies implemented by managers. These business strategies may be influenced by the manager's gender. In this study, the manager's gender is used as a factor to determine the level of commitment to ICT training of tourism managers in the Spanish region of Extremadura. The study also examines their satisfaction with the ICT training they have received, their preferences regarding training providers,

DOI: 10.4018/979-8-3693-1119-6.ch002

and their perceptions regarding how well ICT knowledge supply meets demand in this region. Online questionnaire data from a sample of 238 tourist lodgings were collected. Inferential statistical analysis was applied. The results suggest that the values for the majority of the ICT training variables considered in this study do not differ between companies managed by men and women.

INTRODUCTION

The term *human capital*, which emerged in the mid-20th century, can be defined as the set of experiences and knowledge acquired throughout life through education and training (Becker, 1964; Schultz, 1961). Laroche et al. (1999) broadened this concept by arguing that social attributes, personality and other innate characteristics of individuals also determine their productivity (De la Fuente et al., 2004). Accordingly, innate human capital refers to an individual's natural talent endowed by genetic inheritance, whereas acquired human capital refers to the competencies that an individual develops from the accumulation of experience and from formal or informal education (Schultz, 1993). As part of acquired human capital, education is especially relevant in providing individuals with competent skills (Kasa et al., 2020). Thus, the continuous training of individuals, specifically employees, has become increasingly important over the years (Akther & Rahman, 2021; Jaworski et al., 2018), given the key role of human capital in the development of organisations.

The growing complexity of the environment in which organisations compete forces them to adapt to an era largely defined by technological advances (Kuo et al., 2010). In this environment, the information and communication technology (ICT) training of the members of an organisation is essential because having strong ICT skills is critical to make the most of what ICTs can offer (Yeo & Grant, 2019; Zhang & Lee, 2007). Therefore, training the members of an organisation in this area is vital because it contributes positively to productivity (Dearden et al., 2006). Such training may depend on, amongst other factors, the manager's gender for the following reasons. First, technology education tends to be different between women and men. Specifically, science, technology, engineering and mathematics (STEM) are generally perceived to be the domain of men. As a result, women tend to be less interested in such degrees, which leads to lower female representation in STEM education (Sáinz et al., 2016; Yeo & Grant, 2019). The origin of this lower propensity lies in the predominant gender roles in society (Hetherington, 1965). Second, each gender is associated with a different leadership style that may result in action plans with different approaches (Eagly & Johnson, 1990; Walker et al., 1996). Women's attitude tends to be one of concern for others (Beji et al., 2020), with female managers expected to focus on the welfare of their employees (Feng et al., 2020; Mallin & Michelon, 2011) and, consequently, on their training. However, a review of the literature reveals only one study of the influence of women's presence on the board of directors on employee training (Tran, 2020). This lack of studies highlights the need to investigate this relationship further. Moreover, the cited study revealed a negative relationship.

ICTs are crucial in the tourism industry, which represents a key sector for the economy (Duffus-Miranda & Briley, 2021). ICTs provide tools to improve internal and external operational processes (Alonso-Almeida & Llach, 2013; Cheng & Piccoli, 2002), offering a distribution channel that allows tourism companies to reach a wider market at a lower cost than through traditional channels (Collins et al., 2003). Moreover, through websites, tourism companies can enhance their relationships with customers by generating feedback, which enables optimal management whilst improving corporate image (Cristobal-Fransi et al., 2020). Another key aspect is how ICTs allow and make it easier for users of tourism goods and services to share opinions about their experiences. This sharing greatly benefits companies in the sector, which can improve their internal processes and services quickly and easily, thus encouraging customer loyalty (Anser et al., 2020; Garbin-Praničević & Mandić, 2020).

Considering the importance of the use of ICTs for tourism, the essential nature of ICT training for those who form part of a company in the current business environment and the absence of literature on the relationship between management gender diversity and ICT training, this research focuses on the tourist accommodation sector in Extremadura to meet its objectives. Specifically, this study aims to determine whether there are differences between male-led and female-led companies in terms of commitment to ICT training, degree of satisfaction with ICT training, preferences regarding where to carry out such training, and perceptions of the fit between ICT training supply and demand.

The region of Extremadura, located in southwest Spain, offers a suitable context for this study for the following reasons. First, it is in an emerging phase of the life cycle of its tourism products and services. Its market is still far from becoming saturated and unsustainable, as has occurred in other Spanish tourism markets, especially at certain times of year (Junta de Extremadura, 2017). This region is also characterised by low labour productivity, the loss of its productive framework and the mismatch between educational programmes and labour requirements (Junta de Extremadura, 2023). Therefore, to improve the competitiveness of companies in this region, it is essential to promote an effective use of ICTs, which depends on users' training.

To meet the study aims, data were collected from a survey of 238 accommodation companies in Extremadura. These data were then analysed using statistical inference. The results reveal no differences between male-led and female-led companies in many of the aforementioned ICT training aspects. The exception is the degree of satisfaction with ICT training, with women managers expressing a greater level of satisfaction. Improved STEM education for women in the region could explain these results.

This study makes several contributions. First, to the best of the authors' knowledge, it provides the first evidence of the state of ICT training of employees and managers in Extremadura's tourism sector, the commitment of companies to such training and ratings of the training supply in this area. This knowledge is essential for developing strategies and policies to increase the productivity and competitiveness of the sector. Second, to the best of the authors' knowledge, this study offers the first gender-focused analysis of the role of a company's leader in that company's commitment to ICT training. Thus, the study opens a crucial line of inquiry in the literature in an area where further research is required. That is, the study explores factors that condition ICT training in companies in general and in tourism companies in particular, with the aim of promoting the optimal use of these technologies.

This paper has five sections, the first being this introduction. Section 2 offers a review of the fundamental theories that support the differences in leadership style between men and women. Section 3 discusses the studies of the relationship between women and ICTs, focusing particularly on women's presence in management. Section 4 explains the data collection and method and then presents and discusses the results. Finally, Section 5 outlines the conclusions of the study, the limitations encountered and possibilities for future lines of research.

THEORIES OF DIFFERENCES IN MALE AND FEMALE LEADERSHIP

Numerous studies support the existence of differences between men and women (Croson & Gneezy, 2009; Pratto et al., 1997). These differences can be perceived in management (Cook & Glass, 2018; Krishnan & Park, 2005), giving rise to the adoption of different leadership styles that condition the actions of organisations (Eagly & Johnson, 1990). These gender-based differences between individuals can be explained by three fundamental theories: gender socialisation theory (Chodorow, 1978), transformational leadership theory (Bass, 1998) and upper echelons theory (Hambrick & Mason, 1984). This section presents these theories, which provide the arguments that support the existence of differences between men and women and the existence of differing influences of the manager's gender in the actions of organisations based on these differences.

First, the theory of gender socialisation (Chodorow, 1978) states that men and women adopt different behaviours resulting from the roles they acquire during their development in line with the prevailing social stereotypes (Dawson, 1997).

This theory is based on the premise that the gender identity of each person is constructed from a complex process that begins at the age of around three years and that involves biological, social, cultural and psychological factors (Chodorow, 1978; Ely, 1995). Accordingly, social stereotypes lead to differences between men and women, including the fact that women tend to be more sensitive towards ethics and show greater concern for the needs and welfare of others (Bampton & Maclagan, 2009; Beutel & Marini, 1995; Cumming et al., 2015). They also have a more philanthropic character (Cordeiro et al., 2020; Williams, 2003). Differences are likewise perceptible in people's links with external elements such as technology (Kelan, 2007), where women are associated with a more negative attitude towards technology use (Mulauzi & Albright, 2009; Nord et al., 2017).

In line with these arguments, the differences between men and women mean that managers tend to adopt a certain leadership style depending on their gender. Specifically, women tend to have a transformational leadership style. This leadership style is characterised by being participatory, focusing on the development of subordinates, paying greater attention to the individual needs of workers (Eagly et al., 2003) and encouraging them to place all their efforts in performing the tasks they are assigned (Bass, 1998; Yammarino & Bass, 1990). Companies with a female chief executive officer (CEO) face fewer lawsuits for discrimination (Dadanlar & Abebe, 2020) and have a better relationship with employees because they offer a higher standard of well-being in the workplace (Liu, 2021).

Gender socialisation theory and transformational leadership style theory have led to the emergence of upper echelons theory. According to upper echelons theory, which was developed by Hambrick and Mason (1984), the demographic characteristics, including gender, of the members of the top-level management team influence its decisions. This theory is based on the differences in the values and experiences of men and women, which leads to the adoption of different corporate policies and, ultimately, a differentiated impact on organisational performance (Beji et al., 2020; Uyar et al., 2020). Based on these arguments, many studies have shown the positive influence of a female presence in management on various organisational actions, including those related to corporate social responsibility (CSR) and those that promote greater environmental innovation (Nadeem et al., 2020), greater development of sustainable environmental strategies (Xie et al., 2020), better customer commitment (Ardito et al., 2021) and a better relationship between managers and employees (Li et al., 2018).

GENDER DIFFERENCES IN ICT USE AND ICT TRAINING: A REVIEW OF THE EVIDENCE

This section reviews the literature that supports the existence of relationships between gender and the use and implementation of ICTs, between gender and the importance attached to such tools, and between gender and employee training. The aim of this review is to provide support for the existence of different stances by men and women managers towards ICT training, the focal issue of this study. This review first focuses on these relationships from a general perspective. A specific focus is then adopted to address these relationships in the context of management, which is the area of interest in this study.

First, there are differences between men and women in terms of ICTs (Venkatesh et al., 2000), specifically in relation to attitudes and perceptions, resulting in women being less inclined to use ICTs (Hilbert, 2011; Varank, 2007). However, such differences may be conditioned by where people live. For instance, in certain rural areas, women have been found to be less likely than men to adopt and use technologies (Best & Maier, 2007; Venkatesh et al., 2000). This finding can largely be explained by the existence of certain limiting factors for women, notably the lack of training and ongoing inequalities that continue to exist between women and men in the domestic and work environment. This situation hinders women's access to ICTs, mainly due to a lack of time and low levels of education and income (Best & Maier, 2007; Novo-Corti et al., 2014).

Similar results have also been found in relation to women entrepreneurs, with Mack et al. (2017) reporting that female entrepreneurs are less willing to adopt ICTs than their male counterparts. However, this finding may be due to their lack of knowledge and training in this area because when women entrepreneurs seek the help of business incubators, which provide a possible means of informal learning, they are more likely to use various online applications. Similarly, Hazarika and Chakraborty (2019) found that the low level of ICT use and the lack of ICT competence of female government functionaries in Assam (India) is mainly due to the lack of adequate training to develop the necessary skills to use these technologies. Ma et al. (2020) analysed the use of a particular type of ICT, namely smartphones, according to the gender of farmers. The results of the analysis suggest that male farmers are more likely to use smartphones than their female counterparts. One possible reason for this difference may be that, in rural areas in developing countries, decisions on the purchase of major assets such as smartphones are usually made by men. Therefore, women farmers may have fewer opportunities to access this type of technology.

However, this finding is in contrast to the positive reviews and huge importance that women attach to ICTs (Mulauzi & Albright, 2009; Nord et al., 2017). Studies have shown that women entrepreneurs use ICTs more and more frequently and in a more complex manner, making the most of the competitive advantages that these ICTs provide to enable different types of businesses to develop (Sharafizad, 2016; Ukpere et al., 2014). Mobile phones have been identified as the main ICT used by women entrepreneurs in Ghana because it meets their communication needs but requires a relatively low investment to acquire and maintain (Kwami, 2015). Mulauzi and Albright (2009) found that, in addition to having a positive view of the usefulness of ICTs, professional women in Lusaka (Zambia) increasingly use ICTs, with an optimal level of access. This finding is justified by the fact that professional women have a higher level of education and income and by the study context, namely an urban area that is more developed than rural areas. Nord et al. (2017) also provided empirical evidence that Italian women in their workplaces use ICTs for widely different purposes and experience a range of notable benefits (enhancing communication, forging strong relationships, improving customer service, etc.).

The aforementioned gender differences in the use and importance attached to ICTs are also evident in business management. For instance, Yeo and Grant (2019) argued that the gender of both employees and managers positively contributes to increasing the ability of companies to use ICTs as the proportion of women employees and directors rises. Over the last few years, studies have explored the differences between female and male board members in relation to the use and implementation of ICTs. First, some authors have found that greater gender diversity on boards results in greater use of the corporate website for transparency, corporate governance reporting (Nel et al., 2020) and intellectual capital (Nicolò et al., 2021). This finding is justified on the grounds that a higher proportion of women directors means more effective corporate governance mechanisms, as well as a greater diversity of opinions and values, which improves the quality of the decision-making process.

Similarly, several studies have shown that the number of women on the board of directors is positively related to the disclosure of corporate information and, more specifically, financial information through an organisation's social networks (Basuony et al., 2018). The aforementioned authors justify their findings by arguing that women directors have a positive significant influence on the supervisory functions of the board of directors and, consequently, tend to demand greater transparency for stakeholders (Hannoon et al., 2021).

Based on a sample of companies listed on the London Stock Exchange, Ayman et al. (2019) and Amin et al. (2020) reported that board gender diversity leads to a greater use of Twitter for the disclosure of financial information. This finding is explained by the fact that the presence of female directors means greater board independence, as well as greater attention to the needs of different stakeholders, which in turn leads to a stronger focus on corporate disclosure and the use of far-reaching media.

Finally, there is also evidence of the differences between men and women managers in terms of human resources (HR) and, more specifically, employee training. Studies have shown that companies that have a higher representation of women on the board are more likely to be ranked amongst the best companies to work for (Bernardi et al., 2006; Bernardi & Threadgill, 2010), thanks to their greater engagement with employees (Cruz et al., 2019). However, in the only study of the possible relationship between gender diversity and employee training found by the authors of the present paper, Tran (2020) found that a higher proportion of women on the board of directors does not contribute to employee learning and development. This finding is justified by the possibility that women have a limited ability to provide training to their employees, which may be due to the strong gender inequalities that continue to exist in Vietnam, where the sample was taken.

In conclusion, the literature offers arguments for the existence of differences between men and women in terms of the use of ICTs. Many of these arguments concur in that there exist certain barriers that hinder women's access to technology, notably a lack of training, which to some extent leads to women's low use of ICTs. Although the management literature is still scarce, most of the research in this area shows the differential effect of the presence of women in management on the use of ICTs by companies. That is, there is a positive relationship between female representation amongst managers and the dissemination of corporate information through different ICT media.

Therefore, given the arguments for women managers' greater efforts in HR, the characteristics that distinguish women leaders and their relationship with ICTs, and gender-based differences regarding the adoption of ICTs, the following research hypotheses are tested:

H1: Commitment to the ICT training of employees and managers differs between companies managed by men and those managed by women.
H2: The degree of satisfaction with the ICT training of employees and managers differs between companies managed by men and those managed by women.
H3: Preferences regarding the organisations that provide the ICT training of employees and managers differ between companies managed by men and those managed by women.
H4: Perceptions of the match between the supply and demand of ICT training in Extremadura differ between companies managed by men and those managed by women.

ANALYSIS OF ICT TRAINING IN TOURISM COMPANIES FROM A GENDER PERSPECTIVE: THE CASE OF EXTREMADURA

Sample and Data

To meet the study aims, an emerging Spanish inland tourist destination, Extremadura, was chosen as the study context. A random sample of 238 companies was taken from the population of all tourist lodgings in Extremadura. The sample represents approximately 15% of the population. For the worst case (i.e. p=q=0.50) at a confidence level of 95%, the maximum sampling error when considering both the sample size and the population universe was ± 5.9%.

The data for the study were obtained from an online questionnaire, responses to which were collected between February and July 2020. The items of the questionnaire completed by the sampled lodgings were designed to meet the following requirements:

a) to uncover the degree to which tourism companies are committed to the ICT training of both managers and employees,
b) to investigate the satisfaction of the managers of these lodgings with ICT training and their preferences regarding where the training takes place and
c) to provide insight into the perceptions of possible mismatches between supply and demand in ICT training in the region under analysis.

Once the data had been collected based on these three requirements and before the analysis was performed, the sample was divided into two groups according to the manager's gender. The first group consisted of lodgings where the manager of the tourism company was male, and the second group consisted of lodgings where the manager was female. The first subsample consisted of 110 male managers, and the second consisted of 128 female managers. The balance in the sample sizes resulting from this segmentation by gender ensured the reliability of the comparisons (of both proportions and means) presented in this article.

Methodology

By considering the two previous groups (males and females) in columns and the qualitative variables analysed in this paper (educational level, offer of ICT training, commitment to ICT training, etc.) in rows, the result of this cross-tabulation is a contingency table of i rows and $j = 2$ columns. Besides the description of the values obtained in the cells of this contingency table, the main objective of this paper is to detect possible gender gaps. To achieve this objective, the hypothesis of independence between rows and columns was tested using the chi-square test. This test compares the observed frequencies with the expected frequencies, assuming that the variables appearing in the table are independent. Low values for this test indicate independence, whereas high values indicate an association between the variables in rows and columns. This chi-square test follows an asymptotic normal distribution, a hypothesis that can be accepted given the large sample size.

For the remaining variables analysed in this paper, a 5-point Likert scale was used. Assuming a continuum and a normal distribution along this scale (such as satisfaction with ICT training or ICT training versus training needs), the detection of possible gender gaps was carried out through a t-test of equality of means for male managers and female managers. Given the unknown population variances of these variables for men and women, a test of equality of variances was previously carried out using a Levene test, and this hypothesis was accepted in all cases (equality of variances: Y). Consequently, a t-test was used for independent populations with unknown but assumed equal variances, obtaining the *p*-value associated with the empirical value of this test.

Descriptive Results and Inference Tests

First, before investigating the focal questions of this study, Tables 1 to 3 offer an overview of the educational level of the managers of the analysed companies, the recent commitment of these organisations to training in general and the relationship between these two variables. Companies managed by men are compared with those managed by women in Tables 1 to 3. The following table presents the distribution of the participating managers by educational level, differentiating between male and female managers. Almost half of the managers (46%) had a university education, although a high proportion (approximately 1 in 4) had only a school leaving certificate or compulsory secondary education. The least common educational levels amongst the managers were vocational training (around 18% of the total) and upper secondary education (around 12%).

Table 1. Educational level of managers of the sampled firms

Educational level	Male managers	Female managers
- School leaving certificate or compulsory secondary education	24.5%	21.1%
- Upper secondary education	11.8%	13.3%
- Intermediate vocational qualification	10.0%	8.6%
- Higher vocational qualification	7.3%	10.2%
- University	46.4%	46.8%
Chi-square = 1.098; df = 4; significance = 0.895		

Source: Authors.

The data in Table 1 represent a 4 x 2 contingency table with level of education in the rows and gender in the columns. The value for the chi-square test in this case was 1.098, with an asymptotic significance of 0.895. Consequently, at the 1%, 5% and 10% significance levels, the hypothesis of independence between educational level and gender cannot be rejected. This result implies that the educational level of female managers in tourist accommodation companies in Extremadura is the same as that of male managers. The chi-square test was also performed for the contingency tables presented later in this paper.

The next stage of analysis was to examine the participating managers' perceptions of the importance of the general continuous training of the members of the company in running the business. Thus, the managers were asked to indicate whether training of any type had been provided by the company in the last two years. The results are shown in Table 2. The percentage of managers who had recently held training for their employees or for themselves was only approximately 41%. That is, six out of 10 tourist accommodation companies in Extremadura had not carried out any type of training in the last two years. This situation may represent a competitive disadvantage for the tourism sector of Extremadura, especially given that in the years in question, both public and private business management underwent profound changes that call for the acquisition of new competencies. Although the difference in percentages between male and female managers was conclusive (41.8% for men; 41.4% for women), the chi-square test provided a value of 0.004, with an associated *p* value of 0.949. Hence, there is very strong evidence that there are no statistically significant differences in the commitment to continuous training of tourist accommodation companies in Extremadura according to the gender of the manager.

Table 2. Percentage of managers whose firms offered some form of training in the last two years

Training offered?	Male managers	Female managers
- Yes	41.8%	41.4%
- No	58.2%	58.6%
Chi-square = 0.004; df = 1; significance = 0.949		

Source: Authors.

However, the overall figure of 41% reported above may be masking differences depending on the educational level of the managers, who must ultimately make training-related decisions. Hence, in Table 3, this percentage is broken down by the manager's educational level.

Table 3. Relationship between training initiatives and the manager's educational level and gender (percentage of managers whose companies have offered training by educational level and gender)

Educational level	Male managers	Female managers
- School leaving certificate or compulsory secondary education	19.6%	11.3%
- Upper secondary education	6.5%	5.7%
- Intermediate vocational qualification	4.3%	7.5%
- Higher vocational qualification	4.3%	11.3%
- University	65.3%	64.2%
Chi-square = 3.037; df = 4; significance = 0.552		

Source: Authors.

The differences according to the manager's educational level are evident. Whereas almost two thirds of managers with a university education had run training activities in their companies, less than 20% of managers with any other educational level had done the same. Consequently, university managers show a greater awareness of the importance of continuous training in tourist accommodation companies in this region. Nevertheless, no gender differences were observed, given that the value for the chi-square test was 3.037, with a *p* value of 0.552.

Focusing on the core aims of this research, the analyses presented below address the commitment to ICT training. The results in Table 4 show that only one out of three managers had offered some ICT-related training for employees or themselves. Again, no statistically significant differences were observed between male and female managers (chi-square: 0.590; *p* value: 0.442). Therefore, even though generic continuous training already represents a competitive disadvantage for tourism in Extremadura, continuous ICT training represents an even greater disadvantage, with two out of three tourist accommodation companies in Extremadura having not offered any training in ICTs. In 21st century tourism markets, ICTs represent an essential element in the value chain of tourism companies. However, the percentages observed in the present analysis of the region of Extremadura indicate that this sector is being left behind in the 21st century technological revolution.

Table 4. Percentage of managers whose firms offered some form of ICT training

ICT training offered?	Male managers	Female managers
- Yes	32.7%	37.5%
- No	67.3%	62.5%
Chi-square = 0.590; df = 1; significance = 0.442		

Source: Authors.

Although the percentage of managers who are aware of the importance of ICT training is quite low, further analysis was conducted by specifying different levels of commitment to this type of training. Three levels of commitment were defined:

- *Low commitment* means that no ICT training was taken.
- *Medium commitment* means that there was some ICT training aimed at either the management or employees.
- *High commitment* means that there was some ICT training aimed at both the management and employees.

The results of the responses of the tourism managers are presented in Table 5. Only 9% of tourist accommodation managers in Extremadura had a high commitment to ICT training. Moreover, ICT training was more common amongst managers than amongst employees, given that the percentage of respondents with a medium commitment to having carried out some training aimed at managers varied between 21% for men and 26% for women, whereas a medium commitment to training aimed at employees was only 2.7% in companies managed by men and 3.1% in companies managed by women. The similarity of the percentages presented in Table 5 provide an intuitive indication of the hypothesis testing, confirmed by the chi-square test, namely the absence of a gender gap in the commitment to ICT training of managers in Extremadura.

Table 5. Managers' commitment to ICT training

Commitment	Male managers	Female managers
- Low	67.3%	62.5%
- Medium (only managers)	20.9%	25.8%
- Medium (only employees)	2.7%	3.1%
- High (managers and employees)	9.1%	8.6%
Chi-square = 0.853; df = 3; significance = 0.837		

Source: Authors.

Further analysis was conducted to complement the previous analysis, given that ICT skills cover a very wide range of knowledge. Accordingly, the commitment to ICT training was broken down into several specific aspects of ICT, including social media management, databases, spreadsheets/word processing/presentations, web positioning and mobile applications. The results of this disaggregated analysis are shown in Table 6. In general, the commitment to training in these specific areas was very low, given that the percentage of managers who showed a medium or high commitment was very low in some cases and virtually non-existent in others. The highest levels of commitment to training were in social media management and web positioning, whereas the lowest levels were in database management, cloud storage and mobile applications. Furthermore, the chi-square tests reveal that, in all cases, this level of commitment by ICT training area did not differ significantly between male and female managers. Thus, the results clearly highlight the need to raise awareness amongst tourism managers in this region of how important it is for both themselves and their employees to acquire new ICT management skills so that the tourism sector in Extremadura can keep pace with the technological revolution of the last few years.

Table 6. Managers' commitment to ICT training by training area

Commitment	Male managers	Female managers
Social media management - Low - Medium (only managers) - Medium (only employees) - High (managers and employees) Chi-square = 2.646; df = 3; significance = 0.449	77.3% 15.5% 2.7% 4.5%	70.4% 23.4% 3.1% 3.1%
Databases - Low - Medium (only managers) - Medium (only employees) - High (managers and employees) Chi-square = 1.236; df = 2; significance = 0.539	86.4% 11.8% 0.0% 1.8%	90.6% 8.6% 0.0% 0.8%
Spreadsheets, word processing and presentations - Low - Medium (only managers) - Medium (only employees) - High (managers and employees) Chi-square = 2.111; df = 3; significance = 0.550	84.6% 12.7% 0.0% 2.7%	85.9% 10.2% 1.6% 2.3%

Source: Authors.

Another interesting question for analysis is the level of satisfaction with the ICT training received, differentiating between training for managers and training for employees. The managers were asked to rate this satisfaction on a scale ranging from 0 (*complete dissatisfaction*) to 5 (*complete satisfaction*). Assuming a continuum along this Likert scale, the results reveal the mean and standard deviation of this rating. The statistical results are presented in Table 7. In the case of training for managers, the mean satisfaction was 3.333 points for male managers and 3.771 for female managers. To determine whether the difference between these mean scores was statistically significant, a *t*-test for equality of means was performed. The *t* value was -1.910, with a bilateral significance of 0.06. Consequently, although the result is not significant at the 1% or 5% significance level, at the 10% significance level, the satisfaction of female managers in their ICT training is significantly higher than that of male managers.

Table 7. Degree of satisfaction with ICT training

Satisfaction	Male managers	Female managers
Training received by managers - Mean - Standard deviation	3.333 1.195	3.771 0.905
Difference of means: -0.438; t-test: -1.910; equality of variances: Y; df = 82; significance = 0.060		
Training received by employees - Mean - Standard deviation	3.476 2.462	3.419 2.385
Difference of means: 0.057; t-test: 0.129; equality of variances: Y; df = 50; significance = 0.898		

Source: Authors.

Regarding training for employees, the mean satisfaction score was practically identical in companies run by men (3.476 points) and companies run by women (3.419). In fact, the result of the *t*-test was very close to 0 (0.129), and the *p* value was very close to 1 (0.898), indicating the absence of differences by gender.

Another aspect of the analysis involved studying the providers of the ICT training received by the managers and employees of the tourist accommodation companies in this region. The data presented in Table 8 indicate that the two large public providers of tourism training in the region, the University of Extremadura (with its Degree in Tourism) and the School of Hospitality and Agrotourism of Extremadura (with its training aimed mainly at employees in this sector), have a very small share of the ICT training market in the region. This market is heavily dominated by private training and other training organisations. Whereas more than 61% of male managers and around 54% of female managers who had taken training in ICT received this training from private training providers, only 5.6% of male managers and 2.1% of female managers received their training at the University of Extremadura. An even more striking finding is that none of the women managers consulted (128 in total) had been involved in training provided by the School of

Hospitality and Agrotourism of Extremadura for themselves or their employees. These results show a clear need for these two public training institutions in Extremadura to develop a training offering that enables the managers and employees of tourist accommodation companies in this region to acquire ICT skills. For the purposes of comparing companies with managers of different genders, companies run by men mostly used private training centres (61.1%), whereas those run by women mostly used other training organisations (58.3%).

Table 8. Providers of ICT training for employees and/or managers (multiple response)

Training provider	Male managers	Female managers
- University of Extremadura	5.6%	2.1%
- Vocational training	2.8%	4.2%
- School of Hospitality and Agrotourism of Extremadura	5.6%	0.0%
- Private	61.1%	54.2%
- Other	44.4%	58.3%

Source: Authors.

The analysis concludes with an examination of the managers' opinions in relation to the extent to which the current training supply in the region meets the ICT training needs of the companies in the sector. The managers were asked to rate the suitability of the training in relation to different training organisations in the region on a scale ranging from 0 (*not at all suitable*) to 5 (*completely suitable*). Once again, assuming a continuum along this Likert scale, the mean ratings and the corresponding standard deviations for both male and female managers were calculated. The results are shown in Table 9.

Table 9. Degree to which ICT training meets the training needs of the firms in this sector

Training provider	Male managers	Female managers
University of Extremadura - Mean - Standard deviation	2.218 1.391	2.078 1.418
Difference of means: 1.140; t-test: 0.767; equality of variances: Y; df = 236; significance = 0.444		
Vocational training - Mean - Standard deviation	2.236 1.368	2.094 1.389
Difference of means: 0.142; t-test: 0.795; equality of variances: Y; df = 236; significance = 0.427		
School of Hospitality and Agrotourism of Extremadura - Mean - Standard deviation	2.318 1.401	2.258 1.353
Difference of means: 0.060; t-test: 0.338; equality of variances: Y; df = 236; significance = 0.736		
Private - Mean - Standard deviation	2.255 1.449	2.352 1.499
Difference of means: -0.097; t-test: -0.506; equality of variances: Y; df = 236; significance = 0.614		

If "x_+3"

Public employment service of Extremadura (SEXPE) - Mean - Standard deviation	1.818 1.396	1.938 1.344
Difference of means: -0.120; t-test: -0.671; equality of variances: Y; df = 236; significance = 0.503		
Other - Mean - Standard deviation	2.027 1.384	2.117 1.525
Difference of means: -0.090; t-test: -0.472; equality of variances: Y; df = 236; significance = 0.637		

Source: Authors.

In general, the managers did not report that the ICT training supply in the region meets the needs of the sector, with mean scores ranging from 1.8 to 2.3 points. Nevertheless, the training providers with the highest scores in terms of suitability were the School of Hospitality and Agrotourism of Extremadura (2.318 for men; 2.258 for women) and private training providers (2.255 for men; 2.352 for women). According to the managers, The Extremadura Public Employment Service (SEXPE) had the training offering that was by far the least well suited to the demands of the sector in terms of skills acquisition (1.818 for male managers; 1.938 for female managers). Finally, the gender analysis of these scores based on *t*-tests reveals no significant differences between the opinions of male and female managers.

In conclusion the results generally do not provide support for the hypotheses. With the exception of satisfaction with the training received by managers and the preference for certain training organisations, the statistical evidence indicates that there are no differences according to the manager's gender in the analysed variables relating to the ICT training of employees and managers.

A possible explanation for this finding may relate to the study context, given that most of the managers in the sample had a high level of education that was very similar across the two genders (e.g. 46.4% of men and 46.8% of women were university graduates). In Spain and Extremadura, more than half of university graduates are women (54% across Spain and 55% in Extremadura in 2021). Although the percentage of women graduates in STEM degrees is lower in both cases, it is higher in Extremadura than across Spain and has increased in recent years, reaching 41% in 2021 (Spanish Ministry of Education and Professional Training, 2022). Consequently, the STEM education of women in the region has improved, which may imply that they perform to the same level as men in terms of ICT training. This lack of difference in performance is the result of eliminating one of the biggest barriers impeding women's relationship with technology, namely a lack of education, as noted by several authors (Best & Maier, 2007; Novo-Corti et al., 2014).

Hence, there were no significant inequalities between women and men that meant that women would have less access to ICTs and therefore a negative predisposition towards technologies, as shown in previous studies (Best & Maier, 2007; Venkatesh et al., 2000). Likewise, this similarity in the educational level of managers, the characteristics of the sector and the geographical context (i.e. an emerging, uncompetitive market) might have meant that male and female managers' perceptions of ICT training needs were similar in the analysed companies. Ultimately, this situation would condition the importance they attach to such training, as reflected in the very similar results with respect to the training activities offered (see Table 4).

CONCLUSION, LIMITATIONS, AND FUTURE LINES OF RESEARCH

This study presents an analysis of 238 tourism companies in Extremadura. Data on these companies were obtained from a survey and were analysed using statistical inference in order to meet the research aims. Specifically, the study aimed to establish whether, depending on the manager's gender, there are differences in terms of a company's commitment to ICT training, both in general and in specific training areas. The study also aimed to determine whether there are differences between male-led companies and those led by women regarding satisfaction with ICT training, preferences in terms of training providers and perceptions of the degree to which ICT training supply meets demand in the region of interest.

According to the results, two out of three tourist accommodation companies in the region of Extremadura did not provide any ICT training in the last two years. Moreover, of the companies that did offer such training, the managers were the main recipients. Therefore, the analysis implies that most tourist lodgings in Extremadura have a low commitment to ICT training. Also, the ICT training activities focused mainly on social media management and web positioning. Training on database management, cloud storage and mobile applications was provided to a lesser extent.

Nevertheless, there are no statistically significant differences in commitment to ICT training between companies managed by men and women. Hence, it is not possible to affirm the existence of a gender gap in terms of the commitment to ICT training of managers in Extremadura. This finding can be explained by the similar level of university education of male and female managers in Extremadura. There has also been an increase in STEM degree education among women in the region.

By contrast, in the degree of satisfaction with ICT training, there are statistically significant differences between managers based on gender. Specifically, female managers are more satisfied than their male counterparts. One possible reason for this finding may derive from differences in the decisions regarding the organisations that provide the training. Companies managed by women mainly use training providers that are not tourism training leaders in this region, whereas organisations managed by men tend towards private training. Likewise, the accommodation companies led by women did not use training provided by the School of Hospitality and Agrotourism of Extremadura, which clearly focuses on employees in the sector. In contrast, 5.6% of companies with a male leader took some kind of ICT training there. Finally, the University of Extremadura was used by only 2.1% of the companies managed by women and 5.6% of the companies managed by men.

Consequently, the results are highly relevant for managers of tourism companies, public administrations, ICT training providers and academics. Notably, they reveal the extent of what remains to be achieved in terms of training in this area in organisations that make up a key sector for the regional economy. The results provide insight into what lines of action should be taken in the future to enhance the competitiveness of tourism in Extremadura. These results show the need to investigate the reasons for the lack of commitment to ICT training despite its importance for the development of the sector in the current environment. The goal is to enable the regional government to adopt measures to promote such training in the near future. Moreover, for the managers of these companies, the conclusions highlight the importance of guaranteeing optimal ICT training for all members of the company. These technologies will only be exploited effectively if all members of the company can competently use ICTs. Moreover, sustained competitive advantages will only be created through the optimal use of technological resources.

Those who offer ICT training to tourism companies in Extremadura must take measures to respond to the dissatisfaction of companies in the sector regarding the quality of this training, as reflected by the low degree to which the managers of these companies perceive that the ICT training supply meets the demand for ICT skills. A notable finding is the rating of SEXPE's training offering. Although, amongst its other functions, this organisation implements action plans for labour integration and employment support, its training offering is reportedly the worst suited to the ICT needs of the tourism sector in Extremadura. Finally, this study is of great interest for academics because it shows the need for further investigation into the possible factors that condition ICT training by companies. Research into such factors offers an essential way to provide companies with the tools they need to survive and develop in a highly dynamic context such as the current one. However, this line of research is virtually non-existent.

Despite the relevance of this study, it is worth mentioning its limitations. First, this study was carried out in a region with very specific characteristics. Therefore, the results can only be reliably extrapolated to similar destinations. Second, only the manager's gender was analysed as a key factor in companies' commitment to ICT training. However, there may be other key factors in relation to this type of training. For example, the profile of the recipients of this training, in terms of characteristics such as age or type of contract with the company, may condition the company's investment in their training. The return on investment in training will be greater if employees are younger and their contract is indefinite because permanent employees are considered to be more committed to the company and more capable of using their knowledge. Therefore, as a future line of research, it may be of interest to extend this study to other similar contexts to test the results reported here. Likewise, it would be of interest to perform an in-depth study of the influence of these personal characteristics on companies' implementation of ICT training.

REFERENCES

Akther, S., & Rahman, M. S. (2021). Investigating training effectiveness of public and private banks employees in this digital age: An empirical study. *International Journal of Manpower*, *42*(3), 542–568. doi:10.1108/IJM-04-2021-0240

Alonso-Almeida, M. M., & Llach, J. (2013). Adoption and use of technology in small business environments. *Service Industries Journal, 33*(15–16), 1456–1472. doi:10.1080/02642069.2011.634904

Amin, M. H., Mohamed, E. K. A., & Elragal, A. (2020). Corporate disclosure via social media: A data science approach. *Online Information Review, 44*(1), 278–298. doi:10.1108/OIR-03-2019-0084

Anser, M. K., Yousaf, Z., Usman, M., & Yousaf, S. (2020). Towards strategic business performance of the hospitality sector: Nexus of ICT, e-marketing and organizational readiness. *Sustainability (Basel), 12*(4), 1346. doi:10.3390/su12041346

Ardito, L., Dangelico, R. M., & Messeni Petruzzelli, A. (2021). The link between female representation in the boards of directors and corporate social responsibility: Evidence from B corps. *Corporate Social Responsibility and Environmental Management, 28*(2), 704–720. doi:10.1002/csr.2082

Ayman, A., El-Helaly, M., & Shehata, N. (2019). Board diversity and earnings news dissemination on Twitter in the UK. *The Journal of Management and Governance, 23*(3), 715–734. doi:10.1007/s10997-018-9441-9

Bampton, R., & Maclagan, P. (2009). Does a 'care orientation' explain gender differences in ethical decision making? A critical analysis and fresh findings. *Business Ethics (Oxford, England), 18*(2), 179–191. doi:10.1111/j.1467-8608.2009.01556.x

Bass, B. (1998). *Transformational leadership: Industrial, military, and educational impact*. Lawrence Erlbaum Associates.

Basuony, M. A. K., Mohamed, E. K. A., & Samaha, K. (2018). Board structure and corporate disclosure via social media: An empirical study in the UK. *Online Information Review, 42*(5), 595–614. doi:10.1108/OIR-01-2017-0013

Becker, G. S. (1964). *Human capital: A theoretical and empirical analysis, with special reference to education*. University of Chicago Press.

Beji, R., Yousfi, O., Loukil, N., & Omri, A. (2020). Board diversity and Corporate Social Responsibility: Empirical evidence from France. *Journal of Business Ethics, 173*(1), 133–155. doi:10.1007/s10551-020-04522-4

Bernardi, R., & Threadgill, V. (2010). Women directors and corporate social responsibility. *Electronic Journal of Business Ethics and Organizational Studies, 15*(2), 15–21.

Bernardi, R. A., Bosco, S. M., & Vassill, K. M. (2006). Does female representation on boards of directors associate with Fortune's "100 best companies to work for" list? *Business & Society*, *45*(2), 235–248. doi:10.1177/0007650305283332

Best, M. L., & Maier, S. (2007). Gender, culture and ICT use in rural South India. *Gender, Technology and Development*, *11*(2), 137–155. doi:10.1177/097185240701100201

Beutel, A. M., & Marini, M. M. (1995). Gender and values. *American Sociological Review*, *60*(3), 436–448. doi:10.2307/2096423

Cheng, C., & Piccoli, G. (2002). Web-based training in the hospitality industry: A conceptual definition, taxonomy, and preliminary investigation. *International Journal of Hospitality Information Technology*, *2*(2), 19–33. doi:10.3727/153373402803617737

Chodorow, N. (1978). Mothering, object-relations, and the female oedipal configuration. *Feminist Studies*, *4*(1), 137–158. doi:10.2307/3177630

Collins, C., Buhalis, D., & Peters, M. (2003). Enhancing SMTEs' business performance through the Internet and e-learning platforms. *Education + Training*, *45*(8/9), 483–494. doi:10.1108/00400910310508874

Cook, A., & Glass, C. (2018). Women on corporate boards: Do they advance corporate social responsibility? *Human Relations*, *71*(7), 897–924. doi:10.1177/0018726717729207

Cordeiro, J. J., Profumo, G., & Tutore, I. (2020). Board gender diversity and corporate environmental performance: The moderating role of family and dual-class majority ownership structures. *Business Strategy and the Environment*, *29*(3), 1127–1144. doi:10.1002/bse.2421

Cristobal-Fransi, E., Daries, N., Martin-Fuentes, E., & Montegut-Salla, Y. (2020). Industrial heritage 2.0: Internet presence and development of the electronic commerce of industrial tourism. *Sustainability (Basel)*, *12*(15), 5965. doi:10.3390/su12155965

Croson, R., & Gneezy, U. (2009). Gender differences in preferences. *Journal of Economic Literature*, *47*(2), 448–474. doi:10.1257/jel.47.2.448

Cruz, C., Justo, R., Larraza-Kintana, M., & Garcés-Galdeano, L. (2019). When do women make a better table? Examining the influence of women directors on family firm's corporate social performance. *Entrepreneurship Theory and Practice*, *43*(2), 282–301. doi:10.1177/1042258718796080

Cumming, D., Leung, T. Y., & Rui, O. (2015). Gender diversity and securities fraud. *Academy of Management Journal*, *58*(5), 1572–1593. doi:10.5465/amj.2013.0750

Dadanlar, H. H., & Abebe, M. A. (2020). Female CEO leadership and the likelihood of corporate diversity misconduct: Evidence from S&P 500 firms. *Journal of Business Research*, *118*, 398–405. doi:10.1016/j.jbusres.2020.07.011

Dawson, L. M. (1997). Ethical differences between men and women in the sales profession. *Journal of Business Ethics*, *16*(11), 1143–1152. doi:10.1023/A:1005721916646

De la Fuente, Á., Ciccone, A., & Doménech, R. (2004). *La rentabilidad privada y social de la educación: un panorama y resultados para la UE*. Fundación Caixa Galicia, Centro de Investigación Económica y Financiera.

Dearden, L., Reed, H., & Van Reenen, J. (2006). The impact of training on productivity and wages: Evidence from British panel data*. *Oxford Bulletin of Economics and Statistics*, *68*(4), 397–421. doi:10.1111/j.1468-0084.2006.00170.x

Duffus-Miranda, D., & Briley, D. (2021). Turista digital: Variables que definen su comportamiento de compra. *Investigaciones Turísticas*, *21*(21), 1–21. doi:10.14198/INTURI2021.21.1

Eagly, A. H., Johannesen-Schmidt, M. C., & Van Engen, M. L. (2003). Transformational, transactional, and laissez-faire leadership styles: A meta-analysis comparing women and men. *Psychological Bulletin*, *129*(4), 569–591. doi:10.1037/0033-2909.129.4.569

Eagly, A. H., & Johnson, B. T. (1990). Gender and leadership style: A meta-analysis. *Psychological Bulletin*, *108*(2), 233–256. doi:10.1037/0033-2909.108.2.233

Ely, R. J. (1995). The power in demography: Women's social constructions of gender identity at work. *Academy of Management Journal*, *38*(3), 589–634. doi:10.2307/256740

Feng, X., Groh, A., & Wang, Y. (2020). Board diversity and CSR. *Global Finance Journal*, *100578*(October), 100578. doi:10.1016/j.gfj.2020.100578

Garbin-Praničević, D., & Mandić, A. (2020). ICTs in the hospitality industry. *Tourism (Zagreb)*, *68*(2), 221–234. doi:10.37741/t.68.2.9

Hambrick, D. C., & Mason, P. A. (1984). Upper echelons: The organization as a reflection of its top managers. *Academy of Management Review*, *9*(2), 193–206. doi:10.2307/258434

Hannoon, A., Abdalla, Y. A., Musleh Al-Sartawi, A. M. A., & Khalid, A. A. (2021). Board of directors composition and social media financial disclosure: the case of the United Arab Emirates. In *The big data-driven digital economy: Artificial and computational intelligence* (pp. 229–241). Springer. doi:10.1007/978-3-030-73057-4_18

Hazarika, M., & Chakraborty, J. (2019). Women in Local E-Governance. *Proceedings of the 12th International Conference on Theory and Practice of Electronic Governance*, (pp. 457–460). ACM. 10.1145/3326365.3326425

Hilbert, M. (2011). Digital gender divide or technologically empowered women in developing countries? A typical case of lies, damned lies, and statistics. *Women's Studies International Forum, 34*(6), 479–489. doi:10.1016/j.wsif.2011.07.001

Jaworski, C., Ravichandran, S., Karpinski, A. C., & Singh, S. (2018). The effects of training satisfaction, employee benefits, and incentives on part-time employees' commitment. *International Journal of Hospitality Management, 74*, 1–12. https://www.educarex.es/pub/cont/com/0004/documentos/Programa_Operativo_Fondo_Social_Extremadura_2014_2020-1.pdf. doi:10.1016/j.ijhm.2018.02.011

Junta de Extremadura. (2017). *Plan turístico de Extremadura 2017-2020*. Turismo Extremadure. https://www.turismoextremadura.com/viajar/shared/documentacion/publicaciones/PlanTuristicoExtremadura2017_2020.pdf

Junta de Extremadura. (2023). *Programa Operativo en el marco del objetivo de inversión en crecimiento y empleo*. Junta de Extremadura. https://www.juntaex.es/documents/77055/1158713/Programme_2014ES05SFOP016_9_1_es.pdf/fcc13324-df36-896d-4e6f-b455fec55e33?t=1676359990908

Kasa, M., Kho, J., Yong, D., Hussain, K., & Lau, P. (2020). Competently skilled human capital through education for the hospitality and tourism industry. *Worldwide Hospitality and Tourism Themes, 12*(2), 175–184. doi:10.1108/WHATT-12-2019-0081

Kelan, E. K. (2007). Tools and toys: Communicating gendered positions towards technology. *Information Communication and Society, 10*(3), 358–383. doi:10.1080/13691180701409960

Krishnan, H. A., & Park, D. (2005). A few good women—On top management teams. *Journal of Business Research, 58*(12), 1712–1720. doi:10.1016/j.jbusres.2004.09.003

Kuo, T. H., Ho, L. A., Lin, C., & Lai, K. K. (2010). Employee empowerment in a technology advanced work environment. *Industrial Management & Data Systems, 110*(1), 24–42. doi:10.1108/02635571011008380

Kwami, J. D. (2015). Gender, entrepreneurship, and informal markets in Africa: Understanding how Ghanaian women traders self-organize with digital tools. In J. D. Kwami (Ed.), *Comparative Case Studies on Entrepreneurship in Developed and Developing Countries*. IGI Global. doi:10.4018/978-1-4666-7533-9.ch002

Laroche, M., Mérette, M., Ruggeri, G. C., Laroche, M., Mérette, M., & Ruggeri, G. C. (1999). On the concept and dimension of human capital in a knowledge-based. *Canadian Public Policy*, *25*(1), 87–100. https://econpapers.repec.org/RePEc:cpp:issued:v:25:y:1999:i:1:p:87-100. doi:10.2307/3551403

Li, J., Zhang, Y., Chen, S., Jiang, W., Wen, S., & Hu, Y. (2018). Demographic diversity on boards and employer/employee relationship. *Employee Relations*, *40*(2), 298–312. doi:10.1108/ER-07-2016-0133

Liu, C. (2021). CEO gender and employee relations: Evidence from labor lawsuits. *Journal of Banking & Finance*, *128*, 106136. doi:10.1016/j.jbankfin.2021.106136

Ma, W., Grafton, R. Q., & Renwick, A. (2020). Smartphone use and income growth in rural China: Empirical results and policy implications. *Electronic Commerce Research*, *20*(4), 713–736. doi:10.1007/s10660-018-9323-x

Mack, E. A., Marie-Pierre, L., & Redican, K. (2017). Entrepreneurs' use of internet and social media applications. *Telecommunications Policy*, *41*(2), 120–139. doi:10.1016/j.telpol.2016.12.001

Mallin, C. A., & Michelon, G. (2011). Board reputation attributes and corporate social performance: An empirical investigation of the US Best Corporate Citizens. *Accounting and Business Research*, *41*(2), 119–144. doi:10.1080/00014788.2011.550740

Mulauzi, F., & Albright, K. S. (2009). Information and Communication Technologies (ICTs) and development information for professional women in Zambia. *International Journal of Technology Management*, *45*(1/2), 177–195. doi:10.1504/IJTM.2009.021527

Nadeem, M., Bahadar, S., Gull, A. A., & Iqbal, U. (2020). Are women eco-friendly? Board gender diversity and environmental innovation. *Business Strategy and the Environment*, *29*(8), 3146–3161. doi:10.1002/bse.2563

Nel, G., Scholtz, H., & Engelbrecht, W. (2020). Relationship between online corporate governance and transparency disclosures and board composition: Evidence from JSE listed companies. *Journal of African Business*. doi:10.1080/15228916.2020.1838831

Nicolò, G., Sannino, G., & De Iorio, S. (2021). Gender diversity and online intellectual capital disclosure: Evidence from Italian-listed firms. *Journal of Public Affairs*, *2706*. doi:10.1002/pa.2706

Nord, J. H., Riggio, M. T., & Paliszkiewicz, J. (2017). Social and economic development through Information and Communications Technologies: Italy. *Journal of Computer Information Systems*, *57*(3), 278–285. doi:10.1080/08874417.2016.1213621

Novo-Corti, I., Varela-Candamio, L., & García-Álvarez, M. T. (2014). Breaking the walls of social exclusion of women rural by means of ICTs: The case of 'digital divides' in Galician. *Computers in Human Behavior*, *30*, 497–507. doi:10.1016/j.chb.2013.06.017

Pratto, F., Stallworth, L. M., & Sidanius, J. (1997). The gender gap: Differences in political attitudes and social dominance orientation. *British Journal of Social Psychology*, *36*(1), 49–68. doi:10.1111/j.2044-8309.1997.tb01118.x

Schultz, T. W. (1961). Investment in Human Capital. *The American Economic Review*, *51*(1), 1–17.

Schultz, T. W. (1993). The economic importance of human capital in modernization. *Education Economics*, *1*(1), 13–19. doi:10.1080/09645299300000003

Sharafizad, J. (2016). Women business owners' adoption of information and communication technology. *Journal of Systems and Information Technology*, *18*(4), 331–345. doi:10.1108/JSIT-07-2016-0048

Spanish Ministry of Education and Professional Training. (2022). *Educabase. Series históricas de estudiantes universitarios desde el curso 1985-1986*. Estadisticas. http://estadisticas.mecd.gob.es/EducaJaxiPx/Tabla.htm?path=/Universitaria/Alumnado/EEU_2022/Serie/GradoCiclo//l0/&file=HIS_Egr_GradCiclo_Rama_CA.px

Tran, T. Q. (2020). Identifying female leadership and performance in small and medium-sized enterprises in a transition economy: The case study of Vietnam. *Asian Economic and Financial Review*, *10*(2), 132–145. doi:10.18488/journal.aefr.2020.102.132.145

Ukpere, C. L., Slabbert, A. D., & Ukpere, W. I. (2014). The relevance of modern technology usage on the business ventures of Kenyan women entrepreneurs. *Mediterranean Journal of Social Sciences*, *5*(10). doi:10.5901/mjss.2014.v5n10p58

Uyar, A., Kilic, M., Koseoglu, M. A., Kuzey, C., & Karaman, A. S. (2020). The link among board characteristics, corporate social responsibility performance, and financial performance: Evidence from the hospitality and tourism industry. *Tourism Management Perspectives*, *35*(7), 100714. doi:10.1016/j.tmp.2020.100714

Varank, I. (2007). Effectiveness of quantitative skills, qualitative skills, and gender in determining computer skills and attitudes: A causal analysis. *The Clearing House: A Journal of Educational Strategies, Issues and Ideas*, *81*(2), 71–80. doi:10.3200/TCHS.81.2.71-80

Venkatesh, V., Morris, M. G., & Ackerman, P. L. (2000). A longitudinal field investigation of gender differences in individual technology adoption decision-making processes. *Organizational Behavior and Human Decision Processes*, *83*(1), 33–60. doi:10.1006/obhd.2000.2896

Walker, H. A., Ilari, B. C., McMahon, A. M., & Fennell, M. L. (1996). Gender, interaction, and leadership. *Social Psychology Quarterly*, *59*(3), 255–272. doi:10.2307/2787022

Williams, R. J. (2003). Women on corporate boards of directors and their influence on corporate philanthropy. *Journal of Business Ethics*, *42*(1), 1–10. doi:10.1023/A:1021626024014

Xie, J., Nozawa, W., & Managi, S. (2020). The role of women on boards in corporate environmental strategy and financial performance: A global outlook. *Corporate Social Responsibility and Environmental Management*, *27*(5), 2044–2059. doi:10.1002/csr.1945

Yammarino, F. J., & Bass, B. M. (1990). Long-term forecasting of transformational leadership and its effects among naval officers: Some preliminary findings. In K. E. Clark & M. R. Clark (Eds.), *Measures of leadership* (pp. 151–169). Center for Creative Leadership.

Yeo, B., & Grant, D. (2019). Exploring the effects of ICTs, workforce, and gender on capacity utilization. *Information Technology for Development*, *25*(1), 122–150. doi:10.1080/02681102.2017.1383876

Zhang, J. J., & Lee, S.-Y. T. (2007). A time series analysis of international ICT spillover. *Journal of Global Information Management*, *15*(4), 1–19. doi:10.4018/jgim.2007100104

Chapter 3
Analysis of the Strategies of the Nibco Company From Reynosa to Compensate Intellectual Capital During the COVID-19 Pandemic

María Blanca González Salazar
Tamaulipas Autonomous University, Mexico

Jaime Gerardo Malacara
Tamaulipas Autonomous University, Mexico

Olegario Méndez Cabrera
https://orcid.org/0000-0002-0126-4775
Tamaulipas Autonomous University, Mexico

Daniel Avila-Guzman
https://orcid.org/0009-0008-9547-7544
Tamaulipas Autonomous University, Mexico

ABSTRACT

An analysis of the strategies of the NIBCO Company of Reynosa to compensate intellectual capital during the Covid-19 pandemic is presented. The objective is to know what are the reasonings that led the company to implement compensation strategies in favor of its intellectual capital in response to the COVID-19 pandemic and its possible impacts on its productivity. A non-experimental, descriptive, and cross-sectional methodological design is used. Information collected through the method of interviews with managers and administrators of the same is analyzed. It is concluded that the company reacted favorably towards its intellectual capital, strengthening it through a scheme of additional compensation so that the staff can face greater financial and social security capacity, the effects of this new disease on health, and the disruption of daily forms and lifestyles.

INTRODUCTION

Over the last few years, the pandemic caused by Covid-19 has had great impacts on the various sectors of the life of the Mexican population. Since its appearance in the country during the month of February 2020, at which time the first case of contagion was detected, until the current moment, a multiplicity of effects have been documented. It should be noted that the most specific ones are directly related to what refers to the medical and health aspects, but there are also those related to lifestyle, social coexistence in various public spaces, during daily dynamics inside the home, in school education, economy, and finally in employment.

The last two aspects have widely notable implications, for disorganizing not only directly the individuals affected by the disease, but also by measurements that are imposed by the national government of Mexico and by local governments, in reference to the interruption of financial activities considered as non-essential and the so-called necessary isolation, which lies in not emerging from home. Associated with this, the interruption of airport operations that arise between countries and other logistics networks, deprived commercial operations.

The organizations of Mexico have had to confront what is an environment of uncertainty, because Covid-19 turned out to be a newfangled or perhaps an unknown disease that in an extremely hasty manner managed to become a pandemic and which, although certain vaccines have already emerged that have been applied, no real certainty is generated regarding when it will end creating an unfavorable impact related to society and the economy in general. In that period, organizations have had to make decisions that are dizzying and disruptive in order to guarantee their persistence in the market, especially if it is subject to the liquidity capacity.

Several of these decisions have been motivated mainly by the prevailing need to achieve the true survival of the various organizations, which have been to the detriment of each of the workers. They have also managed to include the partial closure of the various operations, thus reducing what accounts for the level of salaries demanded by employees, the correct cancellation of benefits that have not been considered in the law, the devaluation of the work plan, the temporary interruption of work, the instruction to carry out work at home, modifications in the line of business, the change of personnel for technology to minimize costs, among others.

There are very few organizations that have taken a direction opposite to that previously mentioned, by implementing or launching compensatory measures for the benefit of their workers, due to the various adverse health-related effects directly related to the Covid-19 pandemic, stability, and rising costs of living. One of these organizations is NIBCO, which is established specifically in Reynosa, Tamaulipas, which, in addition to the various benefits in money and in kind that it ordinarily provides to its staff for the work that is being earned, at the same time, it saw fit to achieve the generation and granting of an additional compensation scheme that results from the appearance of Covid-19.

Under this context, it is of great need to understand the various considerations subsequent to such business provisions that show that, in an increasingly complicated and insecure environment such as the one caused by the appearance of the Covid-19 pandemic, it is possible to pursue a business vision that allows the consolidation of its market approach, the care and motivation of intellectual capital, understood as the various intangible assets which maintain, over a long-term horizon, both benefits or profits, as well as the growth and market value of the organization.

Likewise, the description of the case of NIBCO and the various factors that make it viable for this organization, which forms an essential part of the maquiladora industry which is directly established on the northern border of Mexico with the United States, also has what relates to the financial and institutional capacity to be able to provide various improvements to its working team. As part of this, it is necessary to decipher whether such favorable measures are going to be expressed as a consequence of a broader motivation, of what amounts to growth in productivity and a real increase in what amounts to the market, and its solidity.

It can be said that one of the main organizations, previously referred to as NIBCO of Reynosa, Tamaulipas, has achieved both the design and the granting of a direct compensation package for its intellectual capital, in the event of the emergence of Covid-19. It is extremely common that in the literature referring to what business and entrepreneurship are, the approach is reached that the primary purpose of organizations is the acquisition of profits or, in other words, the appearance or increase in profitability. This is understood as the discrepancy between income and operating costs, also circumscribing other expenses that have been carried out to achieve what amounts to production in organizations and the correct and timely cancellation of taxes.

Under this idea, it symbolizes that companies matter because of what they produce and through the financial profitability of each of their products without affecting anything else. Despite this, such a vision manages to change in the literature as well as in what becomes practice, at the moment of introducing what becomes the conceptualization of intellectual capital, which imposes that companies are much more than finances, the various facilities as well as the various sales they carry out, being in the same way significant to what is the value generated by the various so-called intangible assets, such as knowledge, the innovation process, what is known as a accumulated experience, the various relationships that arise with multiple clients and suppliers, among others, as the true or only creators of what is known as long-term market sustainability wealth.

The sudden emergence of Covid-19 in Wuhan (China) at the end of 2019 shook all countries worldwide, immediately generating the emergence of broad challenges and obstacles in multiple spaces, among which the business, political, social, family, educational, and cultural aspects. In this, micro, small, medium, and large businesses endured great damage that in many cases turned out to be irreparable, and innumerable losses of people, temporary and permanent closures of jobs, among other consequences, impacting in a way that was never imagined.

Likewise, it should be noted that the survival of some organizations in the face of such an emerging situation because of the appearance of the pandemic depended significantly on their willingness and the correct capacity that allowed many of them to adapt to what were the various changes, also observing that none of these were adequately prepared to face this immense challenge. Despite all this, the intellectual capital that each of the companies had at that time continuously demonstrated that many were able to adapt in a remarkably rapid manner to the various changes that were generated and managed to remain broadly competitive within the markets in which they operated, although this has not been an easy task, they have known how to deal with this situation of global impact that represents the appearance and permanence of Covid-19.

For this reason, the various organizations in the search to achieve real permanence in the market managed to work to try to influence the behavior of individuals directly and effectively within their respective organizations, with the purpose of achieving the promotion of an environment capable of fostering higher levels of productivity. One of the main tools used for this was the various compensations for each of the workers. For this reason, Covid-19 emerged as a direct problem for companies, in which, through compensation, it was possible to achieve in many cases the inhibition of the various effects on their intellectual capital.

These companies have managed to recognize the imperative need for broad horizons of competitiveness, which can generate the institutional capacity to thus be able to adequately confront the various situations that occasionally disrupt both the corporate and business environment. The purpose of this is to achieve success in times such as those produced or generated by the appearance of the Covid-19 pandemic. Companies that have understood this can be considered first world, since years ago they managed to overcome the idea that, the more hours of work they perform, the better results they will achieve.

They know that what they demand is to monitor the human capital that makes production viable in various areas. For this reason, certain organizations achieved the timely establishment of certain direct compensations for each of their workers derived mainly from the impact they have suffered since the pandemic began. It is extremely important both to identify and to know such compensation strategies, which were implemented in favor of the direct care of the intellectual capital of companies.

As Gurría (2018) explains, the various Mexican organizations have, for the most part, the lowest levels of labor productivity in the Organization for Economic Cooperation and Development (OECD), in addition to being the country where each of the workers has dedicated what would be more hours to their workday per year. Therefore, it is necessary to better understand what would be the elements that can determine whether an organization can deteriorate or improve its various levels of productivity, thus considering human capital as a true point that is key to attention to generate and increase what would be the creation of value.

The various consequences of decision-making and the measures that various companies have been implementing, such as temporary closure, reduction or decline of wages and salaries, as well as layoffs, among others, to achieve in this way its survival in the face of the untimely arrival of the Covid-19 pandemic, are widely clear and have been visible in each of the evident effects on both the well-being and job stability of each of its workers. Hence, some of these consequences are withdrawal from the company, loss of motivation to work in the same company, fading of the bond that was established, and finally achieving a decrease in commitment to it, among others.

What is not so clear, and until this day scientific research has not been able to create adequate evidence, that serves as a true parameter or example of learning for other organizations, is what happens and what the effects of their care will be to protect and at the same time try to strengthen their intellectual capital, especially at times in which their well-being is notably threatened by certain factors that can be considered fulminating, being the specific case of the disease and the pandemic caused by the appearance of Covid-19. In this case, such a lack of knowledge, based on what has been the study of experiences that are real, is a truly emerging need when it comes to the business field.

For this reason, the various contributions of this research must serve as a basis to improve the practices carried out by companies in the region and the maquiladora industry. Likewise, with the arrival of the Covid-19 pandemic, the various business visions and business policies of most companies in Mexico could have been made explicit. In addition, some of the measures that were implemented to survive consisted mainly of reducing salaries, cutting staff, doing work at home, and reducing what would be working hours. This could have had an adverse effect on the economic income and also on the quality of life of the workers.

The above are some of the most common actions, various analyses, studies, and academic works dealt with the negative impact of the Covid-19 pandemic on the economy, companies, and employees. Examples of this are Esquivel (2020), Monroy-Gómez-Franco (2021), Hernández and Mar (2020), and Sánchez-Juárez and Aguilar (2020). For research purposes, the positive measures designed and implemented by Mexican companies have received little or no attention, perhaps because they are the least.

Despite this, other organizations took on the task of planning and implementing different strategies, in order to achieve an increase in productivity and competitiveness, as well as to strengthen their working capital. Likewise, Fierro et al (2021) achieved the recovery of some of these strategies, some of which were optimizing their business model and investment in technology. It is of great benefit to know these positive measures and what impact they can have on the company and, mostly, as an example of good business vision and successful business practices.

This research was carried out to identify and understand the impact that the intellectual capital of companies has had due to the appearance of the pandemic derived from Covid-19. Likewise, the result of the research has benefits for the company NIBCO of Reynosa, Tamaulipas, with the purpose to achieve extensive improvements in its various compensation strategies implemented and, in turn, increasing productivity in each one of their employees. With this study, it was also possible to visualize the beneficiaries, the employees, and the improvement in their quality of life and that of their families.

THEORETICAL FRAMEWORK

Intellectual Capital

Intellectual capital as a term was introduced by J. K. Galbraith in 1969. Since then, the conceptualization of intellectual capital has achieved great development in the literature. Despite this, its conceptualization is not yet a finished work. Likewise, the broadest meaning is that it refers to all the intangible assets of a company. Furthermore, it is understood as knowledge assets or as the set of intangible assets of a social, relational, and structural nature of the company. (García Parra, M.; Simo, P.; Sallan, J. M, 2006).

Furthermore, it is viable to understand that intellectual capital translates into intellectual material, knowledge, information, intellectual property, and experiences, which can be capable of creating value, that is, it translates into a brain force that is collectively the which is expressed by the knowledge, skills, values, and attitudes applied directly to business management. For their part, Sánchez et al (2007), while citing Stewart (1998), manage to propose that intellectual capital be properly understood as the aggregation of the diverse knowledge of the organization's employees that grants or provides a certain type of competitive advantage in a direct and timely manner.

Similarly, intellectual capital is the intellectual knowledge of the organization, the intangible information (which is not visible and therefore not collected anywhere) that it possesses and that can produce value. The concept of intellectual capital has been incorporated in recent years, both in the academic and business world, to define the set of non-material contributions that in the information age are understood as the main asset of companies of the third millennium. (Public Accounting, 2020)

For this reason, intellectual capital translates into an important resource and a key piece for an organization to achieve economic, social, and financial success. Becoming a true driver of intangible value in an organization, which thus generates future benefits within it. Furthermore, it becomes the cornerstone of competitive advantage due to its diverse capabilities and innovations.

According to Hernández (2021), referring to intellectual capital will suggest the union of the various capabilities and intangible assets that can be concentrated in a particular way in what becomes the delimited environment, which can be an organization, a public institution, or a university. Usually, the word was coined for private organizations, however, in recent years, this conception has been transposed to what becomes the public space, giving meaning to the concept of the knowledge society, as it is known today.

While Hernández (2021), who cites Stewart (1997), conceptualizes intellectual capital as the intellectual material, knowledge, information, intellectual property, and experience that may be able to be used to create value. In many cases, it is extremely difficult to identify it and even more difficult to distribute it in an effective way, but whoever manages to find it and subsequently exploit it, achieves success.

In this sense, the statement of intellectual capital provided directly by Sarur (2013) is taken as useful, who states that it is "...an asset which is not possible to identify in a physical way and is duly represented by the various worker skills, at any level of hierarchy or position; That is, what knowledge he has, what skills he has managed to develop and what attitudes he manages to reflect in what becomes his job performance, for the direct benefit of the organization. " (p. 39) Thus, for Sarur (2013) intellectual capital can be directly reflected in human capital, which is one of its main dimensions.

Measurement of Intellectual Capital and its Models

Throughout the process of developing intellectual capital as a notion and as a theory, numerous evaluation and measurement models have been established, although they aim to assess intellectual capital in organizations from various approaches or different perspectives, are used to explain how it can be conceived and clarified beyond theory. The various models identified, based on González and Rodríguez (2010), are as follows:

Balanced Business Scorecard by Kaplan and Norton (1992). The main purpose of this model will be the measurement of results through the implementation of financial and non-financial indicators. Thus proposing the presence of various types of intellectual capital, which are mainly clients, financial, internal business processes, and learning and growth. It uses various drivers and output indicators, as well as financial and non-financial indicators, as indicators for measuring intellectual capital. Among the various most important contributions of this model is the comprehensive vision of the various measurement systems for management. Its main limitation, mentioned in the literature, is its cause-effect simplicity;

T. Brooker Brooking (1996). This model is characterized by postulating that the market value of organizations is translated into the sum of the various tangible assets and intellectual capital. Among the main types of intellectual capital, market assets, intellectual property assets, assets focused directly on the individual (humans) and infrastructure assets are proposed. It uses certain qualitative indicators to measure it. Among its main central contributions is that the company's intellectual property is related to corporate objectives. To try to understand its limitations in this way, the following questions are raised: ¿What about the relationships between the blocks? What about temporal considerations? What about quantitative indicators?;

West Ontario Bontis (1996). Its purpose is the cause-effect relationships between elements of intellectual capital and between it and business results. The main types of intellectual capital in this model are human capital, structural capital, and client capital, which agrees with Stewart (1997). This model does not propose indicators, only relationships. Its principal contribution is that the human capital block is a significant clarifying factor for the rest of the elements. To understand the limitations we discuss, the following questions are conceived: What about the explanations of the interrelationships between the blocks, the time horizon, and the indicators.

Canadian Imperial Bank Saint-Onge (1996). This is a model for measuring intellectual capital that is responsible for knowing the relationship between intellectual capital and its correct measurement in organizational learning. The main types of intellectual capital that arise from time to time are financial, customer, structural, and human. This model does not use indicators. Its main contribution is that learning corresponds to knowledge. To reach the limitations, the following questions are conceived: What about the explanations of the interrelationships between the blocks? and the time horizon? and the indicators?

Intangible Assets Monitor Sveiby (1997). This measurement model differentiates between book value and market value. Among the types of intellectual capital, it includes the competence of collaborators, the internal component, and the external component. Working with three types of indicators that are growth, efficiency, and stability. Thus, providing a direct relationship between the blocks and the indicators. In this model the question is asked: What about the time horizon?

Navigator Skandia Edvinsson and Malone (1997). The measurement purpose of said model is the market value of the organization, which is duly integrated by financial capital and intellectual capital. The main types of intellectual capital include financial capital, customer capital, human capital, process capital, and renewal and development capital. Indicators are also proposed, and ratios are added to the traditional indicators, which are characterized by the fact that they evaluate both performance, speed, and quality. This model also considers the various time horizons. The center of the model previously mentioned is the human approach and its correct empirical application. Also proposing a greater and broader development of the various relationships between the blocks and the indicators.

Intelect Euroform (1998). Is a systematic model of analysis and proposal of a measurement model of intellectual capital. Consisting of human, structural, and relational types of intellectual capital. Manages indicators by blocks and by elements. Providing classification and measurement of intellectual capital, time horizon, stocks, and flows. Improves classification and has greater progress of measurement indicators;

Management by Competencies. Bueno (1998). Strategic management by competencies and intellectual capital is outlined as a purpose. Contrast between human, organizational, technological, and relational intellectual capital. It does not use any type of indicators. His various contributions are strategic vision and formulas. In the restrictions the following is consulted: And the time horizon? And the indicators?

Human Capital Ulrich, D. (1998). In this model, human capital becomes the main generator of intellectual capital. It uses competence and commitment as indicators. His contribution is the treatment in correspondence with the individual. Its identified restriction is that there is no presence of indicators.

The Value Explorer Toolkit. Andriessen and R. Tissen (2000). Translates into a model of fundamental competencies. Discrepancies between human, relational, and structural intellectual capital. In this model, there are no indicators and at the same time, it makes a true monetary valuation of intangibles. Among its main limitations are that it only takes into consideration the various fundamental competencies and that it is not adaptable to all organizations.

Nova Camisón et al (2000). Results in a dynamic model. It takes into consideration all stocks and flows. Its classification of intellectual capital includes human, organizational, social, and innovation and learning capital. Using indicators by blocks and groups. In their contributions, it is admitted that calculating the variation of intellectual capital in two periods of time determines the effect of each block in the remaining ones. Among its limitations is a greater difficulty in its empirical validation.

ICBS Viedma (2000). Is a dynamic model which takes into consideration both the competencies and the fundamental activities. Both operations and innovation are included in its intellectual capital classification. It is measured through ratios and benchmarking. It also provides a true strategic vision. Among its main limitations is its complexity and subjectivity.

Finally, the richness of intellectual capital measurement models lies in variation. Each model has a different purpose and meaning of intellectual capital. Likewise, its measurement method reflects a categorization, typology, or classification of intellectual capital that varies, which is reflected in the result of its measurement. No model is free of restrictions. On the contrary, the contributions of each model allow us to form adjustments and form the best of each one. The Human Capital model stands out significantly, Ulrich, D. (1998), as he reflects that human capital is the creator of intellectual capital.

Motivation Theories

During the 1950s, the true development of the various conceptualizations of motivation was achieved. At this time, various theories arose to try to generate a true explanation of its definition and to achieve a contribution of understanding to this particular topic. These theories are Maslow's, content's, and Alderfer's. They are described below:

Maslow's theory. Cited in Huilcapi-Masacon et al (2017), Abraham Maslow established a series of needs experienced by the individual, giving rise to the so-called "pyramid of needs". According to this theory, the satisfaction of needs found at a certain level lead to the next hierarchy. However, there are areas of coincidence between one level and another since there is no complete satisfaction of needs.

Maslow initially indicated five levels of needs and classified them in order of importance. At the base of the pyramid are the basic or primary needs and at the top are the psychological or secondary needs. When vital needs have been met, it is the desires of each individual that will establish the order of needs and may even modify the hierarchy over time. The needs identified by Maslow are:

Basic needs. They are at the first level and their satisfaction is necessary to survive. They are hunger, thirst, clothing, etc.

Security needs. They are located on the second level, they are security and physical protection, order, and stability.

Social or belonging needs. They are related to social contacts and economic life. They are needs of belonging to groups, and organizations.

Status and prestige needs. Satisfaction occurs when the initiative, autonomy, and responsibility of the individual increases. They are needs for respect, prestige, admiration, and power.

Self-actualization needs. They arise from the need to achieve the value system of each individual, that is, to achieve their highest personal aspirations. (s/a, 2021);

Content theory. Motivational theories can be divided between those of content and those of process. The former study and consider aspects that can motivate people, while the latter study and take into account the thought process by which they are motivated.

Within the content motivation theories, we can mention those of Maslow, Alderfer, McClelland, Herzberg, and McGregor (Theory X and Y). However, in this research, only those of Maslow, Alderfer, McClelland, and Herzberg are analyzed, since they focus on determining human needs based on predetermined typologies. This does not happen with theory X and Y where the number of dimensions to be obtained is not known. (Farías Jesús Eduardo, Contreras Mendoza Margarita, 21);

Alderfer's theory. Some authors point out that the typology of needs proposed by being is not based on new elements but is based on Maslow's theory. Even though this is correct, it can be argued that he makes some criticisms of Maslow's theory, which leads to his work being differentiated in 3 aspects:

First of all, reduce Maslow's 5 needs to only 3 of these needs, which are: existence (need for physical well-being), relationship (interpersonal relationships), and growth (personal development and growth).

Secondly, Alderfer argues that in the emergence of a new need, it is not essential that the lower ones have been sufficiently satisfied; and

Thirdly, this author found that the movement of the hierarchy of needs is not only ascending, since people can go back in the hierarchy with the aim to satisfy an already satisfied need.

Herzberg dual factor. Through surveys that investigated people's satisfaction in their jobs, it was determined that well-being is related to personal stimulation, recognition, achievements, and self-realization, called motivating factors. Hygienic factors, which refer to the environment where the worker does his or her work, and the conditions and policies of the organization, influence his or her state of mind. The worker desires autonomy, feedback, and a work environment of primary stimuli.

McClelland's three factors. This theory maintains that people have three characteristics that motivate them toward their goals: achievement, power, and affiliation.

McGregor's Theory X and Theory Y. Under the assumption that one of the characteristics of people is laziness at work, he explains that Theory X in motivation is achieved through controls and punishments, and Theory Y overvalues effort and commitment as motivators.

Expectations theory. Focuses on knowing what the person is looking for within the organization and the way in which they will try to achieve it, because the degree of motivation is determined by what they believe is valuable for them in the goals and incentives.

Goal Setting by Edwin Locke. The value of goals is based on the drive you give them to achieve through: having more attention to your task; mobilizing energy and effort; increasing persistence and helping strategize; and

Stacey Adams Equity. Working motivated and receiving recognition benefits the organization (Consultores, 2021).

Work Motivation

Motivation can be specified in different ways because each individual manages to respond to various stimuli based on their personal situation. As stated by Velaz Rivas (1996), motivation contains numerous meanings, is open to more than one interpretation, and has usually been used to relate to the force of the tendency that promotes behavior, considering not only internal factors but also appropriate external factors.

Therefore, motivation is something that can help any individual stay in action, achieve the necessary processes, and implement the relevant actions to carry out an achievement, objective or satisfy a certain need. For Peña and Villon (2017) motivation is "…the need or desire that activates and directs our behavior, that directs it and underlies any tendency for survival." (p. 179) Motivation keeps people moving and drives them to do more and behave better.

While, in the business field and, more specifically in the workplace, motivation is an essential ingredient for success. It is known that companies that promote motivation and maintain it among their staff obtain better production and financial results. Motivating the people who make up a company, from managers, administrators, and even operators, becomes a positive influence that helps people carry out their tasks with greater assertiveness, security, and the ability to do well.

Hence, it is not only in actions but also in behavior and attitudes. Work motivation is the set of psychological processes that cause the initiation, direction, intensity, and persistence of a person's behavior. It can be stated that work motivation is understood as the internal energy that drives a person to work.

Productivity in Companies

With reference to productivity, it is a measure, according to (Galindo, 2015), of how efficiently work and capital are performed to produce economic value. High productivity implies that a lot of economic value can be produced with little work or capital. An increase in productivity implies that more can be produced with the same thing. In economic terms, productivity is all production growth that is not explained by increases in labor, capital, or any other intermediate input used to produce.

In addition, it can be said that the production factor that most affect productivity and that is commonly thought of is the application of a new production technology, that is, new, more efficient machines. But there are many other factors as important as technology that must be identified and evaluated. To organize everything that affects productivity in a more understandable way, it is very practical to consider the following classification:

Internal factors: all those included within the company and its production processes. They are not necessarily your own. We can mention Trust (Quintero et al. 2020) and Usefulness (Quintero et al 2022) may affect.

External factors: all those that are in the environment or context that surrounds the company and that are related to it.

Own factors: all those that belong to the company and are in direct relationship with the external context. They can be inside or outside the facilities.

Foreign factors: all those that do not have a direct relationship with the company and its environment. They are usually global and macro factors that affect the entire society.

It may seem that internal factors are the same as own factors, and that external factors are the same as foreign factors, but we will see that they are different. To understand it, you have to visualize the company as a system, a team, a tribe, a universe, a whole. In this way, it is understood that many factors are within the company and belong to it, but also that some are internal and are not its own. (Escobar, 2021).

Impact of the Covid-19 Pandemic on Companies

It can be said that the Covid-19 disease is not like other pandemics that humanity has experienced in the past. Since beyond the health, medical, and life repercussions, Covid-19 also became involved and had adverse effects on lifestyle, the forms of social coexistence that were customary, on the economy, and the employment. In these two areas, its impact was, in most cases, extremely devastating, with the complete closure of businesses, the total cessation of employment or the reduction of salaries, and the halting of value chains from beginning to end.

This has also generated, at the same time, an environment of broad uncertainty, in which companies, starting with their owners and managers, but having implications for all the people involved, including suppliers, employees, and customers, have had to rethink the ways of continuing producing and, therefore, to keep their businesses profitable and operating. Although, the hardest hit is the staff, who, at times, live from day to day waiting for weekly or biweekly payments to cover their daily living expenses.

In this scenario, it can be said that companies have had to make decisions that keep their businesses afloat. Some of these decisions have had to do with a short-term vision, in order to guarantee financial cash flow, such as affecting personnel, layoffs, temporary work suspension, salary reduction, reduction in time worked, and cutting benefits and compensations.

Despite this, another long-term vision, related to the future of the company in the post-pandemic stage, has led to decisions to keep the working conditions of its employees unaffected and grant them certain compensations that help them cope with the impact of the disease in their health, their lives and their homes. This is mostly possible in companies with a long operating life, with extensive operating experience, with extensive economic capacity, and that are seeking business permanence over a longer time horizon.

Likewise, the Survey on the Economic Impact Generated by COVID-19 on Companies, prepared by the National Institute of Geography and Statistics (INEGI), is of great relevance. To date, three surveys of this survey have been carried out. The first in April and the second in August, both in 2020. Likewise, the third survey was carried out in the month of February 2021. Among the main results is that 59.6% of companies implemented technical stoppages or temporary closures. Of these, 46.7% did so for 21 or more days.

Next, it is reported that 93.2% of companies had their businesses affected due to the Covid-19 pandemic. The effects are a decrease in income, a drop in demand, as well as a shortage of inputs and/or products. Additionally, some of the measures implemented by companies, according to the survey, are home delivery of orders, special promotions, work at home, online sales, emergency credit or financing, and offering new products or services.

Finally, among the main operational actions designed and carried out by companies are the deferral of payments for services, the transfer of cash, access to new credits, deferral of taxes, deferral of credit payments, loans with subsidized interest rates, tax exemptions or reductions and payroll subsidies.

RESEARCH FOCUS AND SCOPE

This research has a qualitative approach, as well as a descriptive and observational scope. We seek to know how the company NIBCO of Reynosa, Tamaulipas, which is part of the maquiladora industry installed on the northern border of Mexico with the United States, reacted in favor of its intellectual capital to the presence of the

Covid-19 disease, by designing and implement an additional compensation package delivered to its staff.

Likewise, the purpose is to try to understand the possible positive effects of these compensations on staff motivation and company productivity. In this sense, the expected results of this research have to do with knowing, from the context of the NIBCO company, as well as from the perceptions, ideas, and general and administrative decisions of the management and administrative staff of the company in Reynosa, Tamaulipas, what impacts or effects can be observed with the implementation of these compensations.

It is then considered that the contribution of this research is to investigate and reflect, from the light of the data and information obtained by the research methods described in this document, what is the origin of the decisions to create a package of compensations in favor of the intellectual capital of the company in an environment of uncertainty caused by the arrival and presence of the Covid-19 disease, how these compensations were defined, what was expected to be achieved with them and what is considered to be the result obtained afterwards of its application.

REFERENCES

Alama, E. M. (2008). *Capital intelectual y resultados empresariales en las empresas de servicios profesionales de españa*. EPrints. https://eprints.ucm.es/id/eprint/8709/1/T30356.pdf

Barrena-Martínez, J., López-Fernández, M., & Romero-Fernández, P. M. (2016). Efectos de las políticas de recursos humanos socialmente responsables en el capital intelectual. *Intangible Capital, 12*(2), 549-590. https://upcommons.upc.edu/bitstream/handle/2117/87880/Jesus%20Barrena-Mart%C3%ADnez.pdf?sequence=1&isAllowed=y

ConsultoresN. (2021). *Principales.* IDC Online/ https://idconline.mx/laboral/2012/10/04/principales-teorias-de-la-motivacion

Contaduría Pública. (2020). *Responsabilidad.* Contaduria Publica. https://contaduriapublica.org.mx/2020/04/01/responsabilidad-laboral-del-capital-intelectual-en-las-organizaciones/

Escobar, A. M. (2021). *42 Factores.* Webly.com. https://adrianamartinezescobar.weebly.com/42-factores-de-la-productividad.html

Farías, M. L. (2016). *La compensación por competencias y sus efectos sobre la motivación humana. VIII Congreso Internacional de Investigación y Práctica Profesional en Psicología XXIII Jornadas de Investigación XII Encuentro de Investigadores en Psicología del MERCOSUR*. Facultad de Psicología - Universidad de Buenos Aires, Buenos Aires, 2016. https://www.aacademica.org/000-044/356.pdf

Galindo, M. y. (2015). Productividad en serie de estudios económicos. *México ¿Cómo vamos?*, 2.

Garcia Parra, M., Simo, P., & Sallan, J. M. (2006). *Redalyc.org*. Obtenido de https://www.redalyc.org/pdf/549/54920301.pdf

INEGI. (2014). *Productividad total.* INEGI. http://internet.contenidos.inegi.org.mx/contenidos/productos//prod_serv/contenidos/espanol/bvinegi/productos/nueva_estruc/702825068103.pdf

INEGI. (2020). *Encuesta sobre el Impacto Económico Generado por COVID-19 en las Empresas.* INEGI. https://www.inegi.org.mx/programas/ecovidie/

Madrigal, B. E. (2009). Capital humano e intelectual: su evaluación. *Observatorio Laboral Revista Venezolana, 2*(3). https://www.redalyc.org/pdf/2190/219016838004.pdf

Medina-Quintero, J. M., Abrego-Almazán, D., & Ortiz-Rodríguez, F. (2018). Use and usefulness of the information systems measurement. a quality approach at the mexican northeastern region. *Cuadernos Americanos, 31*(56), 7–30. doi:10.11144/Javeriana.cao.31-56.ubwm

Peña, H. C., & Villón, S. G. (2017). Motivación Laboral. Elemento Fundamental en el Éxito Organizacional. *Revista Scientific, 3*(7), 177-192. http://www.indteca.com/ojs/index.php/Revista_Scientific/article/view/181

Quintero, J. M. M., Echeverría, O. R., & Rodríguez, F. O. (2022). Trust and information quality for the customer satisfaction and loyalty in e-Banking with the use of the mobile phone. *Contaduría y Administración, 67*(1), 283–304.

Reynosa, V. H. (2021). *Libro digital 2010.* Reysona. http://reynosaenelbicentenario.blogspot.com/

Sánchez, A. J., Melián, A., & Hormiga, E. (2007). El concepto de capital intelectual y sus dimensiones. *Investigaciones Europeas de Dirección y Economía de la Empresa, 13*(2), 97–111. https://www.redalyc.org/articulo.oa?id=274120280005

Sarur, M. S. (2013). La importancia del capital intelectual en las Organizaciones. *Ciencia Administrativa, 1*, 39-45. https://www.uv.mx/iiesca/files/2014/01/05CA201301.pdf

Teijeiro, M. M., García, M. T., & Mariz, R. M. (2010). *La gestión del capital humano en el marco de la teoría del capital intelectual.* Una guía de indicadores. https://dialnet.unirioja.es/servlet/articulo?codigo=3405054

Tinoco, C. E., & Soler, S. M. (2011). Aspectos generales del concepto "capital humano". *Criterio Libre, 9* (14), 203-226. https://dialnet.unirioja.es/servlet/articulo?codigo=3697483

Valencia, M. (2005). El capital humano, otro activo de su empresa. *Entramado, 1*(2). https://www.redalyc.org/pdf/2654/265420471004.pdf

Velaz Rivas, J. I. (1996). *Motivos y Motivación en la Empresa.* Madrid España: Diaz de los Santos.

Chapter 4
Physical Sciences Teachers Integrating Information and Communication Technologies in Education 4.0:
Exploring Enablers and Constraints

Colani Khoza
University of South Africa, South Africa

Leila Goosen
https://orcid.org/0000-0003-4948-2699
University of South Africa, South Africa

ABSTRACT

The purpose of the study reported on in this chapter is to evaluate how effectively physical sciences secondary school teachers are integrating information and communication technologies (ICTs) in the context of Education 4.0 and one of the northern districts in the city of Tshwane, Gauteng province, South Africa. Against the background of exploring intersectionality and women in science, technology, engineering and mathematics (STEM), the chapter will be exploring enablers and constraints in this regard.

DOI: 10.4018/979-8-3693-1119-6.ch004

INTRODUCTION

This section will describe the general perspective of the chapter and end by specifically stating the **aim and objectives**.

Exploring Intersectionality and Women in Science, Technology, Engineering, and Mathematics

Incorporating the gender perspective and its intersectionality in various areas of knowledge is necessary to determine inequalities, and social exclusions, among others, in addition to strengthening a transdisciplinary and diverse vision for incorporating more women in science. Women are an important asset for research, innovation, and the **future** of global development.

Physical Sciences Teachers Integrating Information and Communication Technology in Education 4.0: Exploring Enablers and Constraints

There is an increasing global call to adopt information and communication technologies (ICTs) in teaching and learning. ICTs have become so essential that the South African government has introduced the e-education policy (Chisango, Marongwe, Mtsi, & Matyedi, 2020). However, for several decades now, researchers in South Africa and elsewhere have continued to present evidence of low levels of learner achievement and underperformance, especially in science and mathematics subjects (Venkat & Mathews, 2019). These low levels of learner achievement are associated with the poor quality of teaching, which has not changed over a number of decades (Mlachila & Moeletsi, 2019). This phenomenon exists despite the integration of information and communication technologies in teaching and learning (Dixon, 2019; Tachie, 2019). The instability and inconsistency of teaching practices in classrooms are not unique to South Africa but have been observed (for decades) in other countries, as well (Mikeska, Holtzman, McCaffrey, Liu, & Shattuck, 2019). Consequently, there has been an upsurge in efforts, locally and internationally, which prioritize the search for strategies to improve the teaching of science subjects (among other subjects) in schools (Arends, Winnaar & Mosimege, 2017; Michos & Hernández-Leo, 2020). It is against this background that ICTs, due to their potential, have come to be a contender to improve the quality of teaching in science classrooms across the globe, including those in South Africa (Gui, Parma & Comi, 2018; Singh, Sharma & Kaur, 2020; Umugiraneza, Bansilal & North, 2018). However, Daya and Laher (2020) noted that what takes place in individual schools indicate that the ICT integration agenda in South Africa is yet to achieve satisfactory results holistically. Therefore, this proposed study seeks to evaluate the integration of ICTs by Physical Sciences teachers in secondary school contexts in South Africa. The investigation will also determine the ICT 'enablers' and 'constraints' Physical Sciences educators are confronted with.

Target Audience

Like that of the book that it proposes to form part of, the **target audience** of this chapter includes researchers, Science, Technology, Engineering and Mathematics (STEM) students and practitioners.

Recommended Topics

From the **recommended topics** suggested for this book, the chapter will focus especially on **Physical Sciences**, but will also discuss Mathematics, Life Sciences, Computer Science, and Health Sciences.

Aim and Objectives of the Study

Women and girls make up half of the world's population. However, structural disparities and lag are evident. According to the international journal article by Chauhan and Rai (2020, p. 9), studies had "shown that just 30 percent of the world's researchers are women because women in STEM fields are less into publication". Along with abridging the gender **gap** in intellectual property, and despite some positive changes, a gender gap in STEM persists around the world. This gap begins in education, fueled by gender stereotypes and expectations regarding women's work. As part of this book, the chapter aims to show women in STEM research advances.

As part of this book, the chapter also looks to reduce all gaps in digital access and skills, sharing knowledge of the unprivileged gender in the STEM world.

Various factors can explain gender gaps in science, including the reconciliation between private and professional life, promotion criteria, and institutional mechanisms, which are often not thought of from a gender perspective. The former deputy president of the Republic of South Africa, Mlambo-Ngcuka (2019, p. 25) lamented that women "are valued very low, and so is their work. … There is a pattern of discrimination against women that" all are expected to address, as everyone acts "to end all forms of discrimination against women."

The aim of the study is to evaluate how effectively Physical Sciences secondary school teachers are integrating information and communication technologies in Education 4.0 in Tshwane North district. The objectives for the study are to:

- determine the nature of ICT integration into the teaching and learning of Physical Sciences by teachers in Tshwane North district.
- examine the attitude of teachers towards the role of ICTs in the teaching and learning of Physical Sciences at secondary school level in Tshwane North district.
- determine the ICT tools, which are used by teachers in Physical Sciences in Tshwane North secondary schools.
- determine the enablers and constraints of integrating ICTs into the teaching and learning of Physical Sciences in Tshwane North secondary schools.

Now that the study discussed in this chapter had been introduced and the research **objectives** stated, the remainder of the chapter can be outlined as being organized as follows:

- The next section orients the reader by providing the **background** and context of the study by presenting reviews of both theoretical and empirical literature related to the study. An international and national perspective on the topic in question will be provided in this section of the chapter. The definitions of key terms will be provided as well.
- The following section will introduce the **problem** the study will focus on. This section of the chapter will provide the rationale for undertaking the research study, a discussion of the **problem** statement and **research questions**, as well as explaining and discussing the research methodology and research design, which will be adopted in the study. Ethical considerations will be described in detail. The **limitations** that may be encountered by the researcher will be indicated.
- Solutions and **recommendations** which may be applicable, are discussed next. Ultimately, the **recommendations** will be based on answers provided to the research questions.
- Suggestions related to **future research directions** will be provided.
- Finally, the chapter will end by providing the **conclusion**.

BACKGROUND

This section of the chapter will provide broad definitions and discussions of the topic on **Physical Sciences Teachers Integrating Information and Communication Technologies in Education 4.0** by **Exploring Enablers and Constraints** and incorporate the views of others (in the form of a literature review) into the discussion to support, refute, or demonstrate the authors' position on the topic.

In this section, the researchers will further review theoretical, conceptual and empirical literature in order locate the research project into a broader framework of relevant theory and research. The conceptual and theoretical approaches used by others in studying related topics will be reviewed. This will help the researcher to decide on an own conceptual/theoretical strategy and on how the proposed study may contribute to improvements in this regard.

Daya and Laher (2020, p. 159), in an Africa education review journal article, reported "on a study that used a quantitative, cross-sectional design" for exploring the influence of educators' access to and attitudes towards Educational Technologies (ET) "in understanding the use and integration of" ET in classrooms in Johannesburg schools.

Theoretical Perspective

This proposed study will be anchored in the use of the Unified Theory of Acceptance and Use of Technology (UTAUT), as a lens for conducting the investigation (Davis, Bagozzi, & Warshaw, 1989). The framework allows individuals to comprehend cognitive processors between the users and show how they respond to adopting and integrating the new piece of technology within their life. Nevertheless, in the context of the proposed study, the piece of technology denotes ICT tools and platforms integrated by Physical Sciences teachers in the classroom.

The theory proposed that teachers should be optimistic about using new technology in their teaching. At the same time, tracking the improvement gained through new technologies can help assess the feedback and the productivity rate. Studies on preservice teachers and teacher educators, respectively, found they have a diverse understanding of ICT use in their teaching and learning, while others expressed discontent on the use of technology (García, Aguaded, & Bartolomé, 2018). In this regard, the prospective user's perception of whether or not using a particular application system will enhance their performance within an organization is important.

A paper published in the proceedings of the South Africa International Conference on Educational Technologies (SAICET) by Goosen and Van Heerden (2017) showed how to go beyond the horizon of learning programming with educational technologies against the background of Computer Science (CS) education.

The article by Gui, et al. (2018, p. 141) in the context of policy and the Internet asked whether public investment in ICTs improve learning performance and provided "a detailed and robust estimate of the impact of three different digital technologies (interactive whiteboards, wireless connections, and mobile devices) on Italian language and mathematics performance in lower secondary schools".

MAIN FOCUS OF THE CHAPTER

Issues, Problems

This section of the chapter will present the authors' perspective on the **issues**, problems, etc., as these relate to the main theme of **Exploring Intersectionality and Women in STEM** and arguments supporting the authors' position on **Physical Sciences Teachers Integrating Information and Communication Technologies in Education 4.0** by **Exploring Enablers and Constraints**. It will also compare and contrast with what has been, or is currently being, done as it relates to the specific topic of the chapter. Recent/authoritative literature on the proposed research **problem** will also be analyzed and discussed.

The book on *Global Perspectives on the Strategic Role of Marketing Information Systems* edited by Medina-Quintero, Sahagun, Alfaro and Ortiz-Rodriguez (2023) indicated that a "level of decision making is concerned with deciding the organization's **objectives**, resources, and policies. A significant **problem** at this decision-making level is predicting" these.

A chapter in the latter book on trust in electronic banking with the use of cell phones for user satisfaction by Medina-Quintero, Ortiz-Rodriguez, Tiwari and Saenz (2023, p. 87) pointed out that mobile "technologies play a transcendental role in the development of organizations" and the banking industry had "become the world's economic engine".

The objective of the research reported on in the chapter by Ortiz, Tiwari, Amara and Sahagun (2023, p. 168) in the latter book was "to determine the critical success factors of a tax collector website in a country with an emerging economy. In" terms of the methodology, a questionnaire was applied to determine the extent of e-government success from an end-user perspective.

The chapter by Barrera, Martinez-Rodriguez, Tiwari and Barrera (2023, p. 118) in the latter book "addressed what smartphones, mobile applications, programming languages, and mobile operating systems are. The development, implementation, and results obtained" are related to a political marketing application ('app') based on citizens.

Davis, et al. (1989, p. 982), in their management science journal article, indicated that computer "systems cannot improve organizational performance if" these are not used. Unfortunately, user acceptance of computer technologies and "**resistance** to end-user systems by managers and professionals" remain **problems**. The latter authors therefore offered a comparison between two theoretical models.

The UTAUT theory proposes strong support for the effective use of technologies. The theory anticipated that technology applied during instructional practices should be learner-friendly, implying that there should be no difficulties during the integration process. In contrast, the theory contends that the teachers' age, awareness of technology use, behavioral intentions, facilitating conditions, and social **issues**, influence teachers' actual usage of technology in their teaching and learning. Similarly, the theory suggests that the institutional, technical, and physical infrastructures require backing from the prevailing technologies. This backing includes internet accessibility in the institution and teacher educators' knowledge on how to use the existing technologies for the advancement of the preservice teacher. In a nutshell, UTAUT is purposely chosen for the proposed study because it calls for a holistic understanding of the other variables affecting teacher educators' perceptions and practices on integrating ICT during Physical Sciences teaching and learning. However, the factors identified in this theory seem relevant to teacher educators when assessing their practices. Ultimately, the proposed study aims to evaluate Physical Sciences teachers' actual practices regarding ICT integration in the teaching and learning process in secondary schools.

Challenges and opportunities regarding usage of computers in the teaching and learning of Mathematics were discussed by Tachie (2019, p. S1) in a South African journal article on education. Many studies had "identified the fact that most mathematics teachers experience **challenges** in using" technologies "in their teaching, and learners also find it difficult to use" these when learning.

"The aim of the research described in" the Iberian journal article on information systems and technologies by Maestre Góngora, Colmenares Quintero and Stansfield (2020, p. 28) was "to at identify, classify, and explore the main concepts and their evolution related to smart technologies." The latter authors applied s systematic study approach towards mapping these concepts, as well as the **challenges** for smart technologies.

Using classroom observations to evaluate science teaching and the implications of lesson sampling for measuring science teaching effectiveness across lesson types were deliberated by Mikeska, et al. (2019, p. 123). "Despite the prevalent use of observational measures in teacher evaluation systems, research" had "only recently begun to take into account how aspects of the instructional environment and lesson sampling design may interact with teachers' scores on these measures."

A "Collective Inquiry with Data Analytics (CIDA) framework" was used by Michos and Hernández-Leo (2020, p. 4) in the context of computers and education to study and support teachers as designers in technological environments. According to Michos and Hernández-Leo (2020, p. 1), the "use of new technologies such as learning analytics by teachers is **challenging** due to the changes they bring to teachers' practices and their pedagogical interventions."

Statement of the Problem

The central **problem** of this study is that despite the critical role of ICT in sectors like banking, construction, transport and communication, it has not been fully adopted in the teaching and learning processes in most developing countries like South Africa. While there is a wide range of innovations in ICT to support effective and quality delivery of educational services, there is considerable lag in South African secondary schools. Evidence of low scientific achievement and underperformance among South African high school learners abounds in the literature (Jita & Munje, 2020). Although technology in education, particularly in the classroom environment, is significant, its application is too scarce in some contexts (Ngao, Sang, & Kihwele, 2022, p. 1). The study reported on in the education sciences journal article by the latter authors "explored the perceptions and practices of teacher educators" about understanding integrating information and communication technologies in teacher education programs. Mobile technologies had "increasingly been used in education for enhancing teaching and learning among students." Ngao, Sang, Tondeur, Kihwele and Chunga (2023, p. 18), in the context of digital education, "reviewed qualitative studies that focused on" transforming an initial teacher education program with mobile technologies to provide a synthesis of such qualitative evidence.

The advent of the Fourth Industrial Revolution provides meaningful opportunities for embracing pedagogic innovation as an integral part of digital transformation (Ramaila, 2021, p. 102). The study by the latter author "examined technology integration in Natural Sciences teaching and learning in South African township schools in the context of education and new developments. An international journal article on higher education by Ramaila and Molwele (2022, p. 14) considered the role of technology integration in the development of 21st century skills "and competencies through technology integration, technology integration in Life Sciences teaching and learning and **challenges** afflicting technology integration in science classrooms."

However, there is a crucial need to bridge the digital divide between under-resourced and well-resourced schools within the broader South African context. **Challenges** stifling meaningful integration of technology in teaching and learning include poor literacy of educators (Johnson, Jacovina, Russell, & Soto, 2016). **Challenges** and **solutions** when using technologies in the classroom were offered by the latter authors.

Meaningful information and communication technology integration in the classroom is hampered by a myriad of factors. These factors include a lack of time, a lack of clarity regarding the South African e-education policy (Department of Education, 2004), a lack of support both in terms of infrastructure and policy, a lack of skills and more focus on the technical aspects, as opposed to pedagogical and theoretical frameworks (Msila, 2015; Vandeyar, 2015). Teacher readiness and information and communications technology use in classrooms were tested by introducing digital technologies (Msila, 2015, p. 1973). More traditional learning materials "would be replaced by digital" technologies. A qualitative South African case study in the context of creative education by the latter author showed that the success of digital technologies in classrooms will depend on teachers' readiness. Utilizing "a case study approach and backward mapping principles to policy implementation," the study reported on by Vandeyar (2015, p. 344) in a British journal article on educational technologies "set out to explore how well district and" provinces' e-learning officials were equipped to act as policy intermediaries ind the reform of e-education in South Africa.

ICT integration in teaching and learning remains a key focus area across the globe. Many companies are investing in ICT infrastructure, equipment and professional development in order to improve teaching and learning in schools (Ramaila, 2021). The current belief is that ICT is an important catalyst and tool for encouraging educational reforms that transform learners into productive knowledge workers.

Technology is a powerful and flexible tool for learning as it has also become an important part of learners' lives beyond and within the classroom (Rabah, 2015, p. 14). A Turkish online journal article on educational technologies by the latter author "investigated teachers' and educational consultants' perceptions of ICT integration in Québec English" schools, specifically with regard "to the benefits and **challenges** of ICT integration" in these. In addition, Rabah (2015) further argued that the primary goal of educational technology within a pedagogical context is to facilitate the teaching and learning process.

There is a critical need to examine the complexity of **barriers** impeding ICT integration in teaching and learning with a view to foster pedagogic innovation within the broader South African context. Doff (2015) showed that e-learning devices have reached too high in developed countries language classes while they are in emerging phase in developing countries. Likewise, Shrestha (2018) pointed out that lack of teachers' confidence in ICTs and knowledge of using them is crucial **barrier**. Moreover, the study by Rana (2018) **concluded** that ICTs implementation in secondary education has a number of problems and the government strategies to overcome these problems are inadequate and potentially unsustainable. In one side, the world is being digitized and in the next side, teachers' motivation, skills, knowledge and attitudes are in question. Despite advancements made in teachers' ICT training, some teachers in South Africa and the Tshwane North district in particular, still find it difficult to integrate ICT tools.

The demand for teachers to integrate ICTs into their teaching has increased due to the ability of ICTs to enhance and improve the teaching and learning of various subjects, including Physical Sciences. Although this is the case, "the readiness of schools to effectively integrate ICT in the teaching and learning, and of teachers in terms of knowledge and skills has not been fully explored" (Ngeze, 2017, p. 424). It is for this reason that the researcher seeks to explore and describe the integration of ICTs by Physical Sciences teachers for the purpose of teaching and learning.

Research Questions

In terms of the rationale thus argued, this study is an attempt to answer the following main research question:

What are the enablers and constraints during the integration of information and communication technologies in education 4.0 by Physical Sciences teachers in Tshwane North district secondary schools?

The following secondary questions will be addressed in the study:

- What ICT tools are used in teaching Physical Sciences in Tshwane North secondary schools?
- What is the nature of ICT integration into the teaching and learning of Physical Sciences by teachers in Tshwane North district?
- What is the attitude of teachers towards the role of ICTs in the teaching and learning of Physical Sciences at secondary school level in Tshwane North district?
- What are the enablers and constraints when integrating ICTs into the teaching and learning of Physical Sciences in Tshwane North secondary schools?

Constraints and Enablers for Integrating Information Technologies when Teaching Physical Sciences

Teaching science through information and communication technologies: 'enablers' and 'constraints'

Jita and Munje (2020, p. 109) urged their readers "to pause and explore the **enablers and constraints** involved." An independent journal article on teaching and learning by the latter authors therefore focused on exploring the "**enablers and constraints** beginning teachers face in teaching science subjects".

The study by Ramaila (2022, p. 359) explored "the role of technology integration as a" means towards promoting self-regulated learning in natural sciences teaching through technology integration. "Key findings demonstrated that technology integration plays a" key role. According to Ramaila (2022), there has to be coherence among factors that affect the integration of technology in teaching and learning. These factors include teacher beliefs, knowledge and goals. Beliefs influence how teachers select and prioritize the goals of learning. In addition, beliefs influence teachers' perceptions of classroom interactions and their decisions about tools to be used in the process of learning. At another pragmatic level, access to technology determines whether teachers will employ technology in their classrooms or not (Farjon, Smits, & Voogt, 2019). Abdu (2018) mentioned that teachers are mainly responsible for the adaptation and implementation of information and communication technologies in the classrooms and if they cannot access these technologies due to poor infrastructure or lack of finances, they cannot create smart environments. Another challenge facing teachers in the educational quest for technology integration is lack of ICT competence (De Vera, Andrada, Bello, & De Vera, 2021). Teachers without technological knowledge find it increasingly challenging to address technological **problems** during teaching and learning. ICT competence is important as it allows teachers to devise and be creative enough in implementing technologies that are specific to their learning environments. Successful implementation of technology integration in the classrooms requires availability of digital tools in schools.

Integrating information and communication technologies in education provides a magical power of sustaining teaching and learning beyond unexpected interruptions. The enormous flow of information and use of technology emanated in all fields worldwide (Hennessy, et al., 2022). Studies have shown the significance of using ICT in teaching and persuading the vital essence of a deep personal understanding of ICT (Bai, Wang, & Chai, 2021).

Several Physical Sciences learners in secondary schools in Africa and South Africa in particular believed that it is difficult to comprehend some topics because teachers mostly use the conventional methods of teaching (Guido, 2013). Previous studies also reveal that learners had poor performance in Physical Sciences and other science subjects due to the continuous use of traditional methods of teaching (Agbele, Oyelade, & Oluwatuyi, 2020). Traditional strategies like demonstration, student-centered learning, **problem**-based learning and project-based learning have several benefits in the teaching and learning of Physical Sciences however they have not been found to be effective in improving knowledge acquisitions nor developing interest in learners (Ugwuanyi & Okeke, 2020). In tandem with that, research had indicated that the integration of information and communication technology into the Physical Sciences curriculum has the capability of simplifying the abstract content as well as creating interest in learners and consequently improving the quality of education (Ndihokubwayo, Uwamahoro, Ndayambaje, & Ralph, 2020).

Limitations and Delimitations of the Study

Limitations of a research study are factors that the researcher has no control over (Creswell, 2014). The study will be limited to Tshwane North secondary schools. Therefore, the findings will mostly be applicable and beneficial to the Tshwane North schools only. A quantitative methodology will be used. Therefore, it will not be possible to fully explore **issues** in-depth in order to get rich and thick insights on the phenomena in question. Including both quantitative and qualitative methodologies will enable greater insights to be gained.

Delimitations are the boundaries of the study which reflects aspects of the study which the researcher can control. Conceptually, the study will be confined to the aspect of the integration of ICTs in the teaching and learning of Physical Sciences. Geographically, the study will be confined to Tshwane North secondary schools. The target population will be managed and limited due to time and budgetary constraints. Only research respondents who meet the inclusion requirements of the study will be involved in the study.

RESEARCH METHODOLOGY AND DESIGN

Research methodology is an analytical approach to performing research. This section presents the research strategy that will be used for this investigation. The section includes a presentation of the research design, methodology, study site, target audience, sampling plan, and sample size. The section includes a chapter overview, data collection instruments, data analysis procedures, and measurements of validity and reliability.

Research Approach

The proposed study will adopt an exploratory and descriptive approach which will follow a quantitative design. The philosophical and theoretical standpoint in this research is informed by the pragmatic paradigm and social constructivist theory which aims to explore and describe the manner in which Physical Sciences teachers are integrating ICTs in Tshwane North district. For achieving the objective, exploratory and descriptive quantitative design will be used. In the proposed study, exploratory and descriptive designs will be triangulated. Exploratory research is used if a researcher wants to have a better understanding of a **problem** or phenomenon. Descriptive designs are used to explain and understand some phenomena by answering the questions how and what. The descriptive design will be attractive because it provides accurate data.

SOLUTIONS AND RECOMMENDATIONS

This section of the chapter will discuss **solutions and recommendations** in dealing with the **issues** or problems presented in the preceding section.

Solutions

In South Africa, ICT integration of ICT in the teaching of Physical Sciences is regarded as a tool to allow teachers to explain content in a more comprehensible way (Ramnarain & Moosa, 2017, p. 1). The latter "study investigated the use of interactive computer simulations in" correcting the "misconceptions held by Grade 10 South African learners on electric circuits."

Information and communication technologies have been integrated into Physical Sciences curriculum in both developing and developed countries (Wood & Blevins, 2019, p. 1). "Practical skills in science education, defined as those developed through the observation, demonstration, manipulation, and application of scientific principles," are valued even when substituting the practical teaching of physics with simulations for the assessment of practical skills as part of an experimental study.

However, there are few studies assessing the benefits of using educational software in teaching physical education and possibles challenges that teachers might face. Therefore, the proposed study will explore the benefits of ICT integration followed by **challenges** militating against the integration of ICT into Physical Science education and provide possible **solutions** for the successful integration of ICT into Physical Sciences education.

Clearly, it had been demonstrated that some of the benefits, **challenges**, and **solutions** related to ICTs applied in physics education include that these can assist to make Physical Sciences education less difficult, more applicable, connected to real life and authentic, as well as increasing opportunities for own investigations by the teachers and learners (Ellermeijer & Tran, 2019, p. 35).

Recommendations

There are several factors, which influence the integration of ICT in the teaching of Physical Sciences by teachers. Teachers have a crucial role to play in terms of the evaluation of and **recommendations** regarding the relevant kinds of technologies, as well as figuring out how best to use them to improve classroom teaching and learner performance. As such, teacher knowledge concerning ICT usage in the classroom is critical (Spangenberg & De Freitas, 2019).

FUTURE RESEARCH DIRECTIONS

This section of the chapter will discuss **future** and **emerging trends** and provide insight about the **future** of the theme of **Exploring Intersectionality and Women in STEM**, from the perspective of the chapter focus on **Physical Sciences Teachers**

Integrating Information and Communication Technologies in Education 4.0 by **Exploring Enablers and Constraints**. The viability of a paradigm, model, implementation **issues** of proposed programs, etc., may also be included in this section. **Future research directions** within the domain of the topic will finally be suggested.

Ortiz-Rodriguez, Medina-Quintero, Tiwari and Villanueva (2022, p. 261), as part of a book suggesting **futuristic emerging trends** for *sustainable* development and *sustainable* ecosystems, in their chapter on sharing, retrieving, and exchanging legal documentation across an e-government ontology indicated that the "electronic government is a new application field" of the semantic web, and such "ontologies play a key role in the development of the" semantic web.

In line with the topic of this chapter, Goosen (2018) showed how *sustainable* and inclusive quality education can be achieved through research-informed practice on information and communication technologies.

"Teachers play an important role in the provision of quality education. The variety of classroom practices they use in interacting with learners play a critical role in the understanding of mathematical concepts and overall performance in Mathematics." The South African journal article on education by Arends, et al. (2017, p. 1) therefore provided a reflection on the **Trends** in International Mathematics and Science Study (TIMSS) 2011 in terms of teacher classroom practices and Mathematics performance in South African schools.

The article by Umugiraneza, et al. (2018, p. 2) addressed "the use of technology in teaching" and learning mathematics and statistics in KwaZulu-Natal schools. Recent advances in technologies had unlocked entirely new **future directions** for education **research**.

CONCLUSION

This section of the chapter will provide a discussion of the overall coverage and concluding remarks.

In conclusion, this chapter provided an overview of the research study, which will be conducted by the first author once approval had been granted. This write-up provided the **introduction** and research **objectives**. This section of the chapter also provided an outline, which will guide the structure of the study.

In terms of the **background** to the study, a brief review was conducted to provide a critical summary and assessment of the range of existing literature and knowledge in the field of study. The literature review assisted in providing background and insights into previous work. The key concepts in the study were further operationalized and conceptualized from previous literature.

This was followed by formulating the statement of the **problem** and research questions, as well as the rationale and significance of the study. More importantly, the chapter presented the methodological and philosophical orientations, which will underpin conduct in the study. It was established that pragmatism, constructivist paradigms and an exploratory-descriptive quantitative design will be employed in the study. Reliability and validity aspects of the study were provided and discussed. Additionally, the ethical considerations, limitations and delimitation of the study were provided.

REFERENCES

Abdu, A.-K. (2018). A review of technology integration in ELT: From CALL to MALL. *Language Teaching and Educational Research*, *1*(1), 1–12.

Agbele, A. T., Oyelade, E. A., & Oluwatuyi, V. S. (2020). Assessment of students' performance in physics using two teaching techniques. *International Journal of Innovation and Scientific Research*, *7*(7), 55–59. doi:10.51244/IJRSI.2020.7702

Arends, F., Winnaar, L., & Mosimege, M. (2017). Teacher classroom practices and Mathematics performance in South African schools: A reflection on TIMSS 2011. *South African Journal of Education*, *37*(3), 1–11. Advance online publication. doi:10.15700/saje.v37n3a1362

Bai, B., Wang, J., & Chai, C. S. (2021). Understanding Hong Kong primary school English teachers' continuance intention to teach with ICT. *Computer Assisted Language Learning*, *34*(4), 528–551. doi:10.1080/09588221.2019.1627459

Barrera, R. M., Martinez-Rodriguez, J. L., Tiwari, S., & Barrera, V. (2023). Political Marketing App Based on Citizens. In *G. P. Systems*. IGI Global. doi:10.4018/978-1-6684-6591-2.ch008

Bartolomé-Pina, A., García-Ruiz, R., & Aguaded, I. (2018). Blended learning: overview and expectations. *REVISTA IBEROAMERICANA DE EDUCACION A DISTANCIA (REID)*, *21*(1), 33-56.

Chauhan, A. G., & Rai, S. (2020). Abridging Gender Gap in Intellectual Property. *Prestige International Journal of Management and Research*, *8*, 8–11.

Chisango, G., Marongwe, N., Mtsi, N., & Matyedi, T. E. (2020). Teachers' perceptions of adopting information and communication technologies in teaching and learning at rural secondary schools in Eastern Cape, South Africa. *Africa Education Review*, *17*(2), 1–19. doi:10.1080/18146627.2018.1491317

Creswell, J. W. (2014). Research design. In Qualitative, quantitative, and mixed methods approaches (International student ed.). SAGE.

Davis, F. D., Bagozzi, R. P., & Warshaw, P. R. (1989). User acceptance of computer technology: A comparison of two theoretical models. *Management Science, 35*(8), 982–1003. doi:10.1287/mnsc.35.8.982

Daya, A., & Laher, S. (2020). Exploring the influence of educators' access to and attitudes towards educational technology on the use of educational technology in Johannesburg schools. *Africa Education Review, 17*(1), 159–180. doi:10.1080/18146627.2018.1490154

De Vera, J. L., Andrada, M. D., Bello, A., & De Vera, M. G. (2021). Teachers' competencies in educational technology integration on instructional methodologies in the new normal. *Lukad: An Online Journal of Pedagogy, 1*(1), 61–80.

Department of Education. (2004, September 2). White Paper on e-Education: Transforming Learning and Teaching through Information and Communication Technologies (ICTs). *Government Gazette* (26734), pp. 3 - 46.

Dixon, K. (2019). Access, capital, and the digital divide in a rural South African Primary School. In Stories from Inequity to Justice in Literacy Education: Confronting Digital Divides (pp. 15-33). Routledge.

Doff, P. A. (2015). *Integrated instruction in ELT*. Cambridge University Press.

Ellermeijer, T., & Tran, T. B. (2019). Technology in teaching physics: Benefits, challenges, and solutions. In *Upgrading Physics Education to Meet the Needs of Society* (pp. 35–67). Springer. doi:10.1007/978-3-319-96163-7_3

Farjon, D., Smits, A., & Voogt, J. (2019). Technology integration of pre-service teachers explained by attitudes and beliefs, competency, access, and experience. *Computers & Education, 130*, 81–93. doi:10.1016/j.compedu.2018.11.010

García, R., Aguaded, I., & Bartolomé, A. (2018). The blended learning revolution in distance education. *Revista Iberoamericana de Educación a Distancia, 21*(1).

Goosen, L., & Van Heerden, D. (2017). Beyond the Horizon of Learning Programming with Educational Technologies. In U. I. Ogbonnaya, & S. Simelane-Mnisi (Ed.), *Proceedings of the South Africa International Conference on Educational Technologies* (pp. 78 - 90). Pretoria: African Academic Research Forum.

Gui, M., Parma, A., & Comi, S. (2018). Does public investment in ICTs improve learning performance? Evidence from Italy. *Policy and Internet, 10*(2), 141–163. doi:10.1002/poi3.170

Guido, R. M. (2013). Attitude and motivation towards learning physics. [IJERT]. *International Journal of Engineering Research & Technology (Ahmedabad)*, *2*(11), 2087–2093.

Hennessy, S., D'Angelo, S., McIntyre, N., Koomar, S., Kreimeia, A., Cao, L., Brugha, M., & Zubairi, A. (2022). Technology use for teacher professional development in low-and middle-income countries: A systematic review. *Computers and Education Open*, *3*, 100080. doi:10.1016/j.caeo.2022.100080

Jita, T., & Munje, P. N. (2020). Teaching science through information and communication technologies: 'enablers' and 'constraints'. *The Independent Journal of Teaching and Learning, 15*(2), 107-120.

Johnson, A. M., Jacovina, M. E., Russell, D. G., & Soto, C. M. (2016). Challenges and solutions when using technologies in the classroom. In *Adaptive Educational Technologies for Literacy Instruction* (pp. 13–32). Taylor and Francis. doi:10.4324/9781315647500-2

Maestre Góngora, G. P., Colmenares Quintero, R. F., & Stansfield, K. (2020). Mapping concept and challenges for smart technologies: A systematic study approach. *Iberian Journal of Information Systems and Technologies*, *32*(8), 28–40.

Medina-Quintero, J. M., Ortiz-Rodriguez, F., Tiwari, S., & Saenz, F. I. (2023). Trust in Electronic Banking With the Use of Cell Phones for User Satisfaction. In *Global Perspectives on the Strategic Role of Marketing Information Systems* (pp. 87–106). IGI Global. doi:10.4018/978-1-6684-6591-2.ch006

Medina-Quintero, J. M., Sahagun, M. A., Alfaro, J., & Ortiz-Rodriguez, F. (Eds.). (2023). *Global Perspectives on the Strategic Role of Marketing Information Systems*. IGI Global. https://www.igi-global.com/book/global-perspectives-strategic-role-marketing/302625 doi:10.4018/978-1-6684-6591-2

Michos, K., & Hernández-Leo, D. (2020). CIDA: A collective inquiry framework to study and support teachers as designers in technological environments. *Computers & Education*, *143*, 103679. *Advance online publication*. doi:10.1016/j.compedu.2019.103679

Mikeska, J. N., Holtzman, S., McCaffrey, D. F., Liu, S., & Shattuck, T. (2019). Using classroom observations to evaluate science teaching: Implications of lesson sampling for measuring science teaching effectiveness across lesson types. *Science Education*, *10*(3), 123–144. doi:10.1002/sce.21482

Mlachila, M., & Moeletsi, T. (2019). Struggling to Make the Grade: A Review of the Causes and Consequences of the Weak Outcomes of South Africa's Education System. *International Monetary Fund (IMF). Working Papers*, *19*(47). https://www.elibrary.imf.org/openurl?genre=articlel&issn=1018-5941&volume=2019&issue=047&artnum=A001

Mlambo-Ngcuka, P. (2019). Minimum Wage & Fair Wage Practices. *Legal Momentum*, 25-28. https://www.legalmomentum.org/sites/default/files/wwbor/wv-toolkit-nys-25-28.pdf

Msila, V. (2015). Teacher readiness and information and communications technology (ICT) use in classrooms: A South African case study. *Creative Education*, *6*(18), 1973–1981. doi:10.4236/ce.2015.618202

Ndihokubwayo, K., Uwamahoro, J., Ndayambaje, I., & Ralph, M. (2020). Light phenomena conceptual assessment: An inventory tool for teachers. *Physics Education*, *55*(3), 035009. doi:10.1088/1361-6552/ab6f20

Ngao, A., Sang, G., Tondeur, J., Kihwele, J. E., & Chunga, J. O. (2023, June). Transforming Initial Teacher Education Program with Mobile Technologies. A synthesis of qualitative evidences. *Digital Education Review*, (43), 18–36. doi:10.1344/der.2023.43.18-34

Ngao, A. I., Sang, G., & Kihwele, J. E. (2022). Understanding teacher educators' perceptions and practices about ICT integration in teacher education program. *Education Sciences*, *12*(8), 549. doi:10.3390/educsci12080549

Ngeze, L. V. (2017). ICT integration in teaching and learning in secondary schools in Tanzania: Readiness and way forward. *International Journal of Information and Education Technology (IJIET)*, *7*(6), 424–427. doi:10.18178/ijiet.2017.7.6.905

Ortiz-Rodriguez, F., Medina-Quintero, J. M., Tiwari, S., & Villanueva, V. (2022). EGODO ontology: sharing, retrieving, and exchanging legal documentation across e-government. In *Futuristic Trends for Sustainable Development and Sustainable Ecosystems* (pp. 261–276). IGI Global. doi:10.4018/978-1-6684-4225-8.ch016

Ortiz-Rodriguez, F., Tiwari, S., Amara, F. Z., & Sahagun, M. A. (2023). E-Government Success: An End-User Perspective. In Global Perspectives on the Strategic Role of Marketing Information Systems (pp. 168-186). IGI Global.

Rabah, J. (2015). Benefits and Challenges of Information and Communication Technologies (ICT) Integration in Québec English Schools. [TOJET]. *The Turkish Online Journal of Educational Technology*, *14*(2), 24–31.

Ramaila, S. (2021). Technology Integration in Natural Sciences Teaching and Learning in South African Township Schools. [Lisboa, Portugal: inScience Press.]. *Education and New Developments*, 102–105. doi:10.36315/2021end022

Ramaila, S. (2022). Promoting Self-Regulated Learning in Natural Sciences Teaching Through Technology Integration. *Education and New Developments*, *359-363*, 359–363. doi:10.36315/2022v1end081

Ramaila, S., & Molwele, A. J. (2022). The Role of Technology Integration in the Development of 21st Century Skills and Competencies in Life Sciences Teaching and Learning. *International Journal of Higher Education*, *11*(5), 9–17. doi:10.5430/ijhe.v11n5p9

Ramnarain, U., & Moosa, S. (2017). The use of simulations in correcting electricity misconceptions of grade 10 South African physical sciences learners. *International Journal of Innovation in Science and Mathematics Education*, *25*(5), 1–20.

Rana, K. (2018). *ICT in rural primary schools in Nepal: context and teachers' experiences.* New Zealand: [Unpublished doctoral dissertation, University of Canterbury].

Singh, S., Sharma, R., & Kaur, R. (2020). Teacher competencies for the integration of ICT in post graduate science stream teachers. *Studies in Indian Place Names, 40*(60), 2775-2788.

Spangenberg, E. D., & De Freitas, G. (2019). Mathematics teachers' levels of technological pedagogical content knowledge and information and communication technology integration barriers. *Pythagoras*, *40*(1), 1–13.

Tachie, S. A. (2019). Challenges and opportunities regarding usage of computers in the teaching and learning of Mathematics. *South African Journal of Education*, *39*(S2), 1–10. doi:10.15700/saje.v39ns2a1690

Ugwuanyi, C. S., & Okeke, C. I. (2020). Enhancing University Students' Achievement in Physics Using Computer-Assisted Instruction. *International Journal of Higher Education*, *9*(5), 115–124. doi:10.5430/ijhe.v9n5p115

Umugiraneza, O., Bansilal, S., & North, D. (2018). Exploring teachers' use of technology in teaching and learning mathematics in KwaZulu-Natal schools. *Pythagoras*, *39*(1), 1–13. doi:10.4102/pythagoras.v39i1.342

Vandeyar, T. (2015). Policy intermediaries and the reform of e-Education in S outh A frica. *British Journal of Educational Technology*, *46*(2), 344–359. doi:10.1111/bjet.12130

Venkat, H., & Mathews, C. (2019). Improving multiplicative reasoning in a context of low performance. *ZDM Mathematics Education*, *51*(1), 95–108. doi:10.1007/s11858-018-0969-6

Wood, B. K., & Blevins, B. K. (2019). Substituting the practical teaching of physics with simulations for the assessment of practical skills: An experimental study. *Physics Education*, *54*(3), 035004. doi:10.1088/1361-6552/ab0192

KEY TERMS AND DEFINITIONS

ICT Constraints: Constraint is a constraining condition, agency or force that limits the systems' performance in a given context or environment. In this study, constraints are operationalized as anything that limits or hinders Physical Sciences teachers from integrating ICTs in the teaching and learning process.

ICT Enablers: The term ICT enablers refers to critical success factors or elements that are required to ensure effective integration of ICTs in the teaching and learning of Physical Sciences.

ICT Integration: In the context of this study, ICT integration refers to the extent to which information and communication technologies have been adopted into the school environment and the degree of impact on the classroom pedagogies.

ICT Intensity: ICT intensity refers to the degree, volume or magnitude of the use of ICTs in the teaching and learning process.

ICT Tools: ICT tools refers to hardware and software communication resources such as computers (desktops, laptops), photocopy machines, data projectors, interactive whiteboards, Word Processing, Internet, tape recorders, cell phones and social media apps, specifically WhatsApp which are used for the purpose of teaching and learning.

Information Communication Technologies (ICTs): An umbrella terms referring to a wide range of software and hardware technology components such as computer, telecommunication, internet, video and digital cameras that can be used by teachers to support their work.

Chapter 5
Optimization Model Applied to the Generation of Electrical Energy for a Multi-Region Scenario

Marco A. Santibáñez-Díaz
Universidad Autónoma de Tamaulipas, Mexico

Esmeralda López-Garza
Universidad Autónoma de Tamaulipas, Mexico

René F. Domínguez-Cruz
 https://orcid.org/0000-0001-7001-7543
Universidad Autónoma de Tamaulipas, Mexico

Iván Salgado-Tránsito
Centro de Investigaciones en Óptica A.C., Mexico

ABSTRACT

In this work, an optimization model based on linear programming is proposed applied to the eastern energy generation zone in Mexico. This model is formulated from the division into different regions that make up the study area and allows for scheduling the production of the plants in various time periods, minimizing operating costs. The division of the area consists of four regions where each one has various generation technologies, described with their parameters. The model establishes linear operating restrictions for the operation of the plants and restrictions that guarantee satisfying the demand for each region in each established period, through

DOI: 10.4018/979-8-3693-1119-6.ch005

Copyright © 2024, IGI Global. Copying or distributing in print or electronic forms without written permission of IGI Global is prohibited.

an analysis of the demand of the area, taking into account different costs at the time of generation and allocation of power. The results of the model show the transfers of electrical energy between the regions for an efficient economic dispatch of the area, this being a useful instrument for making decisions with a sustainable perspective in the efficient allocation of energy resources.

INTRODUCTION

Electrical energy is a fundamental resource for humanity to continue developing, which is necessary for economic growth and the increase in the well-being of society. This allows us to have a pleasant environment in homes, the operation of businesses and industries. (SENER, 2019). That is why in countries where their economy is increasing, the demand for electrical energy is also increasing. This is how the United Nations Development Program uses the Human Development Index to determine the development of countries.

In Mexico, the main energy generating company is the Federal Electricity Commission (CFE), which is a public organization that has total management of the national electricity fleet (CFE,2022). The energy generated in the country is conducted through an extension of 752 thousand kilometers of transmission and distribution lines, having a supply range for a total of 190 thousand locations present in the nation. This energy supply means that 97.60% of the national population is covered by electrical energy (Ramos-Gutiérrez et al., 2023). In recent years, there has been an increase in installed capacity in the country due to the increases in electricity demand that occur year after year. Currently, the National Electric System (SEN) has an effective capacity of 88,748 MW belonging to the public and private sectors (Secretaría de Energía, 2021). Many of the plants that make up the SEN are about to reach their life cycle, making it necessary to incorporate new generation plants.

The incorporation of new generation plants, as well as the increase in the demand for electrical energy brings with it a challenge for the administration of resources, at the time of efficient allocation of the loads to be generated in each of the plants that make up the system. This is due to the different variables and parameters that govern the operation of the plants. To have efficient planning, it is necessary to rely on optimization techniques that guarantee the efficient use of resources considering the operating characteristics of the system. Such optimization techniques according to Marquez (2014) have been applied for many years, such as Herrera (2009) for operation cost reduction, greenhouse gas emissions minimization using deep learning algorithms (Renjie Zhu et al., 2023), loss minimization of power through semi-definite programming (Glover 2003), among others.

Economic Dispatch

The generation of electrical energy involves technical and economic variables. This generation must be always ensured and guarantee demand coverage anywhere with acceptable quality at the lowest possible cost (Nuñez, 2020) (Arango et al., 2017). The several generation costs and the high prices of fossil fuels have given an important position to the optimal and economic operation of electrical energy systems. Hence the importance of the ideal allocation for each of the generation plants available in such a way. that the total production costs are the lowest (Lopez et al., 2008) (Chandram et al., 2010). Economic Dispatch is a linear programming problem, which is responsible for the efficient allocation of load between the different electrical energy supply plants that make up the generation system, seeking to minimize operating costs (Liu D. et al., 2013).

There are different variants of the economic dispatch problem have been conducted, as shown in (Zheng et al., 2016) (Manojkumar et al., 2018), which are:

- Economic Dispatch without restrictions: This model consists of an objective function and the equation of the sum of the powers generated from each plant that satisfies the established demand (Arango et al., 2017).
- Economic Dispatch including restrictions incorporates equations that allow taking into consideration the conditions of each generator, establishing operating ranges (Lopez et al., 2008).
- Economic Dispatch without losses: in this model the sum of the energy generations of each plant meets the demand, without including the losses in the transmission lines (Nuñez, 2020).
- Economic Dispatch with losses considers the losses in the transmission lines due to the geographical location of each plant in the system (Liu D. et al., 2013).
- Static Economic Dispatch: consists of the optimization of plants for a given time (Chandram et al., 2010).
- Dynamic Economic Dispatch: optimizes generation plants over a time horizon, where the demands established in each period must be met (Zheng et al., 2016).

This work describes the study of electrical energy generation plants through the Economic Office in one of the areas of Mexico. This study is a linear programming model with the purpose of having the lowest production costs, taking into consideration the operating restrictions of the plants that make up the study system. The model is proposed for a time horizon, in which four time periods are established, and divides the application area into regions to see the energy transfers that are carried out between the areas. This analysis represents a tool for making strategic decisions for efficient load allocation.

METHOD

The economic dispatch implemented in this study is through a linear programming model (Lopez et al., 2022). In this case a multi-region approach is implemented in which the electrical system is divided into regions to establish the plants that belong to it and the energy demand with which this region counts. This generation region is expressed by:

$$r = 1, 2, ..., R$$

Where R is the total number of regions included in the study. Within the regions there are various plants, with diverse types of generation technologies with their own characteristics. These plants are denoted by j, which is:

$$j = 1, 2, 3, ..., J$$

J is the number of plants in the region. The time periods are denoted by k, so the planning horizon consists of the periods:

$$k = 1, 2, 3, ..., K$$

The plants j, incorporated into the system have each of the plants j, cannot operate below their minimum energy generation or above their capacity, being formulated for various periods as:

$$E_{minrj} \cdot v_{rjk} \leq E_{rjk} \leq E_{maxrj} \cdot v_{rjk} \quad \forall r, j, k \tag{1}$$

Being E_{minrj} the minimum energy to be generated in region r, central j, in period k; E_{maxrj} is the maximum energy to generate in region r, plant j in period k, E_{rjk} is the energy to be generated in region r, plant j in period k. v_{rjk} is a binary operating variable whose value of 1 indicates that plant j in region r is operating and 0 indicates that it is not operating.

This energy to be produced in each plant in each period, when moving to the immediately following period, they cannot increase their production above a maximum amount, established as the maximum ramp up U_{rj}, denominated as:

$$E_{rjk+1} - E_{rjk} \leq U_{rj} \tag{2}$$

Where the energy produced in region r, by plant j in period k, must be better than or equal to the maximum ramp up. In the same way, no power plant can lower its energy production above a limit which is called the maximum ramp down F_{rj}:

$$E_{rjk} - E_{rjk+1} \leq F_{rj} \tag{3}$$

It is necessary to implement equations that help account for and control costs that may be incurred, as well as the correct operation of the plants. A plant that is on in a period cannot be off in that same period, therefore:

$$V_{rjk} + Z_{rjk} = 1 \tag{4}$$

Where V_{rjk} is the binary operating variable described above and Z_{rjk} is a binary stop variable that indicates 1 if in region r, central j in period k is off and 0 when not. In the same case, if a plant is in operation in one period and in the next period $k+1$ continues in operation, it cannot start, expressed as:

$$V_{rjk} - V_{rjk-1} \leq Y_{rjk} \tag{5}$$

Where Y_{rjk} is a binary startup variable that indicates 1 when the plant in region r is started, in plant j in period k and 0 when it does not start. Establishing an equation that allows the state conditions to be met given by:

$$v_{jk} - v_{jk-1} + y_{jk} - z_{jk} \leq 0 \tag{6}$$

These conditions described above are the operation of the plants, this model must also satisfy the demand in each region that makes up the system in each of the periods are established according to:

Optimization Model Applied to the Generation of Electrical Energy

$$\sum_{j=1}^{J} E_{rjk} + T_{rk} + T_{rk} = D_{rk} \qquad (7)$$

Where the sum of the energy to be generated from the plants in region r are the main ones in satisfying the demand, T_{rk} are the energy transfers from the surrounding regions, D_{rk} is the demand to be satisfied in region r in the period k. This model's main objective is to minimize the costs of all regions, in all periods, therefore:

$$L = \sum_{r=1}^{R}\sum_{k=1}^{K}\sum_{j=1}^{J}\left(A_{rj}v_{rjk} + B_{rj}E_{rjk} + C_{rj}y_{rjk} + M_{rj}z_{rjk}\right) \qquad (8)$$

Where all the costs of the plants in each of the regions are added, in each of the periods. The parameter A_{rj} is the cost associated with the fixed costs of the generation plant, B_j is the cost associated with the costs variables that each generation plant presents, mostly directly related to the costs of fossil fuels, C_j is the start-up cost that represents the cost incurred by the generation plants when starting up a plant, M_j is the shutdown cost which is generated when a plant is stopped. These costs are accompanied respectively by the variables previously described to account for the corresponding costs, operation (v_{rjk}), energy generation (E_{rjk}), start-up (y_{rjk}) and stoppage $\left(z_{rjk}\right)$. The conditions established to satisfy the different energy demands of each region, in the time intervals that allow long-term planning, establishing in an optimal way the allocation of resources that allows a minimization of the total generation cost by allowing transfers of energy in the regions.

IMPLEMENTATION

Mexico is divided of nine control zones by the National Electrical System, for its generation and distribution in the country (CENACE,2020), as shown in Figure. 1. This study focuses on the eastern area, in which it establishes an optimization model to manage and distribute electrical energy within this study area in an optimal way. Here, the demand can be satisfied in each region required considering the various costs of energy generation.

Figure 1. Areas that make up the Mexican electrical system (SIN) (CENACE, 2020)

The eastern zone of Mexico has a total of eight states of the Mexican Republic which are Chiapas, Oaxaca, Tabasco, Guerrero, Morelos, Puebla, Veracruz, and Tlaxcala. In this case, the eastern area of Mexico was divided into four regions as shown in the following Table 1 and Figure 2.

Table 1. Division into regions of the area

Region	States
Region 1	Veracruz
	Tabasco
Region 2	Chiapas
	Oaxaca
Region 3	Guerrero
	Morelos
Region 4	Puebla
	Tlaxcala

Figure 2. Division of regions in the eastern zone

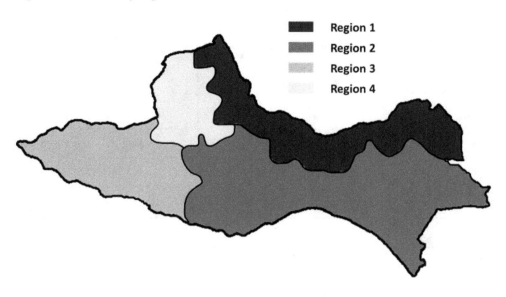

This area has a great diversity of electrical energy generation technologies. The plants in each region of the zone for this study are shown in Table 2.

Table 2. Power plants by region

Region	Power Plants
Region 1	Combined cycle
Region 2	Hydroelectric
Region 3	Hydroelectric
Region 4	Geothermal

This selection was made because they are the type of technology that has the greatest presence in each region. These plants have characteristic operating parameters which are shown in Table 3.

Table 3. Parameters of the power plants [23]

Parameters	Power plant			
	Combined cycle	Hydroelectric	Hydroelectric	Geothermal
E_{min}	1474.5	546.55	1743.82	80.4
E_{max}	2721.06	1394.67	2598.39	301.98
A	90.17	151.46	151.46	522.70
B	16.14	0	0	0.36
C	118.13	0	0	0
M	216	246	246	570
U	800	1000	2000	410
F	800	1000	2000	410

For implementation it is necessary to establish the corresponding demands for the area in each period. The periods established for the study are 4, as shown in Table 4 (CENACE, 2020).

Table 4. Demand in the periods

Period	Demand
Period 1	4876.8
Period 2	4916.1
Period 3	5412.0
Period 4	5810.1

Of this demand shown in Table 4, a percentage corresponds to each of the regions in the established periods (INEGI, 2020).

Figure 3. Percentage of demand for each region

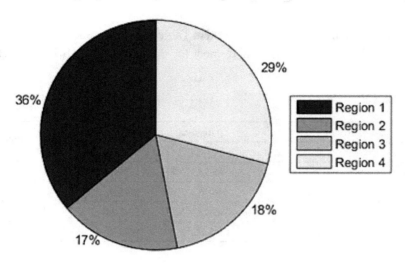

This establishes the demands in each region in the respective period as shown in Table 5.

Table 5. Demand in the periods

Region	Period			
	1	2	3	4
Region 1	1755.64	1769.79	1948.32	2091.63
Region 2	829.05	835.73	920.04	987.71
Region 3	877.82	884.89	974.16	1045.81
Region 4	1425.66	1569.48	1684.92	1425.66

The characteristic parameters of the generation plants shown in table 3, and the demands to be satisfied from Table 5 are incorporated into the described equations (1-8), to obtain the values of the variables that minimize operating costs using MATLAB.

RESULTS AND CONCLUSION

The results shown in MATLAB presented in Table 6 show the energy to be generated in each period in each of the plants to meet the demands of the different regions.

Table 6. Results

Period	Regions				Total
	1	2	3	4	
Period 1	2586.43	546.55	1743.82	0	4876.8
Period 2	2625.73	546.55	1743.82	0	4916.1
Period 3	2721.06	947.12	1743.82	0	5412.0
Period 4	2721.06	1345.22	1743.82	0	5810.1

This model optimally seeks to reduce operating costs. Table 7 shows the combination of the contributions of the plants that make the costs the lowest considering the ramp restrictions that make the allocation of energy complex for generate each one.

Table 7. Costs and contributions of each center in each period

Power plant	1 Period		2 Period		3 Period		4 Period	
	Energy in MWh	Total, cost per plant ($)	Energy in MWh	Total, cost per plant ($)	Energía en MWh	Energy in MWh	Total, cost per plant ($)	Energy in MWh
Region 1 Combined cycle	2586.43	184488.72	2625.73	187291.95	2721.06	194091.76	2721.06	194091.76
Region 2 Hydroelectric	546.55	39844.49	546.55	39844.49	947.12	69046.04	1345.22	98067.53
Region 3 Hydroelectric	1743.82	127125.47	1743.82	127125.47	1743.82	127125.47	1743.82	127125.47
Region 4 Geothermal	0	570	0	570	0	570	0	570
Total per period	4876.8	352028.697	4916.1	354831.931	5412	390833.287	5810.1	419854.777

These results show a greater participation of the plant in region 1 due to it has greater installed capacity compared to the plants in regions 3 and 4, which have lower costs. On the other hand, region 4 is not producing energy due to the operating costs it presents, which makes assigning load not an efficient option, and therefore generates an energy flow between the zones. The energy transfer in the first period can be seen in Figure 4, which shows how region 1 is transferring 282.5 MWh to region 2, to satisfy the demand, it presents. Region 4 receives 548.29 from region 1 and 866 from region 3 in that same period and in this way ensures that the requirements of the study area are met.

Figure 4. Energy transfers between the regions of the zone in period 1

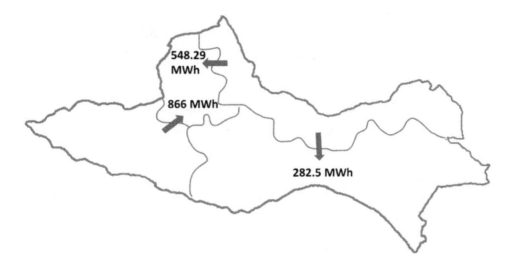

The transfers for the following periods have a very similar behavior, where the regions surrounding zone 4 tend to generate more than the energy demanded in their zone so that in this way the corresponding transfers can be made and thus be able to comply with the requests requested.

This model helps the efficient administration of the resources currently available within the zones when establishing the division of regions. The results show a greater participation of hydroelectric plants, due to their costs, and of combination plants due to their installed capacity. Studies like this are necessary for decision-making on priority issues in national energy matters, because they serve as a sample to detect plants with high costs and see the flow of plants within the area. This kind of study allows for establishing a diagnosis of the situation and the establishment of new generation centers in strategic locations. That allows a change to the distributed generation of electrical energy.

REFERENCES

Arango, D., Urrego, R., & Rivera Rodríguez, S. (2017). Despacho económico en micro redes con penetración de energía renovable usando algoritmo de punto interior y restricciones lineales. Ingeniería y ciencia, 13(25), 123-152.

Centro Nacional de Control de Energía (CENACE). (2020). *Demandas del Sistema Eléctrico Nacional*. CENACE. https://www.cenace.gob.mx/Paginas/Publicas/Info/DemandaRegional.aspx

Chandram, K., Subrahmanyam, N., & Sydulu, M. (2011). Equal embedded algorithm for economic load dispatch problem with transmission losses, *International Journal of Electrical Power & Energy Systems, 33*(3), 500-507. doi:10.1016/j.ijepes.2010.12.002

Comisión Federal de Electricidad (CFE). (n.d.). *Historia de la CFE*. CFE. https://www.cfe.mx/nuestraempresa/pages/historia.aspx

de Energía, S. (2019). *SENER*. Demanda y Consumo.

Glover, F. (2003). Melián Belen. Búsqueda Tabú. Inteligencia Artificial. *Revista Iberoamericana de Inteligencia Artificial*, (19), 29–48.

Gómez, M. (2014). Las metaheurísticas: tendencias actuales y su aplicabilidad en la ergonomía. Ingeniería Industrial. *Actualidad y Nuevas Tendencias, 4*(12), 108-120

Herrera, F. (2009). *Introducción a los algoritmos metaheurísticos*. UGR. https://sci2s.ugr.es/docencia/metaheuristicas/IntMetaheuristicas-CAEPIA-2009.pdf

Informe Sobre Desarrollo Humano. (2022). *Tiempos inciertos vidas inestables: Configurar nuestro futuro en un mundo en transformación*. ISDH.

Instituto Nacional de Estadística y Geografía (INEGI). (2019). *Producto Interno Bruto por entidad federative*. INEGI

Liu, D., Guo, J., Huang, Y., Wang, W., & Wang, P. (2013). A dynamic economic dispatch method of wind integrated power system considering the total probability of wind power. *2nd IET Renewable Power Generation Conference (RPG 2013)*. CrossRef. 10.1049/cp.2013.1823

Lopez, J., Gallego Pareja, L., & Mejía Giraldo, D. Coordinación hidrotérmica de corto plazo con restricciones de red usando un método de punto interior. Ingeniería y Ciencia. ISSN: 1794-9165. Vol. 4 Núm. 8. 2008. Págs. 45-63. Colombia.

López-Garza, E., Domínguez-Cruz, R. F., Martell-Chávez, F., & Salgado-Tránsito, I. (2022). Fuzzy Logic and Linear Programming based Power Grid Enhanced Economical Dispatch for Sustainable and Stable Grid operation in Eastern Mexico. *Energies, 15*(11), 4069. doi:10.3390/en15114069

Manojkumar, T., & Singh, N. A. (2018). Solution of Environmental/Economic (EED) Power Dispatch problem using Particle Swarm Optimization Technique. *2018 International Conference on Control, Power, Communication and Computing Technologies (ICCPCCT),* (pp. 347-351). IEEE. 10.1109/ICCPCCT.2018.8574256

Núñez Jiménez, A. (2020). Despachos Económicos Mercado y Transporte de la Energía Eléctrica. Universidad politécnica de Madrid. España.

Ramos-Gutiérrez. (2012). La generación de energía eléctrica en México. *Tecnología y ciencias del agua, 3*(4), 197-211. https://www.scielo.org.mx/scielo.php?script=sci_arttext&pid=S2007-24222012000400012&lng=es&tlng=es

Secretaria de Energía (2021). *Programa de Desarrollo del Sistema Eléctrico Nacional* 2021-2035.

Zheng, W., Wu, W., Zhang, B., Sun, H., Guo, Q., & Lin, C. (2016). Dynamic economic dispatch for microgrids: A fully distributed approach. *2016 IEEE/PES Transmission and Distribution Conference and Exposition (T&D),* (pp. 1-3). IEEE. 10.1109/TDC.2016.7520068

Zhu, R., Guan, X., Zheng, J., Wang, N., Jiang, H., & Cui, C. (2023). DRL based low *carbon economic dispatch by considering power transmission safety limitations in internet of energy. Internet of Things, 24.* doi:10.1016/j.iot.2023.100979

Chapter 6
Honey Adulterant Detection System Using Fiber Optics Sensors

Mayeli Anais Pérez-Rosas
Unidad Académica Multidisciplinaria Reynosa-Rodhe, Mexico

Leonardo Alvarez-Villarreal
Unidad Académica Multidisciplinaria Reynosa-Rodhe, Mexico

Yadira Aracely Fuentes-Rubio
 https://orcid.org/0000-0002-7385-9794
Unidad Académica Multidisciplinaria Reynosa-Rodhe, Mexico

Rene Fernando Dominguez-Cruz
 https://orcid.org/0000-0001-7001-7543
Unidad Académica Multidisciplinaria Reynosa-Rodhe, Mexico

Luis A. Garcia-Garza
Unidad Académica Multidisciplinaria Reynosa-Rodhe, Mexico

Oscar Baldovino-Pantaleón
 https://orcid.org/0000-0001-7523-1442
Unidad Académica Multidisciplinaria Reynosa-Rodhe, Mexico

ABSTRACT

Honey's valued for nutrition and antioxidants, but adulteration, mainly sugar addition, reduces quality and nutritional value. In this chapter, a detection system for honey adulterated with sucrose syrup is reported using a sensor built with fiber optics. The sensor consists of the union of a segment of non-core multimode fiber (NC-MMF) joined at its ends to two segments of single-mode fiber (SMF). The principle of operation is that, when propagating an optical field in the device, a transmission peak appears at its output due to its filter-like response, the position of which depends on the effective refractive index of the medium surrounding the NC-MMF. Therefore, when different mixtures of adulterated honey are coated on the NC-MMF section, the peak wavelength changes according to the refractive index of the mixture. In this way, adulterated honey can be detected from the shift in wavelength of the transmission peak. The device was tested on a compliant commercial honey brand, exhibiting a linear response with a sensitivity of -0.5417 nm/% in the 1%-5% adulteration range.

INTRODUCTION

Honey is a sweet, viscous substance produced by bees from the nectar of flowers or secretions from certain insects. It is a natural food product that has been used by humans for thousands of years (Zhang & Abdulla, 2022). Bees collect nectar from flowers and the enzymes present in the bee's stomach transform the nectar into honey through a process of regurgitation and evaporation. Once the bees return to the hive, they deposit the honey into wax cells and fan their wings to accelerate the drying process, resulting in the thick, syrupy consistency of honey (Bogdanov, 2012).

Honey is predominantly composed of carbohydrates, primarily fructose, and glucose, which give it its sweetness. It also contains trace amounts of minerals, vitamins, enzymes, antioxidants, and other bioactive compounds that contribute to its potential health benefits (Bogdanov et al., 2008). Has been traditionally used to treat laryngitis, as well as for its antimicrobial, antiviral, and antiparasitic properties. It has been used in traditional medicine and natural remedies for its potential healing, and in the cosmetic industry as an ingredient in skin and hair care products due to its moisturizing and antioxidant properties (Talha et al., 2023). Besides, honey is also used in the food industry as a natural sweetener in foods and beverages, a topping for desserts and breakfast items, or an ingredient in sauces and dressings (Bogdanov, 2012; Talha et al., 2023).

However, honey quality and authenticity pose a challenge due to adulteration. Honey adulteration refers to mixing or altering pure honey with other ingredients or substances to increase the quantity, improve its appearance, and flavor, or for more significant economic gain (Fakhlaei et al., 2020). The adulteration can be categorized into direct and indirect, as depicted in Figure 1. Direct adulteration involves adding a substance directly to the honey, while indirect adulteration happens when the honeybees are given a substance that adulterates the honey (Jaafar et al., 2020).

Figure 1. Honey adulteration categories

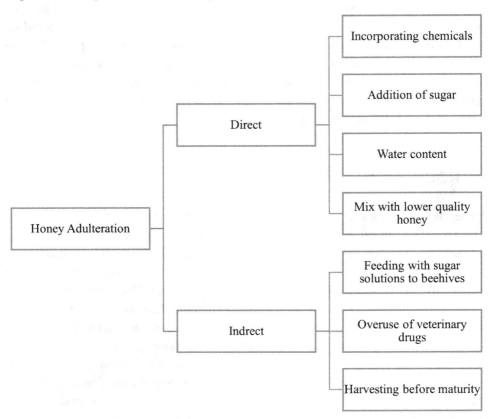

Typically, direct adulteration includes diluting honey with water, adding inexpensive sugars or syrups, mixing with lower quality or unknown-origin honey, or incorporating chemicals such as antibiotics or pesticides to prevent fermentation and prolong shelf life (Fakhlaei et al., 2020; Jaafar et al., 2020). In this sense, sugar addition is the main honey adulteration mechanism (Bogdanov, 2007) due to the use of cheaper and readily available sweeteners, such as cane sugar, beet sugar, glucose, fructose, sucrose, maltose, etc. (Oroian et al., 2018). Adulterated honey changes the biochemical and chemical properties and taste of honey, leading to a reduction in nutritional value and negatively affecting human health (Guler et al., 2014; Soares et al., 2017).

Detecting adulterated honey takes a significant role in the food industry. To address this need, several techniques/methods have been developed for its detection, such as spectroscopy (Mantha et al., 2018), stable carbon analysis (Cinar et al., 2014), chromatography (Wang et al., 2014), and Fourier transforms (FT) Raman spectroscopy (Batsoulis et al., 2005). Although these techniques are effective, they require adequate laboratory instruments, do not provide real-time measurements, and are expensive.

In contrast, fiber-optic-based sensors have been developed for various applications due to their notable advantages over conventional sensors, including small size, fast response, immunity to electromagnetic interference, remote and on-site sensing capabilities, and resistance to harsh environments (Yin et al., 2017). In this regard, only one tapered silica microfiber sensor has been reported for detecting adulterated honey based on different glucose concentrations (Isa et al., 2017). However, as it is a tapered sensor, the fabrication process is neither simple nor repeatable.

In this work, we present an application of a fiber optic sensor based on multimodal interference with SMS configuration for the detection of honey adulterated with sucrose. The sensor is capable of detecting concentrations of sucrose syrup from 1% to 5% in commercial brand honey and exhibits a linear response.

THEORETICAL DESCRIPTION

This section dives into the world of optical fibers and their application in the monitoring of a common material in the food industry, honey. Understanding the theoretical foundations behind this research is essential to contextualizing and appreciating the interplay between these two seemingly distinct but merging elements in a fascinating combination of optics and food analysis.

This section is divided into two different parts, each of which is dedicated to laying the necessary foundations to understand the development and results of this study.

In the first part, the generalities of optical fibers are addressed; this knowledge is crucial to understanding how optical fibers become valuable tools for monitoring and transmitting information. It begins with the generalities of optical fiber, such as its basic structure and how they function as light guides, the essential components of an optical fiber, including the core and the cladding. The optical phenomena and laws that allow light to travel through fibers will be delved into. It concludes with a focus on the phenomenon of Total Internal Reflection (TIR). It explains in detail how TIR allows light to remain within the fiber core, without significant intensity losses. This phenomenon is fundamental for the efficient transmission of data through optical fibers and plays an essential role in honey monitoring.

The second part of this section focuses on the generalities of the material under study: honey. To understand how fiber optics are used as a monitoring tool for this fluid, it is essential to have a solid understanding of the properties of honey. The key areas that will be explored in this section include rheological properties, optical properties, and other relevant characteristics, such as chemistry, density, viscosity, and other aspects that influence its behavior.

The above is with the purpose of establishing a solid base of knowledge in the areas of optical fibers and the properties of honey. These insights are essential to understanding how fiber optics become a powerful tool for honey monitoring and how optical principles are applied in this research. With this theoretical basis, we are prepared to address the experimental development and results of this study.

Fiber Optic Fundamentals

When an incident light ray encounters the interface between two materials, each with a different refractive index (RI), it can undergo both reflection and transmission. Under specific conditions, the light ray may be entirely reflected at the interface, without any part of it entering the second medium (Hecht, 2017). In other words, refraction may not occur. To illustrate this, consider the diagram depicted in Figure 2. Multiple rays are shown emanating from a light source within material *a*, characterized by a certain RI η_a, at various angles of incidence. These rays interact with the interface of medium *b*, which possesses an RI η_b, of $\eta_a > \eta_b$.

Figure 2. Total internal reflection phenomenon occurs if $\eta_b < \eta_a$

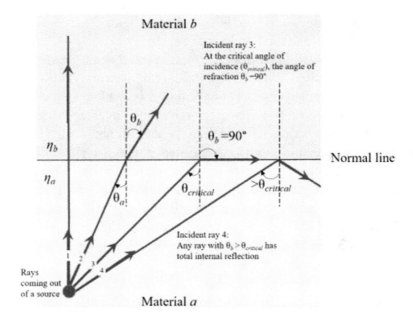

As evident, when the angle of incidence of the light ray increases, the transmitted ray deviates further from the normal line. Notably, there exists a specific angle of incidence at which the refracted ray travels parallel to the interface. This particular angle is known as the critical angle. Beyond the critical angle, for incident angles greater than this value, the light beam ceases to transmit into the second medium, and the interface acts as a reflective surface. Consequently, the ray remains confined within material A and is entirely reflected by the interface. This phenomenon is referred to as total internal reflection (TIR) and occurs only when the ray encounters a material with a lower RI than the one it originates from (Young et al., 2009)

The way to calculate the critical angle for two given materials is through Snell's Second Law, equating $\theta_b = 90°\,(sen\theta_b = 1)$, from which we obtain:

$$sen\theta_{critical} = \frac{\eta_b}{\eta_a} \qquad (1)$$

The propagation of light within a long, slender dielectric material is predicated on the Total Internal Reflection (TIR) phenomenon, as depicted in Figure 3. This journey began in 1870 when John Tyndall demonstrated the feasibility of confining and guiding light within a stream of water. However, it wasn't until 1970 that the Corning Glass Works company developed a dielectric filament composed of highly pure silicon dioxide (SiO_2) known as optical fiber, which had the capability to transmit signals with an attenuation of 20 dB/km, rivaling the copper electrical systems of that era. Subsequent research conducted over the following two decades led to the reduction of transmission attenuation to a mere 0.16 dB/km (Hecht, 2017). Figure 3 provides a diagram illustrating the mechanism of light confinement within an optical fiber based on geometric criteria.

Figure 3. Path of a light beam when propagating in an optical fiber

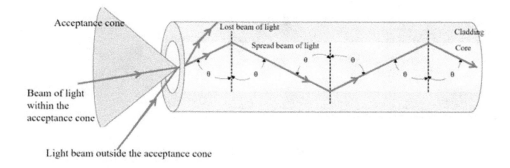

As can be seen, a fiber essentially consists of two concentric solid cylinders, the inner one being the core and the outer one being the cladding. The RI of the core is greater than that of the cladding. In this way, when a beam of light travels through the core and hits at an angle greater than the critical angle at the core-cladding interface, the beam will be completely reflected. Therefore, there will be no losses due to refraction towards the outside, thus propagating through the core through multiple reflections. In this way, light signals are guided that allow data transmission over long distances without loss. It is important to mention that the light beam will propagate in the optical fiber under the aforementioned description, as long as the incident beam coming from the outside of the fiber is contained within a certain solid angle, called the acceptance cone. The light beam that hits the fiber outside of said cone will propagate within the core, but there will be losses of the transmitted signal. This is due to the fact that the beam, upon reaching the core-cladding interface, will do so below the critical angle, so part of the radiation will be transmitted towards the cladding, which causes signal attenuation.

Optical fibers have important characteristics, such as: transmission with low losses, capacity to transport a large amount of information, they are light and small cables, and they have immunity to electromagnetic interference. All of this has made them the main means of telecommunications and not only that, but their alternative use as a sensor device for physical variables has also been explored (Krohn et al., 2014).

As mentioned, an optical fiber has a structure consisting of two concentric cylinders of silicon. In addition to its structure, it is surrounded by an outer cover of a plastic polymer that protects it, as shown in Figure 4.

Figure 4. Structure of the optical fiber

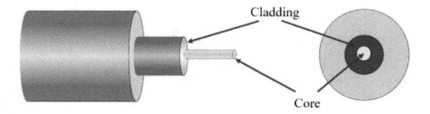

The diameters of the core, cladding and plastic jacket can vary, so there is a wide variety of fibers.

Theoretical Foundations of Optical Sensors based on Multimodal Interference

Goos-Hänchen Effect

A multimodal waveguide can be used as a sensing element because, when a signal propagates in it, part of the guided electromagnetic field penetrates the surrounding medium. This portion of the field that emerges from the waveguide is called the evanescent field and is capable of modifying the propagation of light within the waveguide. To visualize the way in which a waveguide operates as a sensor, it is necessary to consider a description of the propagation of light in terms of rays, shown in Figure 5, where it can be seen that the ray undergoes a total lateral displacement of in the direction of propagation. This phenomenon is known as Goos-Hänchen shift (GHS) and has its origin in phase accumulation in the TIR process.

Figure 5. Geometric description of the Goos-Hänchen (GH) displacement within a waveguide of length L. In it, the evanescent field is the part of the guided field in the core that emerges towards the coating

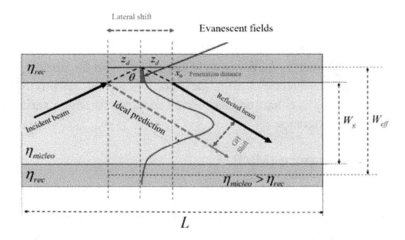

As seen in Figure 5, the lateral displacement indicates that the light penetrates to a depth given by (Snyder & Love, 1976):

$$x_0 = \frac{z_d}{\tan \theta} \qquad (2)$$

which corresponds to the distance traveled in the coating before being "reflected" by a virtual interface within the coating. In terms of the wavelength λ, the critical angle θ_C, the RI of the core $\eta_{núcleo}$, and the cladding η_{rec}, this penetration depth is equivalently expressed by:

$$x_0 = \frac{\lambda}{2\pi\sqrt{\cos^2\theta_C - \left(\eta_{núcleo}/\eta_{rec}\right)}} \tag{3}$$

According to the analysis reported in the reference (Hunsperger & Meyer-Arendt, 1992), if Equation 2 is compared with the solutions to the wave equation under the wave theory, it is obtained that said solutions predict evanescent fields whose penetration constants are related to the depth of penetration x_0 of the ray.

The beam propagates in multiple modes, where each mode has an evanescent field associated with different penetrations into the coating. In such a way that the higher-order modes are less confined and, therefore, have a more extended evanescent field. This, in turn, results in each mode traveling with a different propagation constant, which causes them to accumulate different phases as they propagate. In this way, all modes interfere constructively and destructively along the waveguide; this is multimodal interference.

One of the advantages of sensing via the evanescent field in an MMI situation is that all modes interact, to a greater or lesser extent, with the cladding and this is reflected in the interference of all modes. For this reason, sensitivity to small changes in the coating is enhanced, because all modes sense these variations and report it through interference.

Multimodal Interference (MMI)

The MMI phenomenon occurs in a multimode optical fiber because the origin of the phenomenon lies in the interference of multiple modes. Although the analytical description of the effect changes and is more complex due to the mathematics associated with cylindrical symmetry, it is possible to make an approximation based on considerations similar to those used for a rectangular waveguide (Wang et al., 2008; Zhu et al., 2008).

The analysis begins assuming that we have a standard structure, which consists of an SMF spliced to an MMF section, as shown in Figure 6. It is considered that both fibers are coaxial and that there is no lateral displacement between their centers.

Figure 6. SMF-MMF fiber structure used in simulations to explain the characteristics of MMI devices

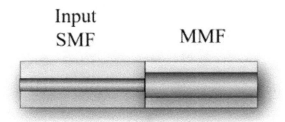

To explain the MMI given the structure of Figure 6, we begin by first calculating the energy coupled from the excitation field to each of the modes supported by the MMF, then the calculations for the propagation constant along the MMF and finally, at each propagation distance, the total field is calculated as the coherent superposition. The analysis presented in this section is based on what was developed in Refs. (Guzman-Sepulveda et al., 2021; Wang et al., 2008; Zhu et al., 2008).

The structure of Figure 6 is considered to have a stepped index profile and are aligned with respect to the propagation axis, without there being a lateral displacement between its cores. At the input plane where both fibers are spliced $(z = 0)$, the light that has propagated through the SMF fiber decomposes within the MMF fiber, it can be written as (Guzman-Sepulveda et al., 2021):

$$E(x, y, 0) = \sum_m c_m F_m(x, y) \tag{4}$$

Where $F_m(x, y)$ is the spatial field distribution and c_m s the field excitation coefficient of the m-th eigenmode.

Due to the circular symmetry of the SMF fiber, the field with which the MMF modes are excited is also radially symmetric. As a result, the excited modes also satisfy the same radial symmetry characteristic by virtue of the energy transfer from the excitation field to each mode, described by the so-called superposition integral. For a radially symmetric situation, the superposition of excited modes in Equation 4 is expressed in terms of a radial coordinate as (Guzman-Sepulveda et al., 2021; Zhao et al., 2011):

$$E(r, 0) = \sum_m c_m F_m(r) \tag{5}$$

The set of eigenfunctions $F_m(r)$ correspond to radially symmetric field distributions (modes LP_{om}) and can be expressed in terms of Bessel functions as follows (Guzman-Sepulveda et al., 2021):

$$F_m(r) = \begin{cases} c_m^{(1)} J_0(u_m \frac{r}{a}), & r \leq a \\ c_m^{(2)} K_0(\omega_m \frac{r}{a}), & r > a \end{cases} \qquad (6)$$

Where a is the radius of the waveguide core; u_m and ω_m are the transverse wave numbers; J_0 and K_0 are the Bessel function of the first type and the modified Bessel function of the second type, respectively; $c_m^{(1)}$ y $c_m^{(2)}$ indicate the amplitude of the electric field in the core and cladding region, respectively.

In this way, as light propagates in the MMF section, the total field at a propagation distance z can be calculated as the coherent superposition of all modes, using the following expression (Wang et al., 2008):

$$E(r,z) = \sum_m c_m F_m(r) \exp(-i\beta_m z) \qquad (7)$$

Where is the propagation constant of the m-th excited mode in the MMF.

The excitation coefficient can be calculated by the superposition integral between $E^{(in)}(r,0)$ y $F_m(r)$ (Zhao et al., 2011):

$$c_m = \frac{\int_0^\infty E^{(in)}(r,0) F_m(r) r\, dr}{\int_0^\infty F_m(r) F_m(r) r\, dr} \qquad (8)$$

Alternatively, it is also possible to estimate the excitation coefficient through the power coupling coefficient η_m. For radially symmetric modes, when the input field covers a small region of the waveguide core, so that the amount of field in the cladding can be neglected, c_m it can be directly related to η_m and the expression is as follows (Guzman-Sepulveda et al., 2021):

$$c_m = \begin{cases} c_m^{(1)} = \sqrt{\eta_m} \\ c_m^{(2)} = \left[\dfrac{J_0(u_m)}{K_0(u_m)}\right] c_m^{(1)} \end{cases} \quad (9)$$

Where η_m, is calculed by (Guzman-Sepulveda et al., 2021):

$$\eta_m = \dfrac{2\left(\dfrac{\omega}{a}\right)\exp\left[-\dfrac{1}{2}\left(\dfrac{\omega}{a}\right)^2 (u_m)^2\right]}{J_0^2(u_m)+J_1^2(u_m)+\left[\dfrac{K_1^2(\omega_m)}{K_0^2(\omega_m)}-1\right]J_0^2(u_m)} \quad (10)$$

With

$$u_m = \left(2m-\dfrac{1}{2}\right)\dfrac{\pi}{2}$$

$$\omega_m = \sqrt{V^2 - u_m^2}$$

The number of modes supported in an optical fiber can be estimated from the normalized frequency, V (Paschotta, 2008):

$$V = \left(\dfrac{2\pi}{\lambda}\right) a\sqrt{n_r^2 - n_c^2} \quad (13)$$

Where is the core radius of the optical fiber, n_r y n_c and is the RI of the core and cladding, respectively, and λ is the free space wavelength.

A value of $V \leq 2.405$ indicates light propagates in a single guided mode, the fundamental mode. In an MMF, V acquires values much higher than this threshold, indicating that the fiber supports multiple propagation modes (Paschotta, 2008). Alternatively, some fiber optic providers use the following expression to calculate the value of V (Thorlabs, 1999-2022):

$$V = \dfrac{2\pi a}{\lambda} NA \quad (14)$$

Finally, for a stepped RI MMF, it is possible to calculate the propagation constant β_m of the m-th mode, with the expression (Guzman-Sepulveda et al., 2021):

$$\beta_m \approx k_0 n_r - \left(2m - \frac{1}{2}\right)^2 \frac{\pi^2}{8k_0 n_c a^2} \qquad (15)$$

Where $k_0 = \frac{2\pi}{\lambda_0}$ and is the magnitude of the vector in free space. The propagation constant β_m, can also be expressed in terms of the effective RI, resulting in the expression $\beta_m = k_0 n_{eff,m}$

An additional phenomenon that needs to be explained is the formation of self-images in the MMI device. And it begins by mentioning that, in restricted symmetric interference, individual images of the input field are generated at effective distances using the expression (Soldano & Pennings, 1995):

$$L = p\left(\frac{3L_\pi}{4}\right) \text{ where } p = 1, 2, 3..... \qquad (16)$$

Where $p = 1, 2, 3,.....$ is the order or index of the self-image and denotes the periodic nature of imaging along MMF, L_π is called the length between the two lowest order modes and is calculated with the expression (Soldano & Pennings, 1995):

$$L_\pi = \frac{4n_{eff} W_{eff}^2}{3\lambda_0} \qquad (17)$$

Where η_{eff} y W_{eff} is the effective RI and the effective diameter of the waveguide, respectively.

As already mentioned, the MMF section has multiple excited modes. The contribution of each mode is determined by the energy content that results from the superposition with the input field (Mohammed et al., 2004; Mohammed et al., 2006; Wang et al., 2008). As the modes travel with their propagation constant, they interfere with each other, creating an interference pattern along the MMF segment.

Fiber Optic Sensors Based on Multimodal Interference

Under symmetric interference conditions, that is, when the MMF is excited at its center by a radially symmetric input field, the spectral response of fiber optic MMI devices is filter-like. It is expressed by the equation (Soldano & Pennings, 1995):

$$\lambda_{peak} = p \frac{\eta_{eff} W_{eff}^2}{L} \qquad (18)$$

The previous equation allows us to calculate the peak wavelength (λ_{peak}) that will replicate the p-th image of the input field of an MMI device with length L, effective RI (η_{eff}) and effective optical diameter (W_{eff}).

Similar to the case of a rectangular waveguide, the effective optical diameter, W_{eff} in a cylindrical waveguide can be estimated by a correction to the physical diameter of the MMF core (W), taking into account evanescent penetration into the cladding (Okamoto, 2021; Soldano & Pennings, 1995):

$$W_{eff} = W + \frac{1}{2}\left(\frac{\lambda_0}{\pi}\right)\left(\eta_r^2 - \eta_c^2\right)^{-\frac{1}{2}}\left[\left(\frac{\eta_c}{\eta_r}\right)^2 + 1\right] \qquad (19)$$

Where η_r y η_c are the RI of the core and cladding, respectively, of the MMF fiber, λ_0 is the free space wavelength, and W is the geometric diameter of the MMF fiber. In fact, (19) can be derived from the formalism for a rectangular guide by averaging the two orthogonal polarizations due to circular symmetry (Soldano & Pennings, 1995). Finally, it is important to mention that, for the design and manufacture of the MMI sensors in this paper, Equation 18 was used in the fourth image ($p = 4$), so that the length of the MMF section to obtain the peak of the response spectral at a desired wavelength, can be estimated by the expression:

$$L_{MMF} = \frac{4\eta_{eff} W_{eff}^2}{\lambda_{peak}} \qquad (20)$$

SMS Structure

The design of the proposed sensor (Figure 7) represents a specific instance of the structure singlemode–multimode–singlemode (SMS), which comprises a section of multimode fiber (MMF) sandwiched between two single-mode fibers (SMFs) (Wu et al., 2021). In this case, a coreless multimode fiber (NC-MMF) is employed, where the surrounding medium around the NC-MMF serves as its cladding. This configuration offers significant sensitivity to the fiber's surroundings, all the while maintaining the sensor's architecture and ensuring a simple fabrication process.

Figure 7. SMS structure of the proposed sensor

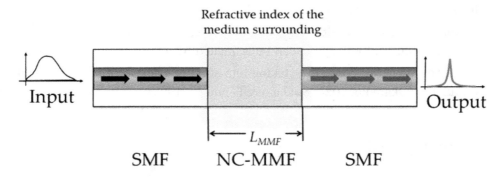

When a beam is made to propagate from the SMF to the NC-MMF, multiple optical modes are excited in this segment and interfere with each other throughout the propagation. Due to this fact, a periodic self-imaging of the input field occurs occasioned by the interference of the optical modes along the NC-MMF (Soldano & Pennings, 1995). For this reason, the NC-MMF fiber must have a specific length to reconstruct the input field to the NC-MMF output.

To select the wavelength of the SMS system, equation 20 is used. Due to the increase of the IR of the liquid surrounding the MMI system, the auto-image construction is modified, so that another wavelength is the one that fulfills this relation established in Equations (16) and (20). Moreover, due to the difference between peak wavelengths for each medium in which the sensor is located, such an effect can be used to evaluate the quality or purity of the surrounding media. In our case, we use this principle to evaluate the honey purity.

Rheological and Optical Properties of Honey

The optical and rheological properties of honey are important for various applications, including honey quality assessment and adulteration detection. These properties are also used to study the composition and structural characteristics of honey, especially in the context of the authenticity and purity of honey, in addition, they are also useful for the design of devices that help to evaluate these parameters (Faustino & Pinheiro, 2021).

Rheological Properties of Honey

The rheological properties of honey can be characterized by measuring its response to applied forces, stress, or deformation. These properties describe how honey behaves like a fluid under different conditions. Based on the references (Bambang et al., 2019; Faustino & Pinheiro, 2021; Machado De-Melo et al., 2017), the following are some common rheological properties of honey and how they can be defined:

Honey is a viscoelastic material, meaning it exhibits both viscous and elastic properties depending on the shear rate or stress applied to it. The rheological properties of honey can vary depending on factors such as temperature, moisture content, floral source, and processing conditions. Here are the primary rheological properties of honey:

1. Viscosity: Viscosity is the resistance of a fluid to flow. Honey is a highly viscous fluid, which means it flows slowly. Its viscosity is influenced by factors such as temperature and moisture content. As temperature increases, honey becomes less viscous and flows more easily.
2. Shear-thinning behavior: Honey exhibits shear-thinning behavior, also known as pseudoplasticity. When subjected to shear stress (e.g., stirring or pouring), the apparent viscosity of honey decreases with increasing shear rate. This property allows honey to flow more readily under applied forces.
3. Thixotropy: Honey is thixotropic, meaning its viscosity decreases over time when subjected to continuous or repeated shear stress and returns to its original viscosity when left at rest. This behavior is often observed when honey is agitated or stirred.
4. Elasticity: Honey possesses some degree of elasticity, meaning it can recover its original shape after being deformed. This property is related to the presence of sugars and proteins in honey.
5. Temperature dependence: The viscosity of honey is sensitive to temperature changes. As the temperature rises, honey becomes less viscous and flows more easily, while lower temperatures increase its viscosity.

6. Newtonian behavior: Although the majority of honey is Newtonian fluids, several varieties of honey have been reported as having fascinating shear-thinning and thixotropic as well as anti-thixotropic behavior.
7. Storage modulus (G'): Honey has a storage modulus (G'), which characterizes its elastic behavior. The storage modulus represents the material's ability to store elastic energy under deformation and is related to the honey's structure.

These rheological characteristics of honey are crucial for assessing its quality and authenticity as well as for understanding how it behaves throughout processing and handling. Rheological tests are frequently performed to evaluate the consistency, stability, and appropriateness of honey for certain uses, such as those in the food industry.

It's crucial to remember that the rheological characteristics of honey might change depending on things like the botanical origin, geographic region, and presence of other ingredients (such as pollen or wax from the honeycomb). As a result, there may be some variation in these qualities among various honey species.

Optical Properties of Honey

The optical properties of honey are of interest due to its ability to interact with light. These properties become important in the design of sensors based on optical fibers. The following references (Bogdanov et al., 2015; Machado De-Melo et al., 2017; Sáenz Laín & Gómez Ferreras, 2000; White & Doner, 1980) mention the optical properties that are key:

1. Refractive Index: The refractive index of honey describes how much the speed of light is reduced when it passes through the honey compared to its speed in a vacuum. The refractive index of honey typically ranges from around 1.4815 to 1.504, increasing when the solid content is high (or water content is low), depending on the temperature and other factors.
2. Birefringence: Honey can exhibit birefringence, which is the property of a material to split a light beam into two orthogonal polarizations as it passes through. Birefringence can occur in honey due to the presence of anisotropic components, such as crystalline sugar particles or other structures.
3. Optical Rotation: Honey can cause the plane of polarization of polarized light to rotate as it passes through the material. This phenomenon is known as optical rotation and is typically caused due to its carbohydrate composition present in honey, primarily sugars. The degree of optical rotation can provide information about the concentration of sugar molecules in the honey. Each sugar has a specific angle of polarized light rotation (specific rotation). Some

sugars rotate the polarized light angle to the left, presenting a negative optical rotation value (fructose), while others rotate to the right, with positive optical activity (glucose). Therefore, the overall value for the optical rotation depends on the concentration of the different honey sugars.
4. Absorption and Scattering: Honey interacts with light through absorption and scattering. Some components in honey can absorb certain wavelengths of light, leading to changes in its color and transparency. Additionally, scattering of light occurs when light interacts with the microstructures or particles in honey, resulting in a diffused appearance.
5. Optical Path Length Variation: Honey's optical path length can vary due to its non-uniform thickness and the presence of suspended particles. This variation in the path length can affect light transmission through the honey.
6. Polarization Properties: The polarization characteristics of light passing through honey can be influenced by its molecular structure and scattering properties. Polarized light can experience changes in its polarization state after interacting with honey.

The refractive index of honey can be used as one of the parameters to verify the quality of honey. Based on the rheological and optic properties, it can be said that the refractive index is influenced by the concentration of dissolved solids, primarily sugars, in the honey. As a result, the refractive index is related to the honey's composition and can provide valuable information about its quality.

Analyzing both properties of honey, we can be concluded that the refractive index can be used to assess the quality of honey in the following ways:

1. Determination of Moisture Content: The refractive index of honey is sensitive to its moisture content. Generally, as the moisture content increases, the refractive index of honey decreases. By measuring the refractive index and comparing it with a reference value for a particular type of honey, it is possible to estimate its moisture content. Honey with high moisture content may be indicative of improper storage or adulteration, as pure and high-quality honey typically has a lower moisture content.
2. Detection of Adulteration: Different types of sugars and syrups have distinct refractive indices. If honey is adulterated with other sweeteners like corn syrup or cane sugar syrup, the refractive index of the honey will deviate from the expected value for pure honey of the same type. Deviations from the standard refractive index can raise suspicion of adulteration and indicate lower quality or authenticity issues.
3. Floral Source Identification: The refractive index of honey can vary based on its botanical origin. Honey from different floral sources may have slightly

different refractive indices due to variations in sugar composition and other compounds. Thus, the refractive index can provide clues about the floral source of the honey, contributing to its quality characterization and authenticity.
4. Honey Dilution and Blending Detection: If honey is diluted with other substances or blended with honey from different sources, the refractive index may be affected. Deviations from the expected refractive index for pure honey of a specific type can suggest that the honey has been diluted or blended, affecting its quality.

It is important to note that the refractive index is a useful tool to assess quality, however, rheological, and optical properties must be considered to avoid any bias in the measurements. In the present research project, it was carried out using the refractive index to identify the adulteration of honey with sucrose syrup. Sample preparation, handling, and measurement were carried out in a controlled environment, to avoid as far as possible errors when measuring.

MATERIALS AND METHODS

Samples Preparation

For the preparation of samples, a commercial brand of honey from Mexico has been used, whose purity was validated by Mexican laws. The pure honey was adulterated by adding commercial brand sucrose syrup at four levels of adulteration, starting with 1%(w/w) to 5%(w/w) in 1% increments, based on the weight fraction (w/w) of Equation 3(Ucko, 2013).

$$\frac{w}{w}\% = \left(\frac{weight-of-solute}{weight-of-solution}\right)100\% \tag{21}$$

Samples were kept at room temperature to avoid the formation of any crystalline material and were shaken for 30 min to ensure homogeneity and avoid complications from natural variations in sucrose concentration.

Subsequently, the refractive index of the samples is measured using a refractometer. Before taking the measurements, the refractometer was calibrated using distilled water and glycerin, according to the manufacturer's calibration instructions.

The refractive index for each sample of sucrose syrup and honey is presented in Table 1.

Table 1. The refractive index of each sample of sucrose syrup and pure honey

% Pure honey	% Sucrose syrup	Refractive index
100%	0%	1.49729
99%	1%	1.49597
98%	2%	1.49333
97%	3%	1.49202
96%	4%	1.49071
95%	5%	1.48811

Sensor Fabrication

The SMS was fabricated according to Equation 20. SMS devices have a section of NC-MMF spliced between two SMFs; the spectral response was designed simply by adjusting the length of the NC-MMF segment. The SMF fibre used is SMF-28 from ®Thorlabs, which has a cladding and core diameter of 125 μm and 8 μm, respectively. The NC-MMF fibre is model FG125LA from ®Thorlabs and has a diameter $W_{eff} = 125 \mu m$ and a refractive index to $n_{eff} = 1.4445$ at an operating wavelength of 1550 nm. All segments were spliced with a Fujikura model ®FSM-60S splicer.

Based on Equation 20 and selecting the fourth self-image $(p = 4)$, the length of the NC-MMF section was calculated to fabricate the sensor for a peak wavelength $\lambda_{peak} = 1488 nm$, so we obtain that the length of NC-MMF is around $L_{MMF} = 60.7 mm$. Subsequently, the sensor head was pigtailed with conventional FC/PC connectors.

Experimental Set-Up

The experimental setup to test the SMS structure is shown in Figure 8. In this scheme, a ®Thorlabs model SLD1550S-A1 superluminescent laser diode is used, it provides a broadband spectrum from 1420 nm to 1650 nm, which is launched on an FC/PC connection cable. The signal is then propagated to the SMS device, collected on a second patch cable, and the transmitted signal is measured with an ®Anritsu model MS9740A optical spectrum analyser.

Figure 8. Experimental setup used to measure the honey sample's adulteration

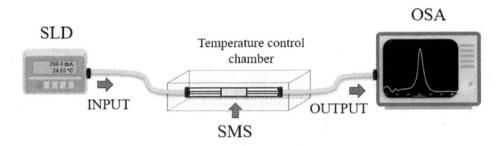

RESULTS

The experimental tests began by placing the sensor in initial conditions, that is, fixed in a container and surrounded by air. Subsequently, the sensor was completely covered with the 5% sucrose syrup sample, and the spectrum of the signal obtained in the OSA was recorded. Later, the sensor is cleaned with vinegar and deionized water; and air-dried to guarantee the same initial conditions for the test. The same process was followed for each sample of sucrose syrup and honey.

As we described before, by changing the medium surrounding the NC-MMF, the constructive interference condition defined by Equation 17, is modified. Consequently, a spectral shift is expected for each sample of sucrose syrup and honey. In Figure 9, shows the spectral response of SMS for the entire samples of sucrose syrup and honey. The spectrum of the sensor in air (initial conditions) is presented, only to show the spectral shift of pure honey compared to the initial conditions.

Figure 9. Spectral response for each sample of sucrose syrup and honey pure

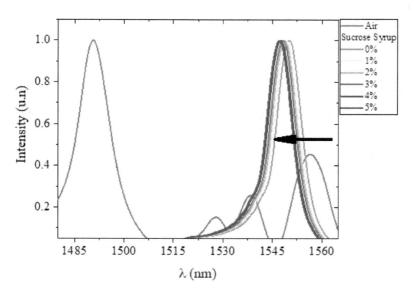

In Figure 10, only the spectral shift is presented for each adulterated honey sample by adding sucrose syrup in percentages from 1% to 5%. In the figure, it is clearly observed that there is a spectral shift to the left as the percentage of sucrose syrup increases.

Figure 10. Zoom-in of the spectra measured for each adulteration concentration

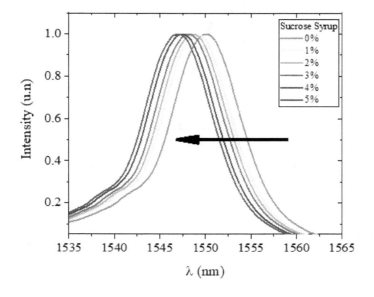

Figure 11 shows the spectral shift of the maximum wavelength, Δλ, as a function of the concentration of sucrose syrup in honey. This displacement is calculated as the difference between the maximum peak wavelengths when the SMS structure is submerged in the sample and its measured position in the air. The negative spectral shift is proportional to the concentration level of the sample. As the amount of sucrose syrup increases, the shift of the wavelength peak decreases. Likewise, in Figure 6, the refractive index of each adulterated sample measured with the refractometer was plotted and a behaviour very similar to the behaviour of the proposed sensor is observed. In both measurement systems (refractometer and SMS), the behaviour is linear, and a sensitivity of -0.54171 nm/% is estimated for the SMS.

Figure 11. Displacement of the wavelength peak for each concentration of sucrose syrup

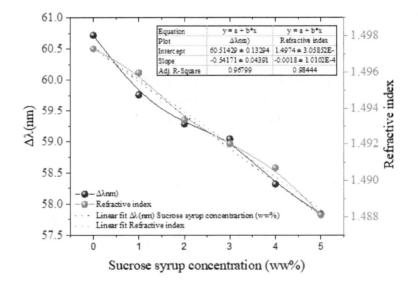

To obtain the error level and the measurement's repeatability, three representative samples were selected: 1%, 3%, and 5%, and their response was measured three times following the same measurement procedure described above, which includes cleaning with vinegar, deionized water, and drying. The standard deviation obtained from all these repetitions is presented in Table 2. We observe that the measurements for small concentrations (1% and 3%) are consistent in each repetition. And, for the maximum concentration (5%), we note a major variation, presumably attributed to the fact that the sucrose syrup level used is the major.

Table 2. Standard deviation to describe the error level and the measurement's repeatability

Sample	Mean	Standard Deviation
1%	1549.2	0.13856
3%	1548.32	0.24
5%	1547.71	0.59003

The information in the Table 2, can be seen in Figure 12.

Figure 12. Wavelength peaks measured for three representative samples (1%, 3% and 5%), to verify the repeatability of the experiment

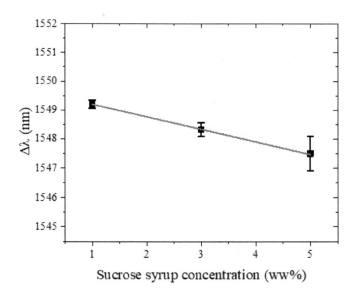

Based on the rheological and optical properties of honey, it is known that temperature affects the refractive index, in addition to influencing its Newtonian behaviour. Based on the rheological and optical properties of honey, it is known that temperature affects the refractive index, in addition to influencing its Newtonian behaviour. However, it is important to know the response of the sensor when applying temperature. For this, experimental tests were carried out, first the highest concentration of sucrose syrup and honey was selected, that is, the 5% concentration. From initial conditions, in air, the sensor was immersed in the selected concentration. The container was placed on a hot plate and the temperature was increased from

25°C to 45°C, in 10°C increments. In this process, the sensor was kept inside the temperature chamber. At each temperature increase, the sample was stabilized for 40 min before recording the spectrum. The results are summarized in Figure 13.

Figure 13. Thermal response reported for a concentration of 5% sugar syrup and pure honey. Measurements were made in the temperature range of 25°C to 45°C in 10°C increments

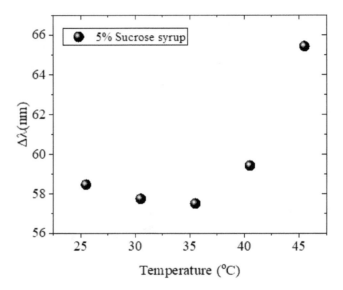

From the results shown in Figure 13, it can be seen that by increasing the temperature, the rheological properties are present, in terms of the dependence on temperature affecting the viscosity of the honey and with it its Newtonian behaviour. All this affects the behaviour of the sensor, and the reading does not present a linear response. Therefore, it is recommended to use the sensor to detect adulteration of honey with sucrose syrup at room temperature 25°C.

CONCLUSION

We are pleased to present the findings of our SMS fibre optic sensor, designed to detect honey adulteration with sucrose syrup in concentrations ranging from 1% to 5%. Rigorous tests were conducted using a commercially approved honey brand, complying with Mexican law for authenticity, and commercial sucrose syrup. Our sensor boasts several advantages, including easy fabrication, use of conventional low-cost fibres, and a linear response, making it a promising tool for quality assessment.

To validate the sensor's accuracy, we compared its results with those obtained from a conventional refractometer. Encouragingly, the response of our proposed sensor closely mirrored that of the refractometer, instilling confidence in its reliability and lack of bias.

Remarkably, our sensor effectively addressed the challenge of measuring adulterated honey, even with its inherent complexity. It is pertinent to acknowledge that honey's rheological properties typically follow a Newtonian behaviour. However, and based on that reported in reference (El-Bialee & Sorour, 2011), we verified that adulterated honey exhibits a non-Newtonian behaviour. This intricacy complicates the assessment of honey quality using solely optical properties, making our sensor's capabilities all the more vital.

Furthermore, our device offers the distinct advantage of real-time measurements, enhancing its suitability for quality control applications in the food industry. This feature significantly piques interest within the food industry as a robust mechanism to monitor honey adulteration levels effectively.

We believe our sensor's potential impact on the food industry is substantial, given its ability to detect adulteration at low concentrations, simplicity of use, and real-time monitoring capabilities. It presents a promising solution to safeguarding the authenticity and quality of honey products in the market. As the issue of honey adulteration remains a concern, our device may serve as a reliable and cost-effective tool for manufacturers and regulatory bodies to uphold the integrity of honey products and protect consumer interests.

ACKNOWLEDGEMENTS

We wish to thank Secretaría de Investigación y Posgrado, Universidad Autónoma de Tamaulipas (internal grant "Expansion of the Research Capacity of the Electronics group at UAM Reynosa Rodhe"), Research Project UAT 2023 (grant UAT/SIP/INV/2023/075) and UAM Reynosa-Rodhe Operational Plan.

REFERENCES

Batsoulis, A. N., Siatis, N. G., Kimbaris, A. C., Alissandrakis, E. K., Pappas, C. S., Tarantilis, P. A., & Polissiou, M. G. (2005). FT-Raman spectroscopic simultaneous determination of fructose and glucose in honey. *Journal of Agricultural and Food Chemistry*, *53*(2), 207–210. doi:10.1021/jf048793m

Bogdanov, S. (2007). Authenticity of honey and other bee products: state of the art. *Bulletin of university of agricultural sciences veterinary medicine cluj-napoca*, 1-8. USAMVLUJ. https://doi.org/http://www.usamvcluj.ro

Bogdanov, S. (2012). *Honey as nutrient and functional food, 100*. Proteins. https://doi.org/http://www.bee-hexagon.net/

Bogdanov, S., Jurendic, T., Sieber, R., & Gallmann, P. (2008). Honey for nutrition and health: A review. *Journal of the American College of Nutrition, 27*(6), 677–689. doi:10.1080/07315724.2008.10719745 PMID:19155427

Bogdanov, S., Lüllmann, C., Martin, P., von der Ohe, W., Russmann, H., Vorwohl, G., Oddo, L. P., Sabatini, A.-G., Marcazzan, G. L., Piro, R., Flamini, C., Morlot, M., Lhéritier, J., Borneck, R., Marioleas, P., Tsigouri, A., Kerkvliet, J., Ortiz, A., Ivanov, T., & Vit, P. (2015). Honey quality and international regulatory standards: Review by the International Honey Commission. *Bee World, 80*(2), 61–69. doi:10.1080/0005772X.1999.11099428

Cinar, S. B., Eksi, A., & Coskun, I. (2014). Carbon isotope ratio (13C/12C) of pine honey and detection of HFCS adulteration. *Food Chemistry, 157*, 10–13. doi:10.1016/j.foodchem.2014.02.006 PMID:24679745

El-Bialee, N., & Sorour, M. (2011). Effect of adulteration on honey properties. *International Journal of Applied Science and Technology, 1*(6). https://doi.org/www.ijastnet.com

Fakhlaei, R., Selamat, J., Khatib, A., Razis, A. F. A., Sukor, R., Ahmad, S., & Babadi, A. A. (2020). The Toxic Impact of Honey Adulteration: A Review. *Foods, 9*(11), 1538. doi:10.3390/foods9111538 PMID:33114468

Faustino, C., & Pinheiro, L. (2021). Analytical Rheology of Honey: A State-of-the-Art Review. *Foods, 10*(8), 1709. doi:10.3390/foods10081709 PMID:34441487

Guler, A., Kocaokutgen, H., Garipoglu, A. V., Onder, H., Ekinci, D., & Biyik, S. (2014). Detection of adulterated honey produced by honeybee (Apis mellifera L.) colonies fed with different levels of commercial industrial sugar (C(3) and C(4) plants) syrups by the carbon isotope ratio analysis. *Food Chemistry, 155*, 155–160. doi:10.1016/j.foodchem.2014.01.033 PMID:24594168

Guzman-Sepulveda, J. R., Guzman-Cabrera, R., & Castillo-Guzman, A. A. (2021). Optical Sensing Using Fiber-Optic Multimode Interference Devices: A Review of Nonconventional Sensing Schemes. *Sensors (Basel), 21*(5), 1862. doi:10.3390/s21051862 PMID:33800041

Hecht, E. (2017). *Optics*. Pearson.

Hunsperger, R. G., & Meyer-Arendt, J. R. J. A. O. (1992). *Integrated optics: theory and technology*. Harvard Press. https://doi.org/https://ui.adsabs.harvard.edu/abs/1992ApOpt.31Q.298H

Isa, N. M., Irawati, N., Rosol, A. H. A., Rahman, H. A., Ismail, W. I. W., Yusoff, M. H. M., & Naim, N. F. (2017). Silica Microfiber Sensor for the Detection of Honey Adulteration. *Advanced Science Letters*, *23*(6), 5532–5535. doi:10.1166/asl.2017.7415

Jaafar, M. B., Othman, M. B., Yaacob, M., Talip, B. A., Ilyas, M. A., Ngajikin, N. H., & Fauzi, N. A. M. (2020). A Review on Honey Adulteration and the Available Detection Approaches. *International Journal of Integrated Engineering*, *12*(2), 125–131. https://doi.org/https://doi.org/10.30880/ijie.2020.12.02.015. doi:10.30880/ijie.2020.12.02.015

Krohn, D. A., Méndez, A., & MacDougall, T. (2014). *Fiber Optic Sensors: Fundamentals and Applications*. SPIE Press. doi:10.1117/3.1002910

Machado De-Melo, A. A., Almeida-Muradian, L. B., Sancho, M. T., & Pascual-Maté, A. (2017). Composition and properties of Apis mellifera honey: A review. *Journal of Apicultural Research*, *57*(1), 5–37. doi:10.1080/00218839.2017.1338444

Mantha, M., Urban, J. R., Mark, W. A., Chernyshev, A., & Kubachka, K. M. (2018). Direct Comparison of Cavity Ring Down Spectrometry and Isotope Ratio Mass Spectrometry for Detection of Sugar Adulteration in Honey Samples. *Journal of AOAC International*, *101*(6), 1857–1863. doi:10.5740/jaoacint.17-0491 PMID:29618406

Mohammed, W. S., Mehta, A., & Johnson, E. G. (2004). Wavelength Tunable Fiber Lens Based on Multimode Interference. *Journal of Lightwave Technology*, *22*(2), 469–477. doi:10.1109/JLT.2004.824379

Mohammed, W. S., Smith, P. W., & Gu, X. (2006). All-fiber multimode interference bandpass filter. *Optics Letters*, *31*(17), 2547–2549. doi:10.1364/OL.31.002547 PMID:16902614

Okamoto, K. (2021). *Fundamentals of optical waveguides*. Elsevier.

Oroian, M., Ropciuc, S., & Paduret, S. (2018). Honey Adulteration Detection Using Raman Spectroscopy. *Food Analytical Methods*, *11*(4), 959–968. doi:10.1007/s12161-017-1072-2

Paschotta, R. (2008). V number. In *Encyclopedia of Laser Physics and Technology* (Vol. 1). Wiley-VCH.

Sáenz Laín, C., & Gómez Ferreras, C. (2000). *Mieles españolas. Características e identificación mediante el análisis del polen.*

Snyder, A. W., & Love, J. D. (1976). Goos-Hanchen shift. *Applied Optics*, *15*(1), 236–238. doi:10.1364/AO.15.000236 PMID:20155209

Soares, S., Amaral, J. S., Oliveira, M., & Mafra, I. (2017). A Comprehensive Review on the Main Honey Authentication Issues: Production and Origin. *Comprehensive Reviews in Food Science and Food Safety*, *16*(5), 1072–1100. doi:10.1111/1541-4337.12278 PMID:33371614

Soldano, L. B., & Pennings, E. C. M. (1995). Optical multi-mode interference devices based on self-imaging: Principles and applications. *Journal of Lightwave Technology*, *13*(4), 615–627. doi:10.1109/50.372474

Talha, M., Imran, M., Ahmad, M. H., Ahmad, R. S., Khan, M. K., Rahim, M. A., & Afzal, M. F. (2023). Honey Composition, Therapeutic Potential and Authentication through Novel Technologies: An Overview. https://doi.org/ doi:10.5772/intechopen.110007

Thorlabs. (1999-2022). *Multimode Fiber Tutorial.* Thorlabs, Inc. https://www.thorlabs.com/newgrouppage9.cfm?objectgroup_id=10417

Ucko, D. A. (2013). *Basics for chemistry.* Elsevier. doi:10.1016/C2013-0-11632-7

Wang, J. M., Xue, X. F., Du, X. J., Cheng, N., Chen, L. Z., Zhao, J., Zheng, J., & Cao, W. (2014). Identification of Acacia Honey Adulteration with Rape Honey Using Liquid Chromatography-Electrochemical Detection and Chemometrics. *Food Analytical Methods*, *7*(10), 2003–2012. doi:10.1007/s12161-014-9833-7

Wang, Q., Farrell, G., & Yan, W. (2008). Investigation on Single-Mode–Multimode–Single-Mode Fiber Structure. *Journal of Lightwave Technology*, *26*(5), 512–519. doi:10.1109/JLT.2007.915205

White, J., & Doner, L. W. (1980). *Honey composition and properties (Vol. 335).*

Wu, Q., Qu, Y., Liu, J., Yuan, J., Wan, S.-P., Wu, T., He, X.-D., Liu, B., Liu, D., Ma, Y., Semenova, Y., Wang, P., Xin, X., & Farrell, G. (2021). Singlemode-Multimode-Singlemode Fiber Structures for Sensing Applications—A Review. *IEEE Sensors Journal*, *21*(11), 12734–12751. doi:10.1109/JSEN.2020.3039912

Yin, S., Ruffin, P. B., & Francis, T. (2017). *Fiber optic sensors.* CRC press. doi:10.1201/9781420053661

Young, H. D., Freedman, R. A., Sears, F. W., Flores, V. A. F., Ford, A. L., & Zemansky, M. W. (2009). *Física universitaria 02*. Addison-Wesley ; Pearson Educación.

Zhang, G. Y., & Abdulla, W. (2022). On honey authentication and adulterant detection techniques. *Food Control*, *138*, 108992. doi:10.1016/j.foodcont.2022.108992

Zhu, X., Schülzgen, A., Li, H., Li, L., Han, L., Moloney, J. V., & Peyghambarian, N. (2008). Detailed investigation of self-imaging in largecore multimode optical fibers for application in fiber lasers and amplifiers. *Optics Express*, *16*(21), 16632–16645. doi:10.1364/OE.16.016632

Chapter 7
Design of Automated Locking Device for Geometry Test Equipment in Fiber Optic Connectors Through Interferometry

Jesus Cruz Garza Moreno
Unidad Académica Multidisciplinaria Reynosa-Rodhe, Mexico

Luz Idalia Balderas García
Unidad Académica Multidisciplinaria Reynosa-Rodhe, Mexico

Lourdes Yajaira García Rivera
Unidad Académica Multidisciplinaria Reynosa-Rodhe, Mexico

Francisco Javier Reyes Mireles
Unidad Académica Multidisciplinaria Reynosa-Rodhe, Mexico

ABSTRACT

In this project, an improvement will be made to reduce the costs for the purchase and repair of measurement fixtures that are used in the equipment that performs the geometry test. This improvement was decided to be implemented since there are constant replacements of measurement fixtures in a brief period, which causes them to have to buy more fixtures because the stock in the warehouse runs out quickly. The stock in the warehouse runs out quickly because the fixtures that are damaged are sent to be repaired by the supplier, therefore, they have an estimated return time. When a measurement fixture is damaged very quickly, it causes it to have to be replaced immediately; that means that the stock is running out because the fixtures that were sent for repair have not yet arrived, causing more to be purchased urgently.

DOI: 10.4018/979-8-3693-1119-6.ch007

Copyright © 2024, IGI Global. Copying or distributing in print or electronic forms without written permission of IGI Global is prohibited.

Design of Automated Locking Device for Geometry Test Equipment

INTRODUCTION

Since the beginning of the internet, it has always sought to improve connectivity and data transmission speed, starting from the premise of improving every day more. to surf the net worldwide, not only required good computer equipment, peripherals, and software. at the beginning of this network, the connectivity was done by the copper cable. for many years copper cable tried to cover the needs of data transfers but once these were surpassed, fiber optics was the innovation that catapulted the internet to new levels and propitiated industry 4.0, all this thanks to the fact that fiber optics has a very low latency and a transmission speed 10 times higher than copper cable (Leiner et al., 1999).

But not everything has advantages when we talk about fiber optics, its main handicaps are the price and its complexity of production, reasons why it has been a slow transition to this recent technology (Rodríguez, 2009).

Also, the telecommunications revolution began with the invention of low-loss optical fiber in 1970, and several enterprises started with production of this innovative product. Nearly 50 years ago, British Telecom's predecessor challenged Corning to develop a fiber that could transmit light with a loss of less than 20 decibels per kilometer. Corning responded by inventing the first low-loss optical fiber. These thin glass yarns were born in the optical communications industry and enabled the rapid explosion of the Internet worldwide (Okoshi, 2012).

Then this enterprise has continually innovated to increase the speed and capacity of optical networks while lowering installation costs. We now offer solutions for growing segments such as fiber-to-the-home, wireless, and hyperscale data centers (Dik Rodriguez & Niola Plaza, 2016; Okoshi, 2012).

After fiber, Corning also created packaging cables and connectors that drastically reduced the cost of installing a network. Today, Corning has manufactured more than one billion kilometers of fiber. We are an industry leader, able to offer our customers integrated solutions that improve their network performance and reduce their costs. Corning gains a thorough understanding of customer challenges, and we use knowledge to develop full-scale solutions that meet our customers' needs (Dik Rodriguez & Niola Plaza, 2016).

The present works aim to an improvement option to help reduce costs in the purchase and sale of measuring fixtures, as well as to help increase their useful life.

To achieve these main aims, a meeting was held with the entire core team of the area that damages the most measuring fixtures, to come up with possible solutions to this problem.

As a member of the test equipment department, it was proposed to create an automated locking system to avoid product manipulation during the geometry test.

This manipulation causes the measuring fixtures to be damaged very quickly, causing them to have to be replaced because they no longer work optimally.

This improvement will help to extend the useful life of the measuring fixtures, helping to avoid the need to replace them constantly and therefore help to reduce costs in terms of purchase and repair of the measuring fixtures.

JUSTIFICATION

In this project, an improvement will be made to reduce the costs for the purchase and repair of measurement fixtures that are used in the equipment that performs the geometry test. This improvement was decided to be implemented since there are constant replacements of measurement fixtures in a brief period, which causes them to have to buy more fixtures because the stock in the warehouse runs out quickly.

The stock in the warehouse runs out quickly because the fixtures that are damaged are sent to be repaired by the supplier, therefore, they have an estimated return time; When a measurement fixture is damaged very quickly, it causes it to have to be replaced immediately, that means that the stock is running out because the fixtures that were sent for repair have not yet arrived, causing more to be purchased urgently

This project will be done in the Test Equipment Department in the production area that makes DROP cables, these fixtures are used in the Interferometry Equipment, and they help the fiber optic connector (product) to be introduced through the fixture and the interferometry equipment to do the geometry test.

The measurement fixture has a part called Iner, which inserts the connector splints and performs the geometry test. One of the most common reasons for damage to fiber optic measurement fixtures is tampering with the product to be tested. That is to say, the fiber optic measurement fixture has a hole (inner) in which a splint (product) is inserted, and the geometry test begins to be performed using the interferometry equipment. In the test, 3 aspects are evaluated, which would be the ROC, Apex, and Protrusion.

These 3 aspects are measured by the interferometry equipment and yield a pass-or-fail result, depending on the parameters established for each product model.

The Apex is the aspect that the operator can manipulate, i.e. when inserting the splint (product) the Apex can be moved so that it marks the test as passing. This manipulation causes the inner to wear out or crack, causing severe damage.

Therefore, as a member of the Test Equipment Department, I will help to make a blocking device that has the purpose of avoiding the manipulation of the product at the time of performing the geometry test on the interferometry equipment using sensors that detect the operator's hand and issue an alert on the screen telling him to remove his hand to proceed with the test. Otherwise, the program will not allow the test to move forward, even if in the middle of the test the operator handles the product, the program will stop the test completely, forcing him to perform it correctly again.

This improvement will help reduce costs in terms of the purchase and repair of fiber optic measurement fixtures for interferometry equipment, as well as extend the useful life of the same. It will also help that when performing the geometry test, it is a more accurate test, avoiding false positives.

OBJECTIVES: GENERAL AND SPECIFIC

General Objective

The main objective is to reduce costs due to the constant replacement of fiber optic measurement fixtures in the interferometry equipment due to damage due to accelerated wear of the same due to poor handling at the time of performing the geometry test, in the production area carried out by Cables Drop in the company Corning Optical Communications S de RL de CV in the city of Reynosa. This will be achieved thanks to the implementation of an automated locking device using sensors, which, when detecting the operator's hand, will activate a padlock in the program, avoiding performing the test on the interferometry equipment.

Specific Objectives

- Avoid constant damage to measuring fixtures for geometry testing equipment.
- Avoid the constant purchase of measurement fixtures.
- Search for the right components to assemble the locking device
- Analyze which production lines are the ones that damage the most fiber optic measurement fixtures.
- Implement the locking device on the line that damages the most measurement fixtures and compare them with the others.

CHARACTERIZATION OF THE AREA

The area where this project will be carried out is in the production area that manufactures DROP cables, which area is the one that replaces the most fiber optic measurement fixtures due to damage.

This area currently has 13 production lines, which are divided as follows depending on the type of product they make:

Table 1. Line identification in the area producing DROP cables

Line	Model
DROP 7	Legacy
PUSHLOK 8	Push-lock
PUSHLOK 9	Push-lock
PUSHLOK 10	Push-lock
2 TELUS FIBERS	Legacy 2 fibers
DROP 11	Legacy
DROP 12	Legacy
PUSHLOK 13	Push-lock
HYB 1	Hybrid
HYB 2	Hybrid
HYB 3	Hybrid
Flexible / Inline	Inline 2-4 fibers
Xtension 1	Legacy 2 fibers

As can be seen in Table 1, the identification of the 13 lines that run the area is shown, in which only HYB 1, HYB 2, HYB 3, and Flexible/Inline run in such a way that they occupy two sides to process the product, that is, on one side they work one end, while the other side of the conveyor works another end. Therefore, these lines require 2 interferometry equipment to be able to run your product. This brings us to the fact that the area in total has 17-floor geometry test equipment.

PROBLEMS TO BE SOLVED BY PRIORITIZING THEM AND OPPORTUNITIES FOR IMPROVEMENT

Doing a visual inspection of the geometry test station, we saw that several aspects that corresponded to the Test Equipment department could be improved, which was made a list to be able to follow up and thus have the station and the equipment in optimal conditions for the ergonomics of the operator.

Design of Automated Locking Device for Geometry Test Equipment

Table 2. List of opportunities for improvement

N	Type	Area of Opportunity	Impact
1	5s	Maximo's Unlabeled Equipment	Low
2	5s	Lever less equipment	High
3	Safety	Equipment with missing support (leg)	High
4	Improvement	Equipment with incorrect power supply	High
5	Improvement	Equipment with block not suitable for the model to be tested	High
6	Improvement	Equipment with USB cable in poor condition	High
7	Improvement	Dirty camera equipment	High
8	Improvement	Damaged servo control equipment	High

Table 2 shows all the opportunities for improvement that we as a test team department were able to close.

SCOPE AND LIMITATIONS

Scopes

By executing this project by the test equipment maintenance department, the company Corning Optical Communications S of RL de CV will benefit.

Through it, the area that produces DROP cables will be the first area to benefit from the implementation of the improvement. The aim is to implement a blocking system at the affected station to reduce the constant replacement of fiber optic measurement fixtures.

Limitations

It should be clarified that this project will only be implemented in one line for the time being, due to the structure and design of the locking system, it will mainly seek to reduce the measurement fixtures are easily damaged, once that problem is attacked, it will proceed in detail to see other aspects such as ergonomics for the operator, etc.

THEORETICAL BACKGROUND

Fiber Optic

Fiber optics is a means of transmitting data employing photoelectric pulses through a wire constructed of transparent glass or other plastic materials with the same functionality. These threads can be almost as thin as a hair and are precisely the medium of transmission of the signal (Dik Rodriguez & Niola Plaza, 2016).

A light signal is transferred from one end of the cable to the other through these very thin cables. This light can be generated by a laser or an LED, and its most widespread use is to transport data over long distances since this medium has a much higher bandwidth than metal cables, lower losses, and higher transmission speeds (Dik Rodriguez & Niola Plaza, 2016).

The Apex Parameter

Apex Offset for APC connectors is the combination of two factors: polish angle and key error. When troubleshooting an APC process that is resulting in poor apex offset values, we need to identify which component (angle, key error, or both) is the primary contributor. "Usually," Angle is the culprit (especially when it comes to tapered APC splints, for reasons we'll discuss later) (Rao & Jackson, 2000; Rochelau, 2016).

Understanding and controlling the characteristics of PC splints end geometry is quite simple and intuitive. A radius is ...... a radio. If you want to increase the radius of a splint, you simply need to buff it with less pressure or use a harder backing pad while polishing. If you want to decrease the radius, you should buff it with more pressure or use a softer backing pad. The Apex is determined simply by how perpendicular the splints is to the polishing surface; a splint with a lower apex value means that the splints is placed more perpendicular to the polishing surface than a splints with a higher apex value. Simple, easy to understand and apply (Duan & Liu, 2012; Rao & Jackson, 2000; Rochelau, 2016).

We typically measure three geometric parameters: Radius, Apex Offset, and Fiber Height.

Understanding and controlling the geometry values of APC splints becomes a bit more complicated than with PC splints. Not only are the bushings polished at an angle, but that angle must be oriented in a specific rotational orientation (relative to the connector "key"). In addition, APC splints vary in shape (tapered tip and stepped tip). Controlling angle and apex values on tapered-tip splints is much more complicated than with stepped-tip splints (the reason for this is that, when polishing a cone shape, the "footprint" of the surface area being polished increases as more material is removed. With staggered, cylinder-shaped splints, the surface area being polished remains constant, regardless of how much splint material is removed (Rao & Jackson, 2000).

First, let's consider Apex Offset for APC splints:

Apex Displacement for APC Splints

When interpreting APC geometry results to modify the polishing process to improve results, it is important to understand Apex Offset, i.e. that Apex Offset (for PC and APC splints) is the result of two components: angle and key error (Rochelau, 2016).

In the case of PC splints, Apex Offset and Angle (or Angular Offset) are essentially two ways of saying the same thing. The "Apex Offset" value measured by the interferometer is simply the distance (in microns) between the Apex point (the highest point of the radius) and the geometric center of the splints (usually the exact center of the fiber). Ideally, we would want both the apex and the center of the splint to be in the same location: an apex offset value of 0 (Rochelau, 2016).

In real life, of course, nothing is "ideal," so we always have some offsetting value from Apex. But what causes the apex of a radius to be imperfect, and off-center? Angles do. Angles create an apex offset. Apex Offset is the result of angle polishing. The fact that the splints is at an angle to the polishing surface during polishing (for whatever reason, imprecise hole in a polishing fixture, uneven polishing surface, contamination in the outside diameter of the splints, etc.) will cause the vertex of that radius to be cut off fixed from the center of the splint. The greater the angle, the greater the displacement of the apex. There is a mathematical relationship between Angle, Apex Offset, and Radius: Tan (Angle) = Apex / Radius. If we know any two values, we can mathematically calculate the third. This also applies to APC splints but with an added factor: Key error (Rao & Jackson, 2000; Rochelau, 2016).

Because the longitudinal axis of a PC splint is perpendicular to the interferometer chamber, the measured apex compensation value stays constant regardless of the orientation of the splint on the equipment accessory. If you measure the apex displacement of PC splints, and then rotate that splints any amount on the machine attachment and measure again, the value of the measured apex deviation remains the same. The splints do not need to have a specific rotation orientation to the connector wrench. However, with APC splints, we have an angled surface that MUST be oriented at a specific location relative to the connector key (if not, two angled connectors will never mate when connected). Any rotational deviation from this angle-to-key orientation is known as a key error. The causes of key errors can be difficult to identify. Key error is most commonly the result of the polishing device wrench width being significantly larger than the connector wrench width. It can also be the result of poor-quality connector components (usually plastic housings) that do not hold the splints solidly in the proper orientation to the connector key (Rochelau, 2016).

Therefore, Apex Offset for APC connectors is the combination of two factors: polish angle and key error. When troubleshooting an APC process that is resulting in poor Apex offset values, we need to identify which component (angle, key error, or both) is the primary contributor. "Usually," Angle is the culprit (particularly when it comes to tapered APC splints, for reasons we'll discuss later). However, we can certainly take note of the APEX BEARING. Again, the Apex Offset values for APC splints are the result of two components: Angular Offset and Key Error. Angular offset moves the vertex along one axis, and key error moves the vertex along the opposite axis. Interferometer manufacturers differ on which axis the angular compensation component is located, and which is the key error component, but you can check by mounting an APC splints on the interferometer WITHOUT using a keyed adapter, focus until you can see the stripe patterns, and slowly rotate the splints to one side or the other. If the vertex point appears to move up and down, then the key error is only on the Y-axis. If you move from left to right, then the key error is along the x-axis (Duan & Liu, 2012).

Now let's consider that we have an Apex Offset problem in APC splints, and we have determined that the main contributor to the problem is the Angular Offset component. How to solve it? For this, we now need to discuss the effect of Radius on an angled surface, as well as the intricacies of polishing a taper (Rochelau, 2016).

PROCEDURE AND DESCRIPTION OF ACTIVITIES PERFORMED

The main activity to be solved during the project was by employing the automated blocking system, the fiber optic measurement fixtures would stop being damaged to avoid their constant replacement, as well as this would help to avoid the purchase of the same, helping to save costs for the area and the company.

A description of the process where the problem was detected will then be displayed.

Geometry Test Station Process

This station is where the geometry test is performed using the interferometry device.

Figure 1. Interferometry equipment

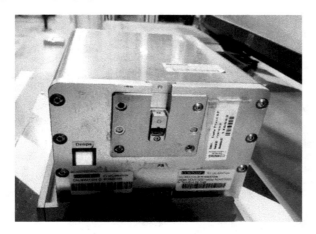

This equipment is made up of several parts, with the measurement fixture being the main part of the equipment that is damaged.

Figure 2. Fiber optic measurement fixture

The connector is inserted in the part marked with a blue circle in Figure 2, this connector when shown on the screen should look as follows.

Figure 3. Blink program for geometry test

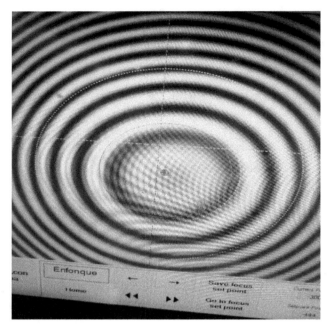

As shown in Figure 3, the connector should be as centered as possible, i.e. the part marked by the red circle in Figure 3 is the face of the fiber and the other images are the spokes of the splints. In this way, the test is done at the geometry test station, where 3 aspects are measured, the apex, the radius, and the protrusion, being that the parameters for each factor would be:

For radius is: 6-12

For apex is: 0-50

Problem Statement

Once we know how the process is performed at the geometry test station, we will focus on detecting the area of improvement at this station. Various tools or ways can be used for this. We, as Test Equipment Maintenance, verify that the IL and BR test equipment and interferometry test equipment are in optimal conditions for processing. So, when you look at the downtimes, you can see the reasons why the time was entered.

Figure 4. Downtimes examples of the geometry test station

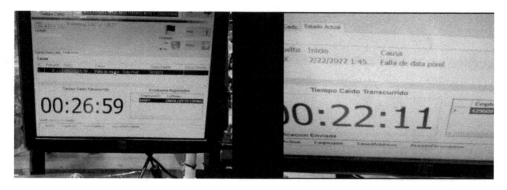

A Pareto diagram was made, to see what the reasons for the downtime at the geometry test were station.

Figure 5. Pareto of the downtime of the geometry test station

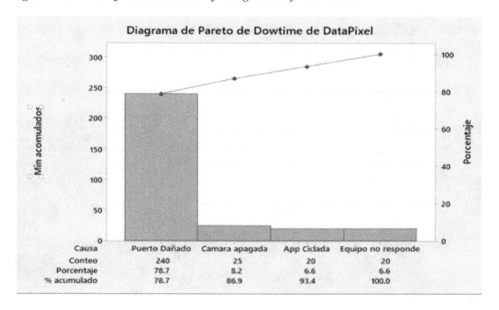

It was concluded that most of them were due to a lack of measurement fixtures for the geometry test equipment, therefore, it led us to another question, why was there a lack of measurement fixtures for the geometry test equipment?

And it was because they had been damaged and were not available in stock, on average between 3 and 4 ports were damaged and even more.

Figure 6. Measurement fixtures damaged in one week

Cantidad	Descripción	Núm. CMMS / ID	Ubicación Anterior	Ubicación Actual	Comentarios
1	Puerto	1122921 03	Drops L5	Bodega	No funcional
1	Puerto	1123378 02	Drops L13	Bodega	No funcional
1	Puerto	1124650 10	Drops L9	Bodega	No funcional

As can be seen in the figure above, 3 lines were affected by a lack of measurement fixtures, causing the lines to be stopped for an indeterminate time and even some lines were undone due to lack of them.

Undoubtedly, this caused a great concern to production due to the increase in damaged measurement fixtures because they had to be purchased more often, which implied an increase in costs, it is worth mentioning that each measurement fixture costs around $700 dollars.

It was seen, that when the failure in the geometry test equipment was reported, some cases were due to the splint breaking and getting stuck in the inner as shown in the following images.

Figure 7. Splint stuck in the measuring fixture

As seen in Figure 7, this happens because the fiber face is not very centered, as shown in the following figure:

Figure 8. Connector with invalid APEX

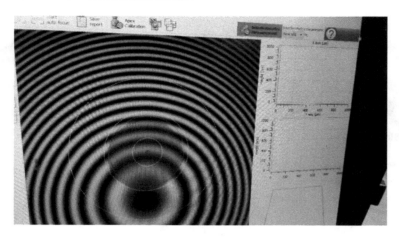

When the operator sees that the product is coming as in Figure 8, he has to cut it and send it to be reworked, but it happens that they do not do that, but they manipulate the connector and try to make the fiber face as centered as possible.

When operators manipulate the connector, it causes the measurement fixture to wear and tear somewhat, and sometimes the splints get stuck as in Figure 7.

Development of the Problem

Figure 9. SWOT analysis

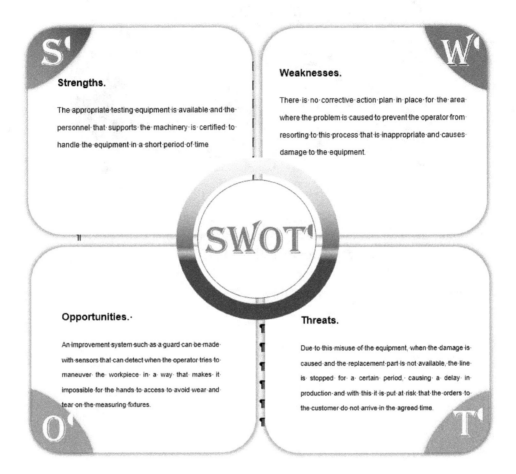

ANALYSIS OF THE PROBLEM USING PDCA

Plan Stage

A meeting was held with the different departments of the Core team to see what could be improved in the geometry test station and prevent the measurement fixtures from being damaged so much. We, as the Test Equipment maintenance department, proposed to make an automated locking device to prevent the operator from tampering with the connector at the inner of the measurement fixture.

Design of Automated Locking Device for Geometry Test Equipment

It should be noted that the objective of this improvement for us as the Test Equipment Department, is to avoid the replacement and constant purchases of measurement fixtures since as mentioned above, each of them costs around $700 dollars.

Therefore, we began with the research of the components that could help us to realize the locking device. We were looking for something simple, that is, we opted for components that are easy to install and thus have simple programming.

Do it Stage

Below are the components that were sent for purchase.

Figure 10. Components for building the improvement

Safety-Curtain-KEYENCE-GL-23F-T

Labjack U3-LV

GL-T11R

OMRON-S82K-00724

Once all these components are obtained, the locking device is assembled, as well as the electronic diagram for its correct operation.

Here's how the locking device would be armed on the geometry test set.

Figure 11. Guard installed on interferometry equipment

In the same way, once the automated locking device has been assembled, the respective programming is conducted in conjunction with the application that performs the geometry test.

As can be seen in the following figure, it was decided to place a guard with sensors, that is to say that the operators have to put their hand near the measurement fixture to be able to manipulate the connector, therefore, we place sensors that when they detect the operator's hand or some other object, the geometry test stops, forcing the operator not to perform the manipulation.

Figure 12. Sensor installed in the interferometry equipment

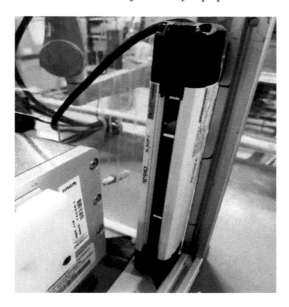

Likewise, this entire device is linked to a small box in which it contains a power supply.

Figure 13. Guard for power supply and wiring system

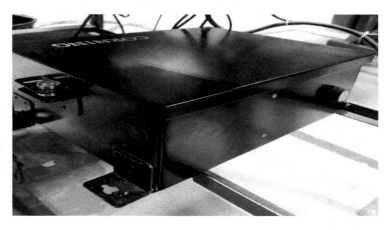

low is a part of the programming code to be used in conjunction with the geometry test application.

Figure 14. Capturing a part of the code for the operation of the enhancement

```csharp
using System;
using System.Collections.Generic;
using System.ComponentModel;
using System.Data;
using System.Drawing;
using System.Linq;
using System.Text;
using System.Threading.Tasks;
using System.Windows.Forms;
using System.IO;
using System.Collections;
using System.Runtime.InteropServices;
using System.IO.Ports;
using LabJack.LabJackUD;
using HWND = System.IntPtr;
using System.Threading;

namespace BlockSFDP
{
    public partial class Form1 : Form
    {
        public Form1()
        {
            InitializeComponent();
        }

        public U3 u3;              //Labjack Variable
        public long lngError;      //Always 0 if no errors in LabJack
        IntPtr handi;
        string titulin;
        int aux = 0;
        bool VentanaEncontrada = false;

        public class MouseClicker
        {
            [DllImport("user32.dll")]
```

It should be noted that the program that managed the test is working based on another program that we call "mascara", this is because the root program does not have the option for an interface where the operator can enter his employee number, scan the tracking serial, etc.

That's why we created what we call an SFDP mask, so that the operator can interact with the program; Several things have been modified to this "mask" so that it works hand in hand with the locking device we put together, so that when the sensors detect an object, a pop-up message is displayed on the test screen indicating that it cannot be continued until the object or hand is removed.

Design of Automated Locking Device for Geometry Test Equipment

Figure 15. Sample of the pop-up message in the app

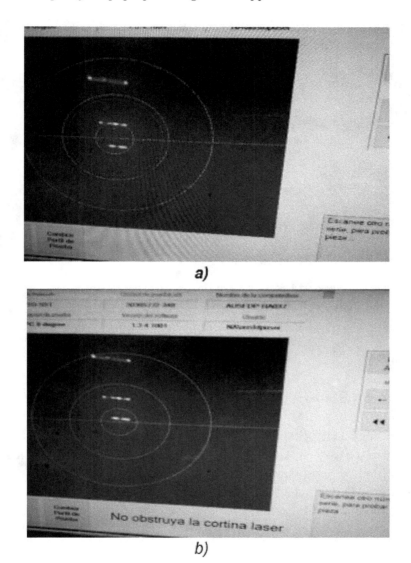

It also shows from another perspective how the automated locking system works.

Figure 16. Operation of the locking system

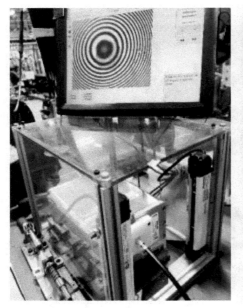 

RESULTS

Verification Stage

Once the automated locking device was implemented, two new measuring fixtures were placed on two different lines. An analysis was made of which line had been reported the most damaged ports, resulting in the production line 10 which manufactures DROP cables being the one that damaged the most measurement fixtures, and likewise, the other new fixture was placed on line 9.

This was done to see which one would wear out the most or get damaged the fastest. It should be noted that the locking device was only implemented on a single line, this is to see if it is possible or not.

After several weeks, data was collected to make a comparison between the two lines.

Next, the results obtained after this project called *Design of Automated Locking Device for Geometry Test Equipment in Fiber Optic Connectors through Interferometry* at the Corning Optical Communications will be presented. A respective comparison will be made with the data obtained before the improvement and after the improvement.

Design of Automated Locking Device for Geometry Test Equipment

Table 3. Measurement fixtures used before and after the upgrade

Date	Measurement Fixture	Days in use	
27/12/2021	1126205 06	9	
05/01/2022	1123697 06	10	
15/01/2022	1123020 08	2	
17/01/2022	1123020 01	10	
27/01/2022	1122921 07	5	
01/02/2022	1125842 20	2	
03/02/2022	1127544 12	6	
09/02/2022	1125841 10	9	
18/02/2022	1125629 10	1	
19/02/2022	1126205 06	9	
28/02/2022	1127543 01	29	
29/03/2022	1124373 09	13	If you install it, look
11/04/2022	1125369 09	24	
05/05/2022	1125629 10	39	
13/06/2022	1116250 05	19	
02/07/2022	1127861 01	16	
Total, days		203	

As can be seen in the table above, a record was made of the measurement fixtures that were replaced and how many days they lasted, before and after the improvement was implemented. The data obtained before the improvement show that this project was monitored for 203 days, and 16 measurement fixtures were used.

Below is a breakdown of the before and after of the improvement in the following tables and graphs.

Production Line 10

Table 4. Measurement fixtures were used before the upgrade

Date	Measurement Fixture	Days in use
27/12/2021	1126205 06	9
05/01/2022	1123697 06	10
15/01/2022	1123020 08	2
17/01/2022	1123020 01	10
27/01/2022	1122921 07	5
01/02/2022	1125842 20	2
03/02/2022	1127544 12	6
09/02/2022	1125841 10	9
18/02/2022	1125629 10	1
19/02/2022	1126205 06	9
28/02/2022	1127543 01	29
Total	11	92

As observed in the table above, it was seen that before implementing the locking device, 11 measurement fixtures were used or replaced, i.e., for 92 days, these fixtures had to be replaced for the reasons mentioned above in other points.

Below is a breakdown of the tables and graphs of the impact of the improvement.

Table 5. Measurement fixtures used after the upgrade

Date	Measurement Fixture	Days in use
29/03/2022	1124373 09	13
11/04/2022	1125369 09	24
05/05/2022	1125629 10	39
13/06/2022	1116250 05	19
02/07/2022	1127861 01	16
Total	5	111

As can be seen, if there was a great impact when the improvement was implemented, as shown that only 5 measurement fixtures were used, with a total duration of 111 days, that is, approximately half of the measurement fixtures were used than when

Design of Automated Locking Device for Geometry Test Equipment

the improvement was not implemented, also the number of days used was a little compared to before the improvement.

Now we will see in the following graph the trend of increasing days in terms of durability of measurement fixtures.

Figure 17. The trend of fixture's durability before and after improvement

As can be seen in Figure 17, as of 29/03/2022 there was an increase in days in terms of durability until the last date captured, compared to previous dates, because as can be seen before the improvement was implemented, for approximately 3 months 11 measurement fixtures were changed, while after implementing the improvement for approximately 4 months, only 5 measurement fixtures were replaced.

As we mentioned in previously, it was mentioned that a comparison would also be made with another of the lines, but without implementing the guard, to see the impact.

Production Line 9

Table 6. Measurement fixtures were used without implementing the in the production line 9 upgrade

Date	Located	Days in use
26/01/2022	1082863 10	0
26/01/2022	1103970 02	15
10/02/2022	1125167 02	25
07/03/2022	1103970 02	5
12/03/2022	1124374 02	3
15/03/2022	1124374 05	4
19/03/2022	1123697 08	6
25/03/2022	1126205 14	17
11/04/2022	1124343 08	5
16/04/2022	1126205 07	23
09/05/2022	1125167 03	4
13/05/2022	1126551 13	9
22/05/2022	1127636 04	1
23/05/2022	1127526 05	1
24/05/2022	1123697 03	0
24/05/2022	5218923 05	20
13/06/2022	1124680 19	13
26/06/2022	1124650 19	3
29/06/2022	1124343 07	8
07/07/2022	1124232 06	1
08/07/2022	1117525 03	10
18/07/2022	1117636 04	8
26/07/2022	1124263 01	9
04/08/2022	1124374 02	14
18/08/2022	1129144 16	2
20/08/2022	1127543 15	9
29/08/2022	1127544 02	9
07/09/2022	1127543 09	0
Total	28	224

As can be seen in Table 6, it can be seen that, during 224 days, 28 measurement fixtures were used, comparing them against the 111 days in which the improvement was implemented in the production line 10, that is, approximately half of the days, there is a difference of 23 fixtures used against the 5, which means that, In twice the time, 10 measurement fixtures would have been used on line 10 according to the data collected.

Financial Impact

To see how much of an impact it had financially, a breakdown was made of how much it cost the area to have a certain number of ports repaired for the 92 days that the line was under observation before the implementation of the improvement.

Table 7. The sum of the total cost to repair damaged fixtures before the upgrade

Fecha	Suma de Precio por unidad reparada (dlls)
27/12/2021 - 02/01/2022	500
03/01/2022 - 09/01/2022	500
10/01/2022 - 16/01/2022	500
17/01/2022 - 23/01/2022	500
24/01/2022 - 30/01/2022	500
31/01/2022 - 06/02/2022	1000
07/02/2022 - 13/02/2022	500
14/02/2022 - 20/02/2022	1000
28/02/2022 - 06/03/2022	500
Total general	**5500**

Figure 18. Cost of having damaged fixtures repaired before the upgrade

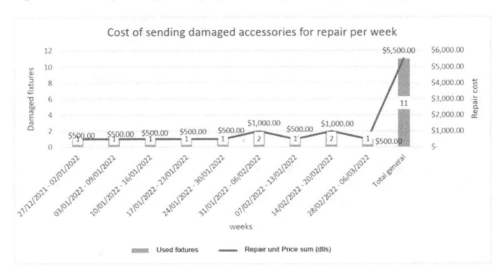

As can be seen during the 92 days, 9 weeks were affected in which the number of 11 measurement fixtures were ordered to be repaired, which is equivalent to a total of $5,500 that it cost the company to repair them.

Now let's see how much it cost the area to have the measurement fixtures repaired that were damaged while using the upgrade.

Table 8. The sum of the total cost to repair damaged fixtures after the upgrade

Fecha	Suma de Precio por unidad reaparada (dlls)
28/03/2022 - 03/04/2022	500
11/04/2022 - 17/04/2022	500
02/05/2022 - 08/05/2022	500
13/06/2022 - 19/06/2022	500
27/06/2022 - 03/07/2022	500
Total general	**2500**

Design of Automated Locking Device for Geometry Test Equipment

Figure 19. Cost of repairing damaged fixtures after the upgrade

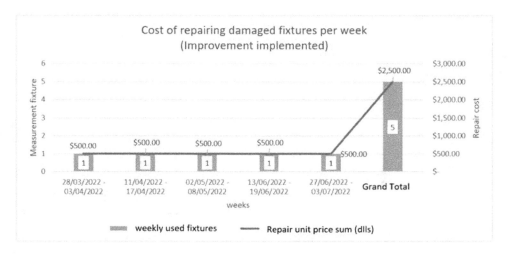

As can be seen in this table and the graph, only 5 weeks of the 111 days that the improvement was tested were affected, as you can see, it practically reduced half of the cost compared to the previous table where the improvement was not yet available that as we previously saw in the table and graph, The service life of the measuring fixtures has been approximately doubled.

We will also see below the data collected in the production 9, which will show how much it cost the area to have the damaged fixtures repaired during a certain time in which the improvement was not installed.

Table 9. The sum of the total cost of damaged fixtures online is 9

Weeks	The sum of the Price per unit repaired	Fixtures Used
24/01/2022 - 30/01/2022	$ 1,000.00	2
07/02/2022 - 13/02/2022	$ 500.00	1
07/03/2022 - 13/03/2022	$ 1,000.00	2
14/03/2022 - 20/03/2022	$ 1,000.00	2
21/03/2022 - 27/03/2022	$ 500.00	1
11/04/2022 - 17/04/2022	$ 1,000.00	2
09/05/2022 - 15/05/2022	$ 1,000.00	2
16/05/2022 - 22/05/2022	$ 500.00	1
23/05/2022 - 29/05/2022	$ 1,500.00	3
13/06/2022 - 19/06/2022	$ 500.00	1
20/06/2022 - 26/06/2022	$ 500.00	1
27/06/2022 - 03/07/2022	$ 500.00	1
04/07/2022 - 10/07/2022	$ 1,000.00	2
18/07/2022 - 24/07/2022	$ 500.00	1
25/07/2022 - 31/07/2022	$ 500.00	1
01/08/2022 - 07/08/2022	$ 500.00	1
15/08/2022 - 21/08/2022	$ 1,000.00	2
29/08/2022 - 04/09/2022	$ 500.00	1
05/09/2022 - 08/09/2022	$ 500.00	1
Total general	$ 14,000.00	28

As can be seen in the table, a total of $14,000 was paid to repair the 28 measuring devices during the 224 days the line was monitored.

CONCLUSION

As has been noted, with the implementation of the improvement, there was a significant change for the area in terms of cost savings, that is to say, we are talking about saving more than half of what it cost them when the improvement was not implemented, and this is thanks to the fact that now the useful life of the measurement fixtures has been doubled Because as seen in the tables and graphs above, we went from using 11 measurement fixtures to only using 5 on average, with a period of about 100 days, that is, approximately 4 months.

This project is useful for the area and the company since with this improvement it is possible to save costs since it is one of the points that every company looks for when producing its products. All this was achieved thanks to the implementation of an analysis and agreement between the entire Core Team of the benefited area, and on the part of us as the Test Team department, it helped us to carry out this project through PDCA which consisted of 4 stages which we were developing throughout this project.

on the other hand, in this project, the automated locking system turned out to be extremely useful, but at the same time, we observed that it has opportunities for improvement in terms of design and cost reduction in terms of components. This project can still be improved to make it more practical to install and use without affecting the ergonomics of the operator.

REFERENCES

Castillo, J. A. (2019). Fiber optics: what it is, what it's used for, and how it works. *Professional Review*. https://www.profesionalreview.com/2019/02/15/fibra-optica-que-es/

Corning. (n.d.). Mercados. *Tecnologías de comunicaciones ópticas: Un flujo de datos sin contratiempos. Corning Optical Communications*. https://www.corning.com/cala/es/markets/Optical-Communications-Market.html

Dik Rodriguez, D. & Niola Plaza, B. (2016). *Análisis y Diseño de la Migración de la Red Actual de Cobre, en la Ruta 13 de la Central Norte de CNT en la Ciudad de Guayaquil*. Red de Fibra Óptica.

Duan, J., & Liu, D. (2012). Influence of kinematic variables on apex offset in polishing process of fiber optic connectors. *Precision Engineering*, *36*(2), 281–287. doi:10.1016/j.precisioneng.2011.10.009

Lee, B. H., Kim, Y. H., Park, K. S., Eom, J. B., Kim, M. J., Rho, B. S., & Choi, H. Y. (2012). Interferometric fiber optic sensors. *Sensors, 12*(3), 2467-2486.

Leiner, B. M., Cerf, V. G., Clark, D. D., Kahn, R. E., Kleinrock, L., Lynch, D. C., & Wolff, S. (1999). *Una breve historia de Internet*. HistInt. http://www.ati.es/DOCS/internet/histint/histint1.html

Malacara, D., & Harris, O. (1970). Interferometric measurement of angles. *Applied Optics*, *9*(7), 1630–1633. doi:10.1364/AO.9.001630 PMID:20076433

Okoshi, T. (2012). *Optical fibers*. Elsevier.

Rao, Y. J., & Jackson, D. A. (2000). Principles of fiber-optic interferometry. In *Optical Fiber Sensor Technology: Fundamentals* (pp. 167–191). Springer US. doi:10.1007/978-1-4757-6081-1_5

Rochelau, D. (2016, March 2). *Polished connector geometries, APC*. Fiber Optic Center. https://focenter.com/es/geometr%C3%ADas-de-conector-pulido-apc-parte-1/

Rodríguez, Y. (2009). *Fibra óptica*. El Cid Editor.

Chapter 8
Vandalism Prevention and Trash Retention System Improvement on Hidalgo County Drainage District Pump Stations

Jesus Cruz Garza Moreno
Unidad Académica Multidisciplinaria Reynosa-Rodhe, Mexico

Luz Idalia Balderas García
Unidad Académica Multidisciplinaria Reynosa-Rodhe, Mexico

Lourdes Yajaira García Rivera
Unidad Académica Multidisciplinaria Reynosa-Rodhe, Mexico

ABSTRACT

The project of redesign and improvement of the trash collection system and vandalism prevention on stationary and portable pumps was implemented by the Welding Department of the Hidalgo County Drainage District No. 1. The purpose of this project is to minimize downtime caused by trash and debris entering the pump stations and the damage caused by vandalism. All this is to reduce flooding risk to the Hidalgo County residents. The Hidalgo County Drainage District No.1 is a government entity dedicated to the cleaning and maintenance of the pluvial drainage system along Hidalgo County—it is located at 902 N Doolittle Rd. in Edinburg Texas.

DOI: 10.4018/979-8-3693-1119-6.ch008

INTRODUCTION

The project of Redesign and Improvement of the Trash Collection System and Vandalism Prevention on stationary and portable pumps was implemented by the Welding Department of the Hidalgo County Drainage District No. 1. The purpose of this project is to minimize downtime caused by trash and debris entering the pump stations and the damages caused by vandalism. All this with the aim of reducing flooding risk to the Hidalgo County residents.

The Hidalgo County Drainage District No.1 is a government entity dedicated to the cleaning and maintenance of the pluvial drainage system along Hidalgo County, it is located at 902 N Doolittle Rd. in Edinburg Texas.

This project contains information collected through the rainy seasons of 2018 to 2021. The main topic in this project is the redesign of the trash collection system and the design and fabrication of cages to prevent vandalism to the Hidalgo County Drainage District portable pump stations. The main goal is to reduce the risk of flooding in Hidalgo County by reducing downtime caused by damages caused by vandalism and damages caused by trash and debris on the stationary pumps.

The most benefited from the implementation of this project would be the residents of the cities that conform The Hidalgo County, especially the ones that live in areas with elevated risk.

The following Project is an improvement to the existing trash and debris collection system on the Hidalgo County Drainage District pump stations, as well as the design and implementation of cages to prevent the portable pump stations from being vandalized.

The main purpose of this project is to reduce the risk of flooding in the cities inside the Hidalgo County area by allowing the water to flow freely through the stationary pump stations, as well as to prevent damage to the portable pump stations caused by vandalism. All this, with the pump reducing downtime on the pump stations.

Every year, Hidalgo County residents and businesses lose millions of dollars because of flooding events. With this simple and cheap improvement, the Hidalgo County Drainage District No1 aims to mitigate as much as possible these losses. To have a better outcome, the implementation of this project covered all the stationary and portable pump stations operated by the Hidalgo County Drainage District No.1. of flooding. Thus, making public this project, other students or engineers can benefit because they might be working in a similar environment and this project even though is simple, can help reduce flooding risk and make the use of pump stations more productive. A slight change in design can make an enormous impact on a whole community.

This project was implemented using fabrication by welding techniques. Measurements of the existing structures were taken, and new guards were designed using what we already had in place. Also, for the portable pump stations we took measurements from the trailers, and pumps and cages were designed depending on the trailer and pump structure.

This project reached all the stationary pump stations as well as the portable pump stations.

THEORETICAL FOUNDATION

According, to **The National Conference of State Legislature**, floods are the deadliest, costliest, and most common form of natural disaster in the United States and the world. And they are caused by a wide variety of natural events. There are two forms to mitigate the risks of flooding, structural and non-structural. The structural forms to mitigate flooding include seawalls, gates, levees, and evacuation routes. The non-structural includes reducing risk by removing people and properties from risk areas (Diggs et al., 2021; Ganesh & Rampur, 2016; Waller & Yitayew, 2015).

The Federal Emergency Management Agency (FEMA), released a report in 2017, called "Innovative Drought and Flood Mitigation Projects" that evaluates four disaster mitigation approaches which include Flood Water Diversion and Storage. This approach states that diverting flood water into wetlands, floodplains, canals, pipes, reservoirs, or other conduits helps mitigate flooding by allowing for a controlled release of water outside the residential and metropolitan areas (Diggs et al., 2021; National Conference of State Legislature, 2019).

With the experience and by observing the problem we concluded that by redesigning the system for trash and debris collection at the pump station we could get a sturdier structure, as well as increase the water flow through the pump's propellers. Also, by observing the cleaning procedures this improvement on the system could give a better view of the work area for the excavator operator, reducing the risk of damaging the structure.

According to the **Merriam-Webster dictionary**, vandalism is "any willful or malicious destruction of public or private property" (Merriam-Webster, 2022).

David Coursen recommends that the implementation of fences, heavy-duty doors, and locks discourage and prevent vandalism (Diggs et al., 2021; Spekkers et al., 2011; Waller & Yitayew, 2015).

In my personal experience working with materials and designing and improving systems to deter vandalism, I have learned what kind of materials are better to work with more efficiently and economically.

COMPANY OVERVIEW

General Overview

Hidalgo County Drainage District No1 (HCDD1) is a government entity focused on the management and maintenance of pluvial drainage in the County of Hidalgo. The company is located at 902 N Doolittle Rd. in the city of Edinburg Texas.

The district develops construction and improvement projects for the pluvial drainage of the County of Hidalgo. The district also provides maintenance to the network of ditches that conform to the drainage system of the County.

"The HCDD No. 1 Debris Removal, Shredding & Mowing Maintenance program is active year-round. The goal of this program is to prevent drainage system blockage, or "clogs" which could potentially cause flooding in surrounding areas and allow for stormwater runoff to flow efficiently during rain events. Shredding & Mowing Maintenance is presently upholding 601.13 miles of channels, of which 285.42 miles are District owned or easement ditches, and the other 315.71 miles are from local irrigation districts. Our maintenance schedule runs on an average of 5 to 6 months cycle year-round" (Ganesh & Rampur, 2016; National Conference of State Legislature, 2019; Waller & Yitayew, 2015).

The district is funded by the collection of property taxes from the County of Hidalgo residents. The actual tax rate is .1051 cents for every $100 of property value. This rate is variable depending on the district's needs.

Company's History

The Hidalgo County Drainage District No1 was created on April 9, 1908, by orders of the Hidalgo County Commissioner's Court which saw the need for an institution to maintain and manage the drainage needs of the County.

The original territory covered by the district was about 508 sq miles, which covered the main cities of Hidalgo County except for the city of Edinburg. On September 15, 1975, another 203sq miles were added to the district for maintenance by order of the Hidalgo County Commissioner's Court. Right now, the district covers 601.13 miles of channels, and it keeps growing according to the County's needs.

MISSION, VISION, AND VALUES

Mission Statement

The mission of the Hidalgo County Drainage District No. 1 is to proactively manage the Hidalgo County Master Drainage System and allow for the efficient exportation of drainage water, to protect life and property for Hidalgo County residents, businesses, and surrounding jurisdictions.

Vision Statement

Our vision is to improve Hidalgo County's Drainage System to enhance long-term economic development opportunities throughout our District by implementing innovative technology in an environmentally conscious manner.

Core Values

- Community driven decisions
- Transparency
- Stewardship of tax dollars
- Commitment to Improving Flood Control
- Collaboration with Local, State, and Federal Entities

PROJECT DESCRIPTION

Background and Problem Definition

Flooding has an enormous impact on society, Infrastructure, agriculture, livestock, and the economy are affected by these natural events. The damages caused by it not all the time are limited to material and economic losses, but on some occasions can also lead to human losses.

Since the main Hidalgo County Drainage District No. 1 main goal is to mitigate flooding caused by rain events, one of the principal assets and tools to alleviate these events is the pumping stations. These pumping stations are located along the levees (an emergency channel property of the Federal Government) as well as the portable pumps, which would be installed in strategic points of the County as needed. To reduce downtime on this equipment and ensure the proper operation of the pumping station is necessary to reduce the amount of trash and debris that runs through the stationary pumping stations as well as to prevent damage to the portable pumps caused by vandalism. In the past, this has been a constant problem for the district, and as a result, extra money from taxpayers must be spent to make the necessary repairs to the equipment on some occasions the affected equipment has increased the risk of flooding while in repair, causing damages to the County's residents' properties as well as public property.

Having considered the problem, the welding department has been asked to redesign the stationary pump station trash collection system, as well as to design and install protective cages for the portable pump trailers to reduce damage caused by vandalism.

GENERAL AND SPECIFIC GOALS

General Goal

The general goal of this project is to reduce downtime, on both, the stationary pumping stations as well as the portable pumping stations caused by either trash and debris accumulation or vandalism. And because of this downtime reduction, the risk of flooding will be reduced as well.

Specific Goals

This is a list of the specific goals that are expected to be achieved by the modification and implementation of this project:

- Reduction of downtime during emergencies
- Reduction in damages caused by vandalism.
- Increased water flow.
- Reduction in cleaning times
- Reduction of damages caused by cleaning of debris and trash.

JUSTIFICATION

Importance

Why is it important to attend to this problem? Since the Hidalgo County Drainage District is a government institution, the main goal is to attend to the community needs concerning flooding management, but also to manage taxpayer's money responsibly. Every time a portable or stationary pump station gets damaged, the district must spend money and resources to fix it in a way that is functional and that it can provide the services that is intended to. All the resources, time, and money spent on equipment repairs can be used on other needs to also help in flooding prevention, and consequently provide a better service to the community.

How the Company Will Be Benefited

If by implementing this project we get to achieve the expected results, the district will benefit by allowing management to dispose of and redirect the money projected for repairs to other equipment, or to improve installations or District-owned ditches.

Also, the men-hours expected to perform these repairs can be used for the repair of other essential equipment. All the time saved on repairs, unexpected maintenance, creation of purchase orders, and cleaning of pump stations would be reflected in savings of taxpayer's money.

Other Benefited Entities

Since the District is a government entity, most of the economic resources come from the taxpayer's contributions. By implementing this project, we not only help to manage taxpayer's money efficiently but also, to keep tax rates low. Which will reflect on a benefit for the County residents.

Even though the initial investment would be large, the community would benefit by preventing flooding, which will damage the taxpayer's property, costing millions of dollars to the community.

The implementation of this project will also benefit other government entities, like cities and County Precincts because if flooding can be prevented, the damages to infrastructure and government property can be reduced.

Outreach and Limitations

Outreach

The main purpose of this project is to cover all the stationary pump stations located along the levees, which are five, as well as the portable pumps, which are twenty. All these pumps are one of the main assets for the district to alleviate flooding problems along Hidalgo County.

The main goal is to mitigate the effects of flooding in the County by reducing downtime on the pump stations due to debris or vandalism.

Limitations

Mechanical Problems

Since all the pump stations work by engine power, the mechanical aspect plays a significant role in the pump station's performance. Year round two persons oversee the maintenance and repairs of the pump stations, to prevent mechanical failure during emergencies. Nonetheless, the unexpected can happen during operations and the performance can be affected by mechanical problems.

Lack of Training

During flooding events the district personnel, like operators, and labor crews are distributed to operate these pump stations, it has happened that they have extremely limited training on how to operate these machines, and consequently, the performance of the pump stations is affected by causing delays.

That downtime caused by debris and vandalism at the pump stations is not the only cause that can affect the pump station's performance, the project is going to be limited by these other variants that can also affect the pump station's performance.

PROJECT DEVELOPMENT

To successfully develop this project, we had to analyze the current condition of the stationary pump stations. Why the stationary pumps first? Because these pump stations can move water faster and because they have a higher priority on the flooding relief program.

These pumps are located at the end of the main ditches, which are connected to the levees, which are the main flooding water reliever of the County.

Figure 1. Original status

Figure 2. Original status

As shown in the first picture (Figure 1) we can observe the actual state of the pump station water entrance, which is clogged with debris and trash. When an excavator is assigned to clean all the trash and debris, the excavator gets located on top of it. We can see the hill is about twenty feet above the metal grill, and about another twenty feet back from the main entrance, at this point, the operator has very limited visibility of the grill, and often they hit it and get damaged, that is one of the problems that can lead to logs or tires getting inside and get the pump's propeller stuck.

In the second picture (Figure 2), we can have a closer look at the entrance, we can observe the logs, tires, and even pieces of construction material, which can cause a malfunction of the pump station. We can also observe how the metal grill is installed just on the rails that run down through the concrete wall. This is another problem we have often, since the rail along the concrete wall is about three inches wide, and about two inches deep, the material on the metal grill must be small enough to get inside the rail. When a flooding event occurs, the pressure that the trash and the water create on the metal grill is too strong that the metal grill often succumbs to it and gets bent, causing it to be moved from its place, and allowing the trash and debris to flow freely through the water pump, and causing the pump's propeller to get stuck.

Having these two problems in mind, we proceeded to redesign the metal grill. This is going to solve these two problems, first, by allowing the operator to have a better visibility of the grill, and minimize damage caused by cleaning the grill. And second, designing the grill strong enough that it can withstand the pressure caused by the water and debris.

After analyzing measurements and the design of the pump station inlet, this is the design we came out with (Figure 3). With this design, we eliminated the problem of the grill collapsing to the water pressure because we introduced a more rigid construction.

The angle iron on the frame is heavy duty 3/8"x4"x6" which is also anchored to the concrete wall with ½" x 10" stainless steel anchors. Also, we increased visibility to the excavator operator reducing damages in the cleaning process.

Figure 3. Design with measurements

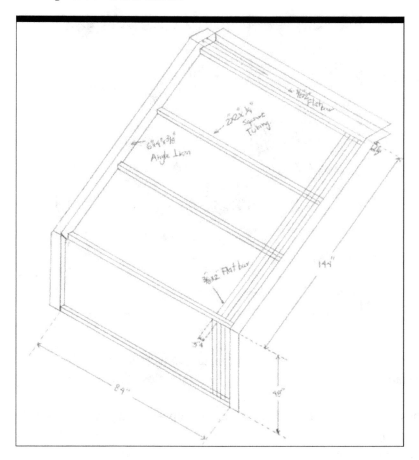

In this image (Figure 4) we can observe the difference between both grills, the old one on the left and the innovative design on the right side.

Figure 4. Original vs. improved

After designing and completing the installation of the new grills on the stationary pump stations, we moved forward to design an enclosed cage to protect the portable pumps.

These are just two of the designs we came up with, they vary slightly depending on the pump and trailer model (Figures 5, and 6). By enclosing the pumps, we can reduce the damage people can make to these pump stations, every year we lose time and money on repairs caused by vandalism. Also, we can protect hoses, and electrical components from weather, which will give us a longer life span and better performance of the pumps. Also, we design the cages with doors that give us access for mechanical repairs and routine maintenance.

Figure 5. Cage design installed

Figure 6. Cage design installed

The cage fully encloses all the mechanical components that can be damaged by people, and it protects de fuel tank, in the past the district had the problem of people stealing and contaminating the fuel, this design helps us protect the fuel from stealing and contamination by throwing garbage or any other contaminant in the tank.

RESULTS AND ANALYSIS

Since rain events do not happen every day, and the portable pumps are not always out on the field is difficult to measure the actual results of the project quantitatively. But after all the fabrication and installation were finished, the only way to prove the results was by observation, as of right now, two years have passed by since the implementation of these changes and improvements, and the results have been positive.

Based on our original goals listed in chapter two this is a list of the accomplished results, note that since there is not a department in charge of analyzing these results, the records of the same are not completely accurate, and have been collected by asking to the mechanic maintenance department, which oversees the pump station maintenance for the assessment of the same. It is not the responsibility of the welding department to collect or study the results of the project:

Damages Caused by Vandalism

The data shown on the following chart is a collection of reports from two years after the installation of the protective cages on the portable pumps. We can observe how the cost in dollars has been declining in these two past years, from over $3500 to less than $500. The reports have been from components and mechanical parts outside the cage, like tires, suction hoses, and trailer jacks.

Figure 7. Damages caused by vandalism graph

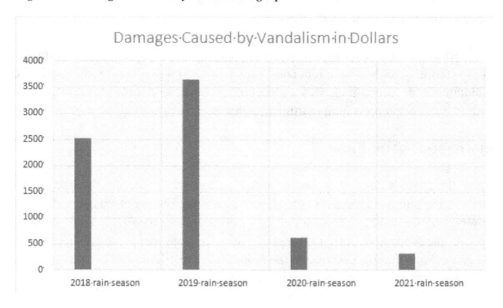

Down Time Caused by Vandalism (Portable Pumps)

These results comprehend the same period, the downtime has been reduced significantly, allowing better operation during emergencies.

Figure 8. Down time caused by vandalism graph

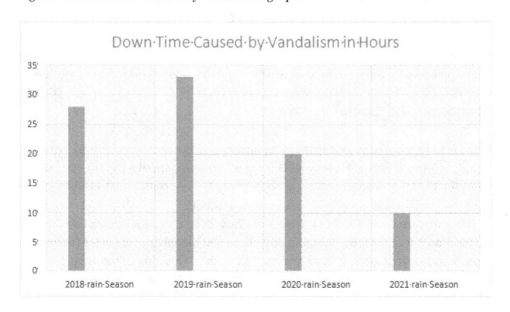

Reduction of Down Time During Emergencies (Stationary Pumps Stations)

The reduction of downtime during emergencies caused by debris entering the pump station gates has been reduced to zero. We had no reports by the mechanic maintenance department or work orders created by supervisors to report damages caused by it, or pump station malfunction due to it.

Increased Water Flow

Since the District does not possess special equipment to measure the water flow through the pump stations, it is difficult to assess the results of this goal. But, by observation we can have an idea that it is working, since the debris tends to move up with the innovative design instead of getting trapped inside the concrete walls, we can assume that the entrance to the pump is less restricted and the water moves with less resistance, by consequence, we have an increased water flow.

Reduction of Cleaning Times and Damages Caused by Cleaning

Again, this is an exceedingly difficult area to measure since the cleaning times vary a lot depending on the type of machine, the operator, and how much debris is in the area. However, it has been reported by operators and supervisors that with the innovative design is easier for them to clean the entrances to the pumps, because it gives them better visibility over the area and because since the walls are not on the way the debris can be removed faster.

As per the damages caused to the grills, we have no reports or complaints of damages caused by cleaning. On a period of two years, the protection grills are still in place and without damages, which results in savings on maintenance costs.

Economic and Social Impact

According to the Texas Department for Insurance, the average claim in Texas for regular insurance during Hurricane Harvey in 2018 was about $18,000, the average claim for flooding insurance was about $119,000, for commercial properties was $222,000 and for automobile insurance was $14,000.

If we analyze these numbers, we can see how of a substantial impact this project can have on our region. By reducing downtime and increasing the water flow on the pump stations we can significantly reduce the risk of flooding in the area. This will not only have a huge economic impact on the Hidalgo County residents, but also will have a social impact, flooding not only destroys property, but it also creates a social and emotional impact on people, sometimes it can even cause human losses and diseases.

By implementing this project, we can save millions of dollars to the insurance companies and residents as well we can contribute to the wellbeing of the people.

CONCLUSION

After analyzing the results obtained with the implementation of this project, we observed that we accomplished most of the primary goals 100%, except for the damages caused by vandalism. By observing the graphs, we can see that the costs and downtime caused by vandalism were reduced, although the damages were not significant, they still affected the pump's performance. Some other measurements were taken to prevent these types of damages in the future, for example, locks were installed on tires to prevent people from stealing them, and trailer jacks were welded instead of bolted on to prevent stealing.

RECOMMENDATIONS

To better the service provided and the response time in emergencies these are my recommendations:

- Implementation of training in the operation of pump stations. This will allow a better response time in case of emergencies.
- Implementation of a maintenance schedule. This will prevent downtime caused by mechanical problems.
- Create an emergency response plan. This will allow a faster response team.
- Acquisition of extra equipment and hoses. In case a malfunction happens on a pump station we can replace it fast, and we can install extra equipment if needed.

REFERENCES

Coursen, D. (1975). Vandalism Prevention. Office of Justice Programs.

Diggs, J., Mikolajczyk, S., Naismith, L., Reed, M., & Smith, R. (2021). *Flood Management in Texas: Planning for the Future*. Texas A&M.

Galloway, G. (2004). *USA: flood management–Mississippi River*. WMO/GWP Associated Programme on Flood Management.

Ganesh, U. L., & Rampur, V. V. (2016). Semi-automatic drain for sewage water treatment of floating materials. *International Journal of Research in Engineering and Technology, 5*(7), 1–4.

Herzon, I., & Helenius, J. (2008). Agricultural drainage ditches, their biological importance and functioning. *Biological Conservation, 141*(5), 1171–1183. doi:10.1016/j.biocon.2008.03.005

Merriam-Webster. (2022). Vandalism. *Merriam Webster Dictionary*. https://www.merriam-webster.com/dictionary/vandalism

National Conference of State Legislature. (2019). *Flood Mitigation*. National Conference of State Legislature. https://www.ncsl.org/research/environment-and-natural-resources/flood-mitigation.aspx#resources

Spekkers, M. H., Ten Veldhuis, J. A. E., & Clemens, F. H. L. R. (2011). *Collecting data for quantitative research on pluvial flooding*. In Proceedings of the 12th International Conference on Urban Drainage, Porto Alegre, Brazil (*Vol. 1116*, p. 461466). Academic Press.

Waller, P., & Yitayew, M. (2015). *Irrigation and drainage engineering*. Springer.

Chapter 9
Digital Inclusion, a Key Element Towards Digital Transformation:
STEM Perspectives

Constanza Alvarado
University ECCI, Colombia

Philippe Aniorte
INDICATIC AIP, Panama

Maria Catalina Ramirez
University of Andes, Colombia

ABSTRACT

New digital economies, globalization of information and knowledge, technological infrastructures (emerging computer and internet revolution) that impose transformation of business models for value creation, suggest challenges in education for innovation, sustainability, and open knowledge, demanding the mastery and development of 21st-century competencies for problem-solving in context, with capacities and skills. As well as new workforce dynamics, disruptive jobs, management of legal aspects (intellectual property), and operations resolved through services and/or "digital transactions" increased in number and intensity, serving users as employees, organizations, government, and digital citizens in general. Such a response does not ensure the integration and social appropriation of ICT, generating a distance, divide, and digital gap (DG), exacerbated in the race for transition on the way to digital transformation (DxTx).

DOI: 10.4018/979-8-3693-1119-6.ch009

INTRODUCTION

The Fourth Industrial Revolution [I4.0] proposed a framework for all domains of society from autonomic computing elements (monitoring, analysis, planning, prediction) collecting information in real time (IBM, 2006). Internet of Everything [IoE] (Bradley, Barbier y Handler; CISCO, 2013), Cyber Physical Systems [CPS] people, data, platforms, processes, based on connected Environment [CE], merging the real and virtual worlds (Lee, Bagheri y Kao, 2015) towards Smart Systems [SS], integrated intelligent devices, platforms, architectures, techno-functional models (Moreno, 2016) in a man-machine relationship that assumes to the former, new competences. Students, citizens, customers in contexts of development and digital transformation [DxTx] (Schwab, 2016). Processes of information exchange "digital transactions" (Cozniuc y Petrisor, 2018) in economies and employment markets, millions of workers are experiencing changes that have profoundly transformed their lives inside and outside of work, as well as their well-being and productivity in relation to what digital services offer and what they deliver (World Bank, 2020, International Monetary Fund, 2020b), deepening that divide (distance) [DG] (Abascal et al., 2016; Longoria et al., 2022).

Digital impact in all scenarios Education, Government, Industry and from there immersed employees, skills, citizens, students (Reisdorf & Rhinesmith, 2020) imposing the question for digital inclusion [DxIx] and its fundamental and transcendent role as it implies an adequate transition, a relevant adaptation in different scenarios of relationship towards/with digital mediations or Information and Communications Technologies [ICT] and its social appropriation (Alvarado et al., 2023). Transition to Industry 4.0 and its applications in organizations and in the different actors of society provided with DxTx understanding connectivity, technological observance and innovation, computer and cyber security, data intelligence, computational autonomy. These elements, foundation for the development of new skills for the development of technological competence and its appropriation (Deloitte, 2019; Kraus, et al., 2019; World Economic Forum, 2020).

Economic, political and social scenarios, rapid technological innovation, acquisition of new technological resources, technological adoption, and urgent development of skills in analytical thinking and innovation, active and collaborative learning, problem solving in context, critical thinking and analysis, creativity, originality and initiative (Nadal & Navarro); leadership and social influence; access, use, monitoring and control of technology; technology design and programming; resilience, stress management, flexibility and reasoning, ideation and problem solving (World Economic Forum, 2020), which should be reflected in education from early training scenarios, new professional profiles for organizations, policies defined by government, and citizens oriented in a collaborative ecosystem, which proposes STEM education and skills as a contributing element to digital inclusion.

Contextualizing elements of convergence to the above, with the need to fix eyes on the education agenda, the recent results of the Program for International Student Assessment [PISA] tests conducted every three years by the Organization for Economic Co-operation and Development [OECD], with the purpose of measuring the skills and knowledge of 15-year-old students in reading, mathematics and science, had an unprecedented drop, compared to the 2018 results. Performance fell by nearly 15 points in mathematics, three times more than in any previous change, and 10 points in reading. In science, the drop was 4 points. Countries such as Germany, Iceland, the Netherlands, Norway and Poland show a drop of 25 points or more in mathematics in 2022. In Colombia, 8 points less in mathematics, 3 in reading and 2 in science, less than in other periods, even so the country has not been able to make a significant leap to get out of the group that is below the OECD average. Scores in mathematics with 383 points, reading with 409 and science with 411 are far from those of the OECD, which are 472, 476 and 485, respectively. The data from the assessment, which includes a total of 81 countries and economies, and their declining performance are not only an impact of the Covid-19 pandemic, the OECD said, as the drop in reading, science and maths scores was evident before 2018.

This work takes some STEM perspectives, from its relevance of application and scope of education, also for the development of competencies that move as a need for training, development, research, participation in strengthening scenarios for broad domains and doings of solving needs from the integration of science technology, engineering and mathematics, organized in an orderly structure of factors associated with the digital divide considered in observation for measurements and decision making towards digital inclusion and digital transformation.

This document presents in five sections the convergent integration of the different STEM perspectives as a fundamental element associated with the understanding of the digital gap (DG) in different scenarios, in search of establishing the basis for key digital inclusion (DI) towards digital transformation (DxTx). *The first one*, presents important topics or problems for STEM issues (perspectives) as a scenario of inclusion and transition to digital transformation. *The second one*, the integration of factors associated with the characterization of the digital gap (base element of the conceptualization of digital inclusion) based on a doctoral dissertation by Timothe Duron in France; *the third one,* a guide from a hierarchy of factors associated with the digital gap in different contexts, factors that intend associated with indicators and measurements, a relationship of remediation proposal to digital inclusion scenarios, *the fourth one*, the emphasis of such factors in terms of STEM mediation in the education scenario; and *the last one*, presentation of results and work in progress and in context.

STEM ISSUES

This section does not attempt to conceptualise STEM, let alone establish a processual formula for how to implement STEM in one direction or another. It is based on broad elements from the late 1990s when the National Science Foundation (2020) presented the notion of the acronym STEM, which stands for Science, Technology, Engineering and Math, with the aim of responding favorably to the challenges that were to come in terms of the development of Information and Communication Technologies [ICT] and what would undoubtedly be the technological revolution 4. 0 from careers called STEM and training new skills in future generations of young people in the United States being the basis of a geopolitical phenomenon in favour of science and technology, established from there educational policies adapted by the United Kingdom and countries in Asia such as Taiwan, Japan, China and Korea; developing high-performance educational systems, creating national policies that allowed the momentum in principle is scenarios of university institutions and industry. An interest in tertiary settings was stimulated to increase enrolment in STEM programs and governments focused the policy agenda for the development of educational and scientific reforms (Blackley & Howell, 2015). Today the STEM concept (National Science Foundation, 2020) pays attention to the expansion of and access to the education ecosystem regardless of background, race, ethnicity, gender, religion and income levels, so that the human capital of new generations from the possibilities of STEM (World Economic Forum WEF, 2020) and citizens take purposeful leadership to reach the training of the future workforce that fulfils human potential (WEF, 2020a). Digital transformation through the exploration of connectivity, experience innovation, cyber security, real-time data intelligence, automation and technology in new fields. These advances are the foundation for the development of new skills to imagine, deliver, and operate new scenarios (Deloitte, 2019; Kraus, et al., 2019). It is recognized that technology, digitization and emerging technologies are close to social relations and, consequently, are places of access to communities, class struggle, gender gap (León, Medina & Zúñiga, 2021).

The literature review aimed at establishing categories of STEM scope work can be observed not only an interest in instrumentalizing STEM as if it were an active educational learning methodology, however the work developed there does not concentrate on the elements of learning detail, it seeks to look at STEM Trend Management its applications and try to establish with digital inclusion sensitivity the STEM impact on Industry 4. 0 (Jiménez, Magaña & Aquino, 2021), as well as the human factors of the new generations in the possibilities of STEM and thus maintain the interest and passion throughout their lives and its impact on the sustainable development of a territory. In the STEM ecosystem that includes geographical, social, political and economic environment that drives innovation, prosperity and global competitiveness of human capital through training in Science, Technology, Engineering and Mathematics, generating access, opportunities, stimuli and tools for participation in the economy of innovation and progress in the face of technological changes, as well as STEM education for the formation of skills, development of business strategies and application of laws that favor the environment in science and technology (Jiménez, Magaña & Aquino, 2021). STEM and innovation agendas to achieve the Sustainable Development Goals [SDGs] (UNESCO, 2017) generate equal access, enhance human rights and strengthen scientific and development prospects as unskilled labor that is cheaper than machines and can replace them, ensuring that boys, girls, men and women are able to develop STEM skills.

Role of everyone (women, men, girls, boys) their skills in Science, Technology, Engineering, and Mathematics [STEM] careers, and DxTx: How can we encourage and empower more everyone to pursue careers in STEM and leverage their skills to drive DxTx in industries and society?" This question addresses the importance of diversity and inclusion in STEM fields (Canu & Alvarado, 2017; Vieira et al., 2023; Bascope et al., 2020) and recognizes the potential impact of women's skills and perspectives on digital transformation efforts (Damiani & Rodríguez-Modroño, 2022; Hanna, 2016).

Which are the possible meanings about the relation between everyone their skills STEM careers and digital transformation [DxTx] such as skills data management, analysis and intelligent data processing, among others) can have several meanings (perspectives) and implication:

- ◇ *Underrepresentation in STEM* historically, women (for example) have been underrepresented in STEM fields. This lack of gender diversity can limit the perspectives and skills available to address complex technological challenges in the era of digital transformation.
- ◇ *Untapped Talent Pool*, encouraging more to pursue STEM careers can tap into a significant talent pool that has been underutilized. For example, Women bring unique skills, insights, and problem-solving abilities to the table.
- ◇ *Innovation and Problem-Solving*, Diverse teams, including STEM skills, can foster innovation and creative problem-solving. Different perspectives can lead to novel solutions and approaches to digital transformation challenges.
- ◇ *Closing the Gender Gap*, Fostering every one participation in STEM and digital roles can help narrow the gender pay gap and promote greater equality in the workforce.
- ◇ *STEM Education*, It highlights the importance of equitable access to STEM education and opportunities for everyone from a young age to prepare them for careers that play a vital role in digital transformation.

- ◊ *Career Advancement,* Encouraging everyone to advance in STEM careers can lead to more female leaders in technology and digital roles, setting an example for future generations.
- ◊ *Economic Growth and digital economies:* Leveraging the full potential skills in STEM can contribute to economic growth (Towsend et al.,2013) by driving innovation, entrepreneurship, and competitiveness in the digital age.
- ◊ *Entrepreneurship Ecosystems*, from STEM initiatives, contributing to the economic development and growth of territories.
- ◊ *Employability for all,* associating STEM skills oriented to DxTx.

With specially attention about **Inclusive Digital Transformation [IDT]**, an inclusive approach to DxTx recognizes the value of diverse skills and perspectives. It ensures that technology solutions are designed to meet the needs of all users, regardless of gender.

The aim is to focus on fundamental elements *that have been observed* from different direct experimentation works in field applications, where Access to Technology, Connectivity, Digital Skills (Perifanou et al., 2021; Idawati & Qismullah, 2019), Educational Resources, Gender Equality, Socioeconomic Equity, Cultural Inclusion, STEM Education, Innovation and Entrepreneurship, Policies and Regulations.

Among other key *dimensions to consider when addressing the relationship between STEM and the digital gap*, concrete steps can be taken to contribute digital inclusion from STEM field and promote reducing disparities about access, participation, and digital social appropriation.

The role of everyone and specially women and their skills in STEM is crucial for advancing DxIx. Her participation in STEM careers is instrumental in advancing DxIx. Their diverse skills, perspectives, and leadership can help create a more inclusive digital society where everyone has equal access to the benefits of technology (UNESCO,2022). Some elements interconnected like women bring unique perspectives and problem-solving approaches to STEM fields (Duque & Canu, 2017; Vieira et al., 2023). This diversity of thought is essential for addressing complex technological challenges and ensuring that digital solutions are inclusive and relevant to a broader population.

Closing the Gender Gap (Meyerhoff & Erhi, 2021), contributes to a more equitable distribution of opportunities in the digital world; Digital Skills (Idawati & Qismullah, 2019); Innovative Solutions, that can address specific needs and challenges faced by women and other underrepresented groups; education and Awarenes, women in STEM can play an active role in promoting STEM education and digital literacy (Dochshanov & Tramonti, 2022; Saetang et al., 2023) among girls and women. Also, inspire the next generation of female scientists, engineers, and technologists (Mahboubi, 2022).

Complementing, other reasons like tech Industry Leadership, women in leadership roles within the tech industry (Guo, Feng & Lin, 2023; George & Paul, 2020) can influence policies and practices that promote digital inclusion. They can advocate for diversity and equity in tech companies, ensuring that products and services are designed with inclusivity in mind.

Actually project work scenarios, among which the following are highlighted, a *Community Engagement* to provide digital skills training, access to technology and support for disadvantaged communities (Gray et al. 2017); *Policy Advocacy*, STEM often engage in community outreach, government (Morte-Nadal & Esteban-Navarro, 2022) and initiatives that aim to bridge the DG to promote DxIx, such as affordable broadband access, digital skills training programs, and measures to address online harassment and discrimination and finally *Research and Data*, researchers in STEM can contribute to DxIx-related studies and data collection efforts by helping to identify barriers and develop evidence-based improvement strategies.

DIGITAL GAP - THE BASIS FOR E-INCLUSION [DxIx]

ICT are a dynamic element of the new economies of development in society in the so-called digital economies (UNESCO, 2021; Alvarado et al., 2023). Therefore, those who, individually and collectively, manage to develop the infrastructure and skills to use them are privileged, have greater decision-making capacity and influence the construction of this society (UNESCO, 2021), which is what the reduction of the distance (Galperín, 2017) towards digital inclusion would consist of (Galperín, 2017).

Bruno Ollivier (2006) points out the digital gap (digital division) refers to a separation, a division caused by digitalization. The digital divide [DG] evokes a fracture, a gap. Each of these words is built on a noun that refers to something that needs to be healed (Plantard, 2021). Such a fracture can become a gap, a distance between two parts that can be brought together, the digital that defines both the origin, in this case the differences in digital terms, and the possible remedy, the advance, "technological progress" (Plantard, 2021). The remedies to the divide are thus entrusted to the information society itself, to the Information and Communication Technologies [ICT] industry and to the European Commission, which has been supporting it since the adoption of the Lisbon strategy in 2000.

Among many social divides, DG (Camacho, 2015), considers the technological gap between communities that have access to ICT and those that do not (UNESCO, 2020), or perhaps what is needed for a society to be digitally inclusive,

"...**the gap** *between the potential of ICT and their social appropriation...*" *(Alvarado et al., 2023).*

in society groups or cultures that attempts to indicate a new understanding of this concept, the factors that can enhance the use of technology as an instrument of development (interrelationships, factors, categories, variables) understood or interpreted from the context, culture and history of the group or community in which they are incorporated, or appropriated, in a complex and diverse way, in the hope that they will flow towards a knowledge society, identified from the principle of inclusion, in which "everyone", wherever they are, should have the possibility to participate; without being excluded from the benefits of the information society (G7, Okinawa Charter on Global Information Society).

Vulnerable communities established in sectors or population groups in institutional, environmental, health, education, co-responsibility, participation, equity, recognition, and multicultural conditions in a state of risk, preventing their incorporation into productive life, development and access to better welfare conditions. DG beyond the sufficient speed with which digital technology is developed, includes factors such as age, gender, economic capacity, ethnicity, employment status, education, and geography, among others that reveal a relationship between the digital divide and social divisions in a broader sense, towards DG and new inequalities in the market (Carrascosa et al., 2021; Digital Agenda for Europe (DAE), 2020).

Plantard in 2021 states that a close study of inequalities in access to computers and the Internet (first level gap), uncovers very contrasting uses of software between social groups (second level), and from this, glaring differences in the interpretation of the information resulting from these uses (third level) and finally, a totally unequal socialisation of digital practices between social groups (fourth level). The question is then whether the gap narrows or shifts (Plantard, 2021). DG is then a revelation of social and economic inequalities that resist the changing facts of the information society, which forces to review the element of digital inclusion, as the social appropriation of ICT (Alvarado et al., 2023) in an intentional, studied, and established way.

FACTORS ASSOCIATED WITH THE DIGITAL GAP

Identification of factors contributing to the so-called DG reviews elements of asymmetry and automated inequality (Cabero, 2014), drawing on international and local literature.

Although there are many factors that can be used to characterize DG, the aim of this article is to focus more specifically on STEM factors. To do so, we build on the thesis work of Timothée Duron, who focused on a cross-cutting factor, perseverance, in the French project Persévérons (Duron et al., 2019, 2022). 3 In this context, we proposed a generic method, applied to observation and evaluation. In this paper, we propose to use it for factors characteristic of the digital divide (DG), and more specifically in the STEM context.

Alvarado et al. in 2023, in their work guidance for actions for the construction of mediation of solutions towards digital inclusion (DxIx) from the observation of the Digital Gap (DG), in different domains or spaces of observation and analysis associated with specific environments, arranged in a matrix consisting of 5 columns and presenting in each row (lines) more than 230 factors identified from the literature review elements associated with the DG that allow the management in Factors associated with it. These can be classified (hierarchized), ordered, organized or grouped into dimensions, categories, subcategories and Scenarios (Context/Field of Study/Field of Application). The hierarchical relationship between dimensions, categories, subcategories and factors (Alvarado & Aniorte, 2023), as shown in Fig. 1:

Dimension (1), the highest level of classification, representing a general or broad aspect to be analyzed or evaluated. **Category (2)**, is an intermediate level that groups related subcategories within a dimension.

Subcategory (3), a more specific level within a category that allows for a more detailed classification. **Factor (4),** is the lowest level of classification and represents a particular aspect or attribute that is assessed or analyzed within a sub-category.

Figure 1. Hierarchical organization of factors
(Authors, 2023)

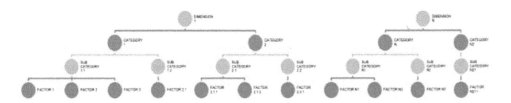

It is important to note that this hierarchy may vary or overlap in **Context/Field of Application (5)** (theme) where it is addressed. The key is to establish a coherent hierarchical structure for organizing the information in a clear and systematic way.

From cross-referencing information, bibliographic reviews and experimental work, the factors emerge structured, grouped and understood on the basis of their attributes or definitions. A matrix that summarizes significant points from the referents, generating a list of descriptors called factors, which suggest an order, classification or grouping, established and in permanent revision that allows associating one or more elements in a line that allows observing the so-called DG, as a consultation tool with more than 200 identified factors. In table 1, a extraction *factors extraction*, is presented:

Table 1. Selection of some matrix factors

Dimension <1>	Category <2>	Sub-category <3>	Factor <4>	Possible Context(s) / Application Field(s) <5>
Technology Access	Technological infrastructure	computers availability	Computers per N inhabitants in rural areas	Education/Classroom
Technology Access	Technological infrastructure	Access to mobile devices Education / Classroom	Percentage of population that owns a mobile device in urban areas	Education/Classroom
Technology Access	Technological infrastructure	Access to mobile devices Education / Classroom	Percentage of population that owns a mobile device in rural areas	Education/Classroom
educational resources access	libraries and community centers Access	Public libraries available	Number of public libraries per N nhabitants	Education/Classroom
educational resources access	libraries and community centers Access	Public libraries available	digital resources and Internet access in public libraries Availability	Education/Classroom
educational resources access	libraries and community centers Access	Public libraries available	digital resources and Internet access in public libraries Availability	Education/Classroom
Technological knowledge and skills	Technological knowledge Level	Basic computer skills	Percentage of population that knows how to use word processing programs	Employability
Technological knowledge and skills	Technological knowledge Level	Basic computer skills	Percentage of population that knows how to use word processing programs	Education/Classroom
Technological knowledge and skills	Technological knowledge Level	Advanced digital skills	Percentage of population that understands data analysis concepts	Education/Classroom
Technological knowledge and skills	Technological knowledge Level	Advanced digital skills	Percentage of population that understands data analysis concepts	Employability
Technological Infrastructure	Developed technologies Capability	Wireless Technologies	High-speed mobile technologies	Products or Services
Technological Infrastructure	Installed Capacity	Basic Resources	Computers Disponibility	Digital Citizenship
Technological Infrastructure	technological tools	technological tools Disponbility	Number of technological tools	Digital Citizenship
Technological Infrastructure	technological tools	technological tools Accesibility	Number of licenses of technological tools	Digital Citizenship
Human-Cultural	Digital Contents	Contents	Language in which it is found	Products or Services
Human-Cultural	Digital Contents	Contents	Language in which it is found	Digital Citizenship

Source. Authors.

Digital Inclusion, a Key Element Towards Digital Transformation

Each Factor then defines an ideal or expected value (expected situation). But several factors can allow to value an indicator or semantically richer information through a formula that allows to evaluate DG (Alvarado & Aniorte, 2023), as shown in the fig. 2.

The information can be consulted by means of dynamic queries on the matrix, meaning that we have implemented it in the form of a database, and furthermore we have built an information system. The TIM method (Duron, 2023) contributes to this characterization by means of a methodological process that makes it possible to observe, measure and calculate values (indicators) that make it possible to evaluate the digital divide and, from there, to elaborate integrative proposals (intentional designs) according to the contexts of remediation towards DxIx.

Figure 2 below shows the possible relationship between factors,

Figure 2. Factors vs. metrics
(Authors)

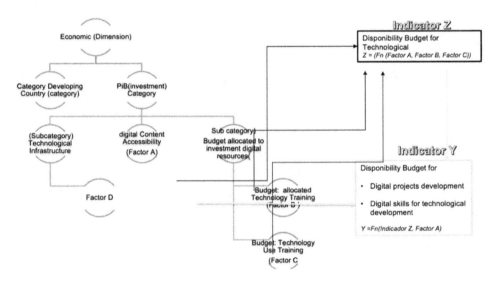

STEM FACTORS IN DIGITAL GAP (DG): MEDIATION EDUCATION FACTORS

How are STEM-related factors integrated into the analysis (observation) Digital Gap?

It should be noted that the criteria for the inclusion of STEM in the hierarchical structure of factors associated with DG arises from consultation specialized literature (repositories) on keywords such as 21st century skills, Education STEM, Governance, Employability for digital transformation (Morakanyane, Grace & O'relly, 2020),

Future Skills, Industry 4.0, Management, Performance among others Jiménez et al, 2022; Magaña, 2021 regarding Management of STEM trends in higher education and their impact on Industry 4.0 (León, Medina & Zuñiga, 2021). Other words such as Improvement, Productivity, STEM Education, STEM Skills and Technology Adoption, Management, Performance Improvement, Productivity, STEM Education, STEM Skills and Technology Adoption, which allowed selecting about 20 articles out of two hundred during the period from 2018 to 2023, considering Business process management, ICT alignment with business processes and rules, enterprise architecture in organizations for digital transformation and digital citizenship (Hinchcliffe, 2015), (Molina et al., 2023; Robledo, 2009a,2022b; Moreno, 2020), (UNESCO, 2017;2021).

In the STEM field, several important issues arise such as the new relationship with current and emerging technologies, their adoption, adaptation and appropriation by very specific users/generators/services/organizations, as well as their concrete appropriation, effective adaptation to the processes linked to the transition towards Digital Transformation (DxTx) (Naranjo et al., 20221). From a holistic point of view, DxTx involves several dimensions and elements linked by cause and effect, benefits and difficulties in a dynamic system, its characterization and understanding based on the factors associated with it, which can explain it widely and diversely and influence it from its own and/or heterogeneous impacts. The work carried out within the framework of the categorization of the matrix of factors associated with GD (Alvarado et al., 2023, Alvarado & Aniorte, 2023) has made it possible to establish different dimensions:

◇ Prospects for management and legal regulation of the field in I4.0 conditions, depending on the accelerating pace of growth in the contexts of education, employability, governance.
◇ Implementation of opportunities for its development in STEM.
◇ Modernization issues in Industry 4.0 conditions, use, availability of technological tools.
◇ Competence training/digital skills (Salinas & de Benito, 2020; Nadal & Navarro).
◇ Educational innovations and diversification of educational services.
◇ STEM skills training in Industry 4.0.
◇ Employability opportunities (offers) with STEM needs.
◇ Digital inclusion, i.e. (inclusive education) access, availability, diversity, among others.

Table 2. Some human factors associated with the digital gap (DG) in the STEM context

Dimension <1>	Category <2>	Sub-category <3>	Factor <4>	Possible Context(s) / Application Field(s) <5>
Gender and Diversity	Gender Equity	Gender Participation	Gender Equality of participation in STEM programs and activities	STEM
Gender and Diversity	Diversity	Minority Inclusion	Minority Inclusion in STEM Activities	STEM
Gender and Diversity	Diversity	Minority Inclusion	STEM opportunities for minorities (marginalized)	STEM
Access to Education and Training STEM	Technological infrastructure	Basic Education	Availability of Educational Institutions STEM Education	STEM
Access to Education and Training STEM	Technological infrastructure	high school education	Availability of Educational Institutions STEM Education	STEM
Access to Education and Training STEM	Technological infrastructure	higher education	Availability of Educational Institutions STEM Education	STEM
Access to Education and Training STEM	Coverage	Basic Education	Number of students with educational STEM access	STEM
Access to Education and Training STEM	Coverage	high school education	Number of students with educational STEM access	STEM
Access to Education and Training STEM	Coverage	higher education	Number of students with educational STEM access	STEM
STEM Education Focus	Curricula	Basic Education	Number of institutional projects emphasis educational STEM	STEM

Continued on following page

Table 2. Continued

Dimension <1>	Category <2>	Sub-category <3>	Factor <4>	Possible Context(s) / Application Field(s) <5>
STEM Education Focus	Curricula	high school education	Number of institutional projects emphasis educational STEM	STEM
STEM Education Focus	Curricula	higher education	Number of institutional projects emphasis educational STEM	STEM
Focus on Education STEM	Investigación	higher education	STEM emphasis projects	STEM
Focus on Education STEM	Coverage	Basic Education	number of women	STEM
Focus on Education STEM	Coverage	high school education	number of special populations	STEM
Focus on Education STEM	Technological Tools	Job-relevant skills and qualifications	Projects labor market defined STEM skills	employability
Focus on Education STEM	Technological Tools	technological skills	digital dispositives use	Education/ Classroom
Focus on Education STEM	Technological Tools	technological skills	communication applications availability	employability
Focus on Education STEM	Technological Tools	technological skills	access networks and information management availabiity	employability
Focus on Education STEM	Technological Tools	disruptive skills	emerging technoligies using	employability
Focus on Education STEM	Technological Tools	disruptive skills	genetic engineering applications using	employability
Focus on Education STEM	Technological Tools	disruptive skills	robotic applications using	Education/ Classroom
Focus on Education STEM	Technological Tools	disruptive skills	genetic engineering applications using	employability
Focus on Education STEM	Technological Tools	disruptive skills	robotic applications using	Education/ Classroom

Continued on following page

Table 2. Continued

Dimension <1>	Category <2>	Sub-category <3>	Factor <4>	Possible Context(s) / Application Field(s) <5>
Focus on Education STEM	Technological Tools	fuerza de trabajo	penetration of disruptive skills (AI)* in the workforce	employability
Policies and Regulations	Digital Inclusion (e-inclusion) Policies	Digital Inclusion (e-Inclusion) Programmes	Number of programmes targeting minority (marginalised) communities	governance

Dimension <1>	Category <2>	Sub-category <3>	Factor <4>	Possible Context(s) / Application Field(s) <5>
Policies and Regulations	Digital Inclusion (e-inclusion) Policies	online health services availability	Percentage of online health services coverage urban area	governance
Policies and Regulations	Digital Inclusion (e-inclusion) Policies	online health services availability	Percentage of online health services coverage rural area	governance
Policies and Regulations	Digital Inclusion (e-inclusion) Policies	public services online availability	Percentage of coverage of public services for people with disabilities	governance
Policies and Regulations	Technology Regulations	Reliable STEM content	Percentage of reliable STEM activities in digital content	governance
Gender Equity STEM	Women's participation	Participation of women in STEM careers	Percentage of women in training in STEM careers in rural areas	Education/ Classroom

Source. Authors.

It is about analyzing how the values of the indicators will be calculated from the values of the factors (the way the rules are formulated), in an automatic experiment, as well as observation (e.g. expert review) in real time and subsequent questionnaires that take massive amounts of information and enter them into an automatic calculation system and allow analysis in context. The definition of the indicators (whose values will be calculated) of the DG, as well as the rules (calculations/formulation) that will allow to give values to these indicators and to track and analyze the key indicators (from an information system) is a work in progress, in different settings, beyond that of education as a classroom. It is being carried out in the framework of an Educational Innovation/Education, 4.0 project, enterprise architecture in an organization and master's thesis in Colombia, such as augmented reality in learning scenarios for mathematics or reading comprehension, as well as strengthening scientific research skills in primary and secondary school students (pupils).

This document presents some elements of the work in a classroom, where diagnosis, design of a Digital Educational Resource (DER), analysis of DG factors observed directly in work sessions with the digital educational resource, considering in its construction computational thinking activities, where STEM elements were considered, a structure of competences associated with statistics, research and computer science (called research areas, computational thinking) within the framework of the educational project of a district educational institution in Colombia, were carried out.

METHOD AND RESULTS

This section presents a general description of the methodological work that allows us to obtain as a result a feed into the large structure of factors associated with DG and to continue observing.

In context or ecosystem STEM the questions in scenarios such as organisations/education/government/governance/employability/digital citizenship, for the human talent considered as a source for innovation, given:

- continuous acceleration of the industrial development cycle, market changes, new knowledge requirements and new technological investments;
- innovation and growth of organizations by developing challenges for holistic and multi-scenario governance of the STEM environment;
- processes of policy change taking place among a wide variety of sectors and actors in a knowledge society, including government, industry and educational institutions;
- linkage towards knowledge production systems imposed by the 4RI disruptive changes to the economy and society, cases such as in South Korea (Jung, 2019) and Sweden (Jacob & Hellström, 2018);
- research and the development and selection of massive common 4RI themes: artificial intelligence, big data, biotechnology, among others, towards a next question:

¿Which are the issues of e-inclusion [DxIx]?

Towards DxTx, from DG observation in scenarios where the exercise is carried out, it is valuable to feed the analysis with metrics and ideal indicators of the defined factors.

Direct observations work in the field, in different contexts, is based on an adaptation and adoption taken by Alvarado et al. (2023) to each case study and this proposes a general framework of four steps, **diagnosis, design of observation mediation instruments, identification of factors, metrics and indicators based on context and analysts' expertise, implementation and analysis of results**, which in the end will feed the cyber-physical system [CPS] model (data, objects, people, services that based on a connected environment) will allow an intelligent decision-making scenario to be proposed.

Specifically in the case of an educational context of a classroom for example, and in the case **of diagnosis**, the aim is to collect socio-economic and cultural population information, associated with DG, also for Digital Competences, Availability of Technological Resources, Accessibility, Digital Educational Resources, Digital Elements Scenarios.

Basic instruments construction for data collection can consist of the following:

◇ Surveys or questionnaires: containing specific questions about the user experience (children, citizens, employees, students). Questions can be related to ease of use, efficiency, overall satisfaction, perceived usefulness, among other relevant aspects. Rating scales (e.g. 1 to 5) to obtain a quantitative measurement of responses.
◇ Interviews or focus groups: Conducting individual interviews or focus groups with users (children, citizens, employees, students) who have used a digital element, or digital educational resource (DER) can provide more detailed and qualitative information about their perception. It can explore their experiences, opinions, and suggestions, and then analyze the data collected to identify common patterns or themes.

Towards Usage *Data Analysis* (DG - Associated Factor element) and **design**:

◇ If the digital resource records usage data, such as interaction time, actions taken or levels completed, you can use this data to assess the level of user participation and engagement. This data can provide an indirect indication of perceived usefulness.
◇ Comparison evaluation, to define the observation medium or scenario, in this case a digital educational resource, with other similar tools available on the market. Comparisons are made based on specific criteria, such as features, functionalities, ease of use, user feedback, etc., to support a decision from the

initial diagnosis to the design of the mechanism/tool/tool/resource in general that allows for gap observation.

It is important to adapt the measurement approach according to ***needs and context/Area of Application***. Also, consider combining different methods to get a more complete picture of the perception of users (children, citizens, employees, students, parents, community leaders, etc.).

Some other examples. For the most part, both indicators (ideal indicator) and formulation need to be established on the ground, in each case. Even if the aim is to eventually have indicators that are cross-cutting and automatic. There may be new factors that emerge from combining one or more factors.

After ***design of the mediating resource (vehicle),*** its ***implementation*** is carried out considering research methodologies focused on observation-action-participation, quantitative-qualitative approach from the relationship of dependent variables and the definition of ideal indicators of factors associated with DG according to the knowledge of the expert in context. Generally, in classroom contexts, a control group and an experimental group are defined. They are calculated from formulations established in the field and for the specific work, ***comparisons are made, and grouped or detailed graphical analyses*** are provided according to the hierarchical structure Dimension/Category/Subcategory/Factor, only for those that were chosen with the initial diagnostic.

CONCLUSION

The theoretical approach proposed in this chapter based on the works of T. Duron, P. Aniorte and L. Gallon and the experimentation through fieldwork, namely the implementation of a Digital Educational Resource (DER) and the direct observation of DG in a classroom context, constitutes a comprehensive and significant contribution that offers valuable insights into DG, its characterizing factors and its relationship with different STEM perspectives. The quantitative-qualitative methodology employed, with control and experimental groups, allowed for a comprehensive evaluation.

The key points are summarized below:

A structured hierarchy of observation of factors, from the TIM method (Duron, 2023) that allows for information gathering, flexibility in the choice of factors after defining measurements (metrics/formulations) and planned ideal indicators, researched with experts. Despite the benefits, the challenge related to access and connectivity are not the only elements associated with GD.

Positive Impact of Digital Educational Resources, the introduction of digital educational resources had a positive impact on student engagement and interest in STEM areas. An increase in motivation and interactivity during activities was observed.

STEM relevance was highlighted, as a significant element associated with the digital divide. While it is a complex ecosystem with multiple perspectives, the exercise adds to the list of factors not only in quantity but also in complexity of measurement and comparison. Students exposed to STEM activities showed greater adaptability to digital tools and a stronger understanding of technology concepts, as well as higher levels of performance in terms of learning outcomes.

The researchers developed several interesting perspectives:

Research Continuum, the research highlighted the need for continuous and adaptive exploration. The constant evolution of technology and social dynamics requires a dynamic approach to ensure the effectiveness and equity of e-inclusion initiatives. It is also worth noting that at the phase corresponding to the design of the resource (not always an educational one), a diagnosis should be sought that allows in context (field work) to establish a vehicle that dynamizes the observation process.

Observations defined from the construction of metrics, formulations, and ideal indicators, with a ***persistent need for expert input*** in context. In drawing conclusions from fieldwork aimed at understanding the factors linked to the digital Gap and proposing decisions for digital inclusion, it becomes clear that the complexity (intricacies) of these factors requires the expertise of professionals who can define relevant metrics, establish appropriate formulations, and design indicators tailored to specific contexts. The complexities observed underline the importance of a nuanced and expert-driven approach when addressing categories associated with the factors.

Need to address Socio-economic inequalities and other dimensions, DG continues to be influenced by socio-economic inequalities.

Considerations for decision-making, a holistic view of the challenges and opportunities associated with implementing fieldwork beyond the educational setting, thus contributing to understanding and addressing the digital divide from a STEM perspective. The next stage of the project will allow us to address more than one district educational institution, seeking to broaden the observation and from there the contribution to an automated tool for data analysis and visualization.

REFERENCES

Abascal, J., Barbosa, S. D., Nicolle, C., & Zaphiris, P. (2016). Rethinking universal accessibility: A broader approach considering the digital gap. *Universal Access in the Information Society*, *15*(2), 179–182. doi:10.1007/s10209-015-0416-1

Alvarado, C., & Aniorté, P. (2023). Un Método para la evaluación de la Brecha Digital: Definición de Factores e Indicadores. El Perfil de Egreso y Competencias Digitales.

Alvarado, C. & Philippe, A. (2023). *Identification de Facteurs Humains associés à la fracture numérique.* EIAH 2023 - Atelier Education 4.0: caractérisation des facteurs humains dans les parcours pédagogiques, LIUPPA Pau, Jun 2023, Brest (France), France.

Bascopé Julio, M., Reiss, K., Morales, M., Robles, C., Reyes, P., Duque, M. I., & Andrade, J. C. (2020). Latin American STEM Policy: A Review of Recent Initiatives on STEM Education in four Latin American Countries. Handbook of Research on STEM Education. Routledge.

Cabero Almenara, J. (2014). Nuevas miradas sobre las TIC aplicadas en la educación. *Andalucía educativa: Revista digital de la Consejería de Educación, 81*

Camacho, K. (2005). La brecha digital. *Palabras en juego: enfoques multiculturales sobre las sociedades de la información*, 61-71.

Canu, M., & Alvarado Mariño, D. C. (2017). *Impacto de talleres de iniciación en robótica sobre la impulsividad en estudiantes de una escuela popular infantil.* Encuentro Internacional de Educación en Ingeniería.

CISCO. (2013). *Inter of Everything.* CISCO. https://www.cisco.com/c/dam/en_us/about/business-insights/docs/ioe-value-index-faq.pdf.

Damiani, F., & Rodríguez-Modroño, P. (2022). *Measuring Women's Digital Inclusion. A poset-based approach to the Women in Digital Scoreboard.* DEMB WORKING PAPER SERIES.

Department of Commerce USA. (2016). *First Reort of the Digital Economy Board of Advisors.* Department of Commerce. https://www.ntia.doc.gov/files/ntia/publications/deba_first_year_report_dec_2016.pdf

DIB. (2023). *Digital Skills as a Tool for Inclusion and Productivity.* DIB. https://www.iadb.org/en/whats-our-impact/RG-T3152

Dochshanov, A. M., & Tramonti, M. (2022). Digital Storytelling And Games To Stem Skills Development. In *EDULEARN22 Proceedings* (pp. 8503-8511). IATED.

Duron, T. (2022). *Modèlisation et détection de la persévérance en milieu scolaire en contexte informatique* [Doctoral dissertation, Pau].

Duron, T., Gallon, L., & Aniorte, P. (2019, April). *Modelling learner's perseverance in education software*. In *Information Systems Education Conference (ISECON 2019)*, USA.

Duron, T., Gallon, L., & Aniorte, P. (2022, July). Detection and classification of dropout behavior. In *FECS'22-The 18th Int'l Conf on Frontiers in Education: Computer Science and Computer Engineering*. Research Gate.

Europe Digital Agenda, E. D. A. (2022). *Digital Competences. DIGCOMP2*, 2.

Feng, S., Magana, A. J., & Kao, D. (2021, October). A systematic review of literature on the effectiveness of intelligent tutoring systems in STEM. In *2021 IEEE Frontiers in Education Conference (FIE)* (pp. 1-9). IEEE 10.1109/FIE49875.2021.9637240

Galperín, H. (2017). *Sociedad digital: brechas y retos para la inclusión digital en América Latina y el Caribe*. UNESCO.

George, B., & Paul, J. (2020). *Digital transformation in business and society*. Springer International Publishing. doi:10.1007/978-3-030-08277-2

Gray, T. J., Gainous, J., & Wagner, K. M. (2017). Gender and the digital divide in Latin America. *Social Science Quarterly*, 98(1), 326–340. doi:10.1111/ssqu.12270

Guo, B., Feng, Y., & Lin, J. (2023). Digital inclusive finance and digital transformation of enterprises. *Finance Research Letters*, 57, 104270. doi:10.1016/j.frl.2023.104270

Hermann, M., Pentek, T., & Otto, B. (2016). Design principles for industrie 4.0 scenarios. In *2016 49th Hawaii international conference on system sciences (HICSS)* (pp. 3928-3937). IEEE.

Hinchcliffe, C. (2015). Citizens and States: considering the concept of citizenship (Doctoral dissertation, University of Oxford).

Idawati, D. E., & Qismullah, F. I. (2019, May). Introducing Stem And Digital Skills In Architectures In Early Childhood Education. In *International Conference on Early Childhood Education* (pp. 1-6). IEEE.

Jiménez-Villarroel, R., Medina-Paredes, J., Castro-Inostroza, A., Chávez-Herting, D., & Castrelo-Silva, N. (2022). Valoración de docentes multigrado sobre un marco que orienta el diseño de unidades STEM integradas. *Revista Científica (Maracaibo)*, (45), 328–344.

Leon, R. J., Medina, D. E. M., & Zúñiga, S. P. A. (2021). Gestión de tendencias STEM en educación superior y su impacto en la industria 4.0. *Journal of the Academy*, (5), 99–121. doi:10.47058/joa5.7

Longoria, I. A. I., Bustamante-Bello, R., Ramírez-Montoya, M. S., & Molina, A. (2022). Systematic mapping of digital gap and gender, age, ethnicity, or disability. *Sustainability (Basel), 14*(3), 1297. doi:10.3390/su14031297

Mahboubi, P. (2022). The Knowledge Gap: Canada Faces a Shortage in Digital and STEM Skills. *CD Howe Institute Commentary, 626.*

(2016). Mastering digital transformation: Towards a smarter society, economy, city and nation. InHanna, N. K. (Ed.), *Mastering Digital Transformation: Towards a Smarter Society, Economy, City and Nation* (pp. i–xxvi). Emerald Group Publishing Limited. doi:10.1108/978-1-78560-465-220151009

Meyerhoff Nielsen, M., & Erhi Makpor, M. (2021, October). Digital inclusion and gender-associated indicators: A critical review of post-2010 literature. In *Proceedings of the 14th international conference on theory and practice of electronic governance* (pp. 123-128). ACM. 10.1145/3494193.3494211

Molina-Izurieta, R., Alvarez-Tello, J., Zapata, M., & Robledo, P. (2023, July). Design of BPM Processes in Higher Education in Ecuador. In *International Conference on Human-Computer Interaction* (pp. 303-310). Cham: Springer Nature Switzerland. 10.1007/978-3-031-35998-9_42

Morakanyane, R., Grace, A. A., & O'reilly, P. (2017). *Conceptualizing digital transformation in business organizations: A systematic review of literature.*

Moreno Zuluaga, M. D. P. (2020). *Guía para identificar los procesos que deben ser automatizados en la transformación digital* [Doctoral dissertation, Universidad EAFIT].

Morte-Nadal, T., & Esteban-Navarro, M. A. (2022). Digital competences for improving digital inclusion in e-government services: A mixed-methods systematic review protocol. *International Journal of Qualitative Methods, 21,* 16094069211070935. doi:10.1177/16094069211070935

Naranjo, G. M. B., Benítez, J. E. M., Freire, S. N. B., Fabián, O., & Jácome, H. (2021). 3.-Factores asociados al rendimiento académico: Un estudio de caso. *Revista EDUCARE-UPEL-IPB-Segunda Nueva Etapa 2.0, 25*(3), 54-77.

Perifanou, M., Economides, A. A., & Tzafilkou, K. (2021). *Teachers' digital skills readiness during COVID-19 pandemic.* Research Gate.

Plantard, P. (2021). La fracture numérique: mythe ou réalité? *Éducation permanente,* (1), 99-110.

Reisdorf, B., & Rhinesmith, C. (2020). Digital inclusion as a core component of social inclusion. *Social Inclusion (Lisboa)*, *8*(2), 132–137. doi:10.17645/si.v8i2.3184

Robledo, P. (2009). *Cloud BPM y la Empresa 3.0*. Apuntes BPM, 1-4.

Saetang, W., Seksan, J., & Thongsri, N. (2023). How academic majors in non-STEM affect digital literacy: The empirical study. *Journal of Technology and Science Education*, *13*(3), 857–868. doi:10.3926/jotse.1791

Salinas, J., & de Benito, B. (2020). Competencia digital y apropiación de las TIC: Claves para la inclusión digital. *Campus Virtuales*, *9*(2), 99–111.

Schwab, K., & Sala-i-Martín, X. (2016, April). *The global competitiveness report 2013–2014: Full data edition*. World Economic Forum.

Vieira, C., Gómez, R. L., Gómez, M., Canu, M., & Duque, M. (2023). Implementing Unplugged CS and Use-Modify-Create to Develop Student Computational Thinking Skills: – A Nationwide Implementation in Colombia. *Journal of Educational Technology & Society*, *26*(3), 155–175. https://www.jstor.org/stable/48734328

Chapter 10
Languages With Artificial Intelligence Applications

Sanjuanita C. Ortiz Valadez
Unidad Académica Multidisciplinaria Reynosa-Rodhe, Mexico

Juan Carlos Huerta Mendoza
https://orcid.org/0009-0005-4713-5759
Unidad Académica Multidisciplinaria Reynosa-Rodhe, Mexico

Vicente Villanueva-Hernandez
Unidad Académica Multidisciplinaria Reynosa-Rodhe, Mexico

Gerardo Tijerina
Unidad Académica Multidisciplinaria Reynosa-Rodhe, Mexico

Daniel Avila-Guzman
https://orcid.org/0009-0008-9547-7544
Unidad Académica Multidisciplinaria Reynosa-Rodhe, Mexico

ABSTRACT

Artificial intelligence (AI) refers to the simulation of human intelligence in machines programmed to think like humans and imitate their actions. The term can also be applied to any machine that exhibits traits associated with a human mind, such as learning and problem-solving. The ideal characteristic of artificial intelligence is its ability to rationalize and take actions that have the best chance of achieving a specific goal. A subset of artificial intelligence is machine learning (ML), which refers to the concept that computer programs can automatically learn from and adapt to new data without the help of humans. Deep learning techniques enable this machine learning by absorbing vast amounts of unstructured data, such as text, images, or video.

DOI: 10.4018/979-8-3693-1119-6.ch010

INTRODUCTION

Nowadays artificial intelligence (AI) has had a considerable impact, with significant advances in different fields such as machine learning, allowing a system to learn by improving autonomously through deep learning and neural networks (Villazón-Terrazas et al, 2020), avoiding being explicitly programmed when processing vast amounts of information as Trust (Quintero et al. 2020) and Usefulness (Quintero et al 2022). Computer vision is another field that has had high growth thanks to the algorithms that are developed so that computers can see, observe and understand significant information from different visual inputs such as digital images and videos, allowing them to take actions or make recommendations based on the analysis of the information. The field of natural language processing (NLP) has also had its significant and constant evolution, because it provides computers with the ability to interpret, understand and manipulate human language, for organizations that have large volumes of voice information and texts, allows you to process, analyze and store them according to your needs. There are more fields that allow the implementation of AI such as expert systems, fuzzy logic, data mining, knowledge engineering, Bayesian networks, reagent systems, among others. In order for these fields to continue developing, it is necessary to use different programming languages that are oriented towards the creation of artificial intelligence. This chapter describes what AI-oriented programming consists of, which key languages can be used to program, each one offering its own characteristics, making it essential to understand when and how to use them. On the other hand, it is also described how the simulation of human language in machines allows us to imitate their way of thinking and performing their actions, based on an interdisciplinary approach such as mathematics, computer science, linguistics, psychology, among others, providing a great benefit for different types of industries. The beginning of artificial intelligence through the first programming languages is something interesting, with autocode being the term used to refer to the family of the first languages descended from autocoding systems whose objective was to increase understandability in machine programming. . For this, Ferranti Mark 1 is one of the first computers that allowed the development of applications for AI, it was the world's first commercially available general purpose electronic computer, which could use two 40-bit words to address the accumulator (register in the which the results of the logical unit are stored), and had secondary storage where an offset value was saved using an additional 20-bit word, thus being one of the requirements to be able to carry out programming oriented to artificial intelligence.

WHAT IS PROGRAMMING ORIENTED FOR ARTIFICIAL INTELLIGENCE?

Artificial intelligence (AI) refers to the simulation of human intelligence in machines programmed to think like humans and imitate their actions. The term can also be applied to any machine that exhibits traits associated with a human mind, such as learning and problem solving.

The ideal characteristic of artificial intelligence is its ability to rationalize and take actions that have the best chance of achieving a specific goal. A subset of artificial intelligence is machine learning (ML), which refers to the concept that computer programs can automatically learn from and adapt to new data without the help of humans. Deep learning techniques enable this machine learning by absorbing vast amounts of unstructured data, such as text, images or video.

Artificial intelligence is based on the principle that human intelligence can be defined in such a way that a machine can easily imitate it and perform tasks, from the simplest to the most complex. The goal of artificial intelligence is to imitate human cognitive activity. Researchers and developers in this field are moving with surprising rapidity in imitating activities such as learning, reasoning, and perception, to the extent that they can be concretely defined. Some believe that innovators will soon be able to develop systems that surpass humans' ability to learn or reason about any subject. But others remain skeptical, because all cognitive activity is imbued with value judgments that are subject to human experience.

As technology advances, previous benchmarks that defined artificial intelligence become obsolete. For example, machines that calculate basic functions or recognize text using optical character recognition are no longer considered to embody artificial intelligence, as this function is taken for granted as an inherent function of the computer. (Frankenfield, 2023)

AI is continually evolving to benefit many different industries. The machines are connected using an interdisciplinary approach based on mathematics, computer science, linguistics and psychology, among others.

LANGUAGES ASSOCIATED WITH ARTIFICIAL INTELLIGENCE APPLICATIONS

Language 1: Python

Python is a high-level programming language used to develop applications of all types. Unlike other languages such as Java or .NET, it is an interpreted language.

Python is an easy language to read and write due to its high similarity to human language. In addition, it is an open source cross-platform language and, therefore, free, which allows you to develop software without limits. Over time, Python has been gaining followers thanks to its simplicity and its wide possibilities, especially in recent years, since it makes it easier to work with artificial intelligence, big data, machine learning and data science, among many other booming fields. (Atha, 2022)

Language Features: Works on multiple platforms; connection to database, easy integration with other programming languages; graphical interface programming support; it is scalable and flexible; simple and easy to understand; difficult to run multiple threads; It does not have good documentation.

Language 2: Java

Java is a simple, object-oriented language that allows the development of applications in several areas, such as security, animation, database access, client-server applications, graphical interfaces, interactive Web pages and mobile application development, among others. One of its main features is the creation of reusable modules, which work without the need to know their internal structure. This allows the user to add new modules, in addition to obtaining programs independent of the platform on which they were developed, thanks to the implementation of the so-called Java Virtual Machine (JVM). (Atha, 2022)

Language features: JAVA is a cross-platform language, executable on most operating systems; complete language, has a wide library and utilities; free distribution software; allows development with databases; It is very functional for mobile application development; language that runs slowly when interpreted; difficult to learn due to its complex syntax.

Language 3: R

The R language is primarily used for statistical analysis, manipulation of large volumes of data, and high-quality graphical representation. R first appeared in 1996 by statistics professors Ross Ihaka and Robert Gentleman at the University of Auckland in New Zealand.

R is the result of a collaborative project that involves thousands of users from all over the world. It currently has one of the richest ecosystems for data analysis, around 1,200 Open Source packages available. Such is its potential that it is the favorite software of any data scientist in the international scientific community. In addition to having a graphical environment with a wide range of classic and advanced statistical tools for the analysis and graphical representation of exportable data. R has great relevance in the areas of Big Data, data mining, Artificial Intelligence and predictive analysis. (Atha, 2022)

Language features: extensive statistical tools; allows the definition of own functions; provides manipulation of code objects from C language; allows growth through packages developed by the user community; It is accessible to the integration of different databases; generates high quality graphics; It has its own documentation format; It is used as a tool for numerical calculations.

Language 4: C++

It is a language designed in 1979 by Bjarne Stroustrup. The intention of its creation was to extend the C programming language mechanism that allows the manipulation of objects, its syntax is inherited from C, it allows the grouping of instructions, it is portable in addition to having a large number of compilers on different platforms and operating systems, It has a large data type such as characters, integers, floating point numbers, booleans and voids.

C++ is ideal for dynamic load balancing, adaptive caching, and developing large data frameworks and libraries.

The vast majority of libraries used for artificial intelligence have been developed in C++ due to its great capacity and efficiency in terms of the operations it performs, which makes it a very powerful language for developers with knowledge of C++.

Apart from having some unique C++ features like memory management, performance features, and systems programming, it definitely serves as one of the most efficient tools for developing rapidly scalable data science and big data libraries. (Chatterjee, 2020)

Language features: Allows code reuse; maintains dynamic load balancing; transparency in memory management; creating solutions in windowed, console mode are fast; supports templates to create your own project types; extensive documentation on the use of artificial intelligence; manages memory effectively.

Language 5: Julia

Developed by MIT in 2012, Julia is a relatively new AI programming language designed to effectively handle expansive numerical analysis and handle large data sets easily. MIT engineers designed Julia taking into account all the requirements of modern AI development. It has remarkable speed, powerful computing power, simple script-like syntax, and much more, helping developers make the best AI programming.

Despite being relatively new, Julia has gained the attention of the development world and already has a thriving community, as well as an ecosystem of machine learning libraries such as TensorFlow.jl, Scikitlearn.jl, Flux, Mocha.jl, and many more (Ortiz-Rodriguez et al, 2006).

An interesting feature of Julia is that it can easily translate algorithms directly from research articles to code, reducing model risk and increasing security. It is a high-performance AI programming language built for modern AI applications and is ideal for developers with experience in Python or R. (Atha, 2022)

Language features: allows own definition of different types of arguments to define the function compartment; integrated package management; designed for parallel and distributed computing; allows calling functions from other programming languages; contain tools for meta programming; allows very effective management of processes through the command line; handles dynamic typing system; can efficiently perform specialized code generation for different types of arguments.

Language 5: Haskell

Haskell's winning attribute is security and speed. Haskell is a modern, purely functional AI programming language with far-reaching advantages in artificial intelligence programming. It has advanced features such as type classes that allow overloading of type-safe operators. Other features are lambda expressions, type classes, pattern matching, type polymorphism, and list comprehension. All of these features make Haskell ideal for research, teaching, and industrial applications. Thanks to its flexibility and error handling capabilities, Haskell is one of the safest AI programming languages. (Atha, 2022)

Language characteristics: its programming is mainly focused on functions based on arguments; It handles two types of parametric and ad hoc polymorphism; types are checked at compile time; uses indentation to structure the code; allows the execution of different processes in the same period of time.

WHAT TYPE OF LANGUAGE WAS MOST USED AT THE TIME?

Simula

Simula, an acronym for Simulation Language, is presented as the first object-oriented programming language created by Norwegian developers Ole-Johan Dahl and Kristen Nygaard in 1962 by determining how programs can model or simulate the world seen by computer users.

According to computer science experts, Simula changed the narrative of programming languages, designing them around objects rather than functions or linear procedures. In essence, with this OOP language, objects could communicate through messages, modeling the traditional idea of receiver and sender.

Its main characteristic is that it can serve as a framework for special application languages, thanks to the fact that it can be easily structured to adapt to specialized problem areas.

There is no doubt that its use led to the introduction of some other programming languages, such as Java, C++ and other new practice-oriented programming languages and systems. Additionally, the general algorithmic language, ALGOL 60, is a subset of Simula 67. (Wikipedia, 2024)

WHAT WAS THE FIRST PROGRAMMING LANGUAGE ORIENTED TO ARTIFICIAL INTELLIGENCE?

Autocode

Autocode is the name of a family of "simplified coding systems", later called programming languages, devised in the 1950s and 1960s for a series of digital computers at the universities of Manchester, Cambridge and London. Auto code was a generic term; The auto codes for different machines were not necessarily related to each other, as are, for example, the different versions of the single Fortran language.

Today, the term is used to refer to the family of early languages descended from the generally similar Manchester Mark 1 autoencoder systems. In the 1960s, the term autoencoder was used more generically to refer to any high-level programming language that used a compiler. Examples of languages called self-coding are COBOL and Fortran. (Wikipedia, 2023)

The first auto code and its compiler were developed by Alick Glennie in 1952 for the Mark 1 computer at the University of Manchester and is considered by some to be the first compiled programming language. Its main objective was to increase comprehensibility in the programming of the Mark 1 machines, which were known for their especially abstruse machine code. Although the resulting language was much clearer than machine code, it was still very machine-dependent. (Mendoza, 2020)

BETWEEN WHAT YEARS DID PROGRAMMING FOCUSED ON ARTIFICIAL INTELLIGENCE BEGINNED?

In the 1940s and 1950s, a group of scientists from several fields (mathematics, psychology, engineering, economics, and political science) began to discuss the possibility of creating an artificial brain. The field of artificial intelligence research was founded as an academic discipline in 1956. (Wikipedia, 2024)

WHAT TYPE OF COMPUTERS WERE USED

Ferranti Mark 1

The Ferranti Mark I, also known as the Manchester Electronic Computer, was the world's first commercially available general-purpose electronic computer. The first machine was delivered to the University of Manchester in February 1951, ahead of UNIVAC I, which was delivered to the United States Census Bureau a month later.

The machine was built by Ferranti of the United Kingdom. It was based on the Manchester Mark I, which was designed at the University of Manchester by Freddie Williams and Tom Kilburn. The Manchester Mark I served as the prototype of the Ferranti Mark I; The main improvements were the size of the primary and secondary memory, a faster multiplier, and additional instructions. (History-Computer, 2023)

WHAT WERE THE REQUIREMENTS OF COMPUTERS FOR PROGRAMMING ORIENTED TO ARTIFICIAL INTELLIGENCE

A 20-bit word was stored as a single dotted line of electrical charges sitting on the surface of a Williams tube display, and each cathode tube stored 64 dotted lines. The main memory consisted of eight tubes, each of which could store a page of 64 comments. The single 80-bit accumulator (A), the 40-bit "multiplier/quotient register" (MQ), and eight "B-lines," or index registers, were stored in other tubes, which was one of the distinguishing features of the design of the Mark 1. The Ferranti Mark 1 could also use two 40-bit words to address the accumulator. An offset value was stored in secondary storage using an additional 20-bit word per tube.

For secondary storage, a 512-page magnetic drum with a revolution period of 30 milliseconds was used, containing two pages per track. The drum had eight times the storage capacity of Manchester's original design. (History-Computer, 2023)

CONCLUSION

Artificial intelligence has become one of the most promising disciplines in the world of technology, supporting different areas such as online shopping by making recommendations to consumers, web searches providing relevant results, personal assistants in the organization of daily activities, automatic translations such as subtitling, real estate with the internet of things, the health sector to detect diseases, vehicles with autonomous driving, cybersecurity using pattern recognition, and some others such as transportation, manufacturing, food, crops, government. In order to have a good result in the implementation of solutions in each of these areas through artificial intelligence, the good choice of the programming language to use is essential and crucial. Each of them that we mention stands out for its unique characteristics. Python is a language that allows you to work with vast volumes of data and is easy to understand due to its high similarity to human language. JAVA implements reusable modules for the development of web-based algorithms interacting with databases in a client-server environment. For the implementation of algorithms with statistical analysis with high-quality graphical representation, the R language has it as its main characteristic. Most of the libraries used in artificial intelligence programming are developed in the C++ language, which makes it a good option for implementation in data science and big data solutions due to its great capacity and efficiency in carrying out operations. For solutions with a high need for calculations at an efficient speed, the JULIA language is very promising and has been built to develop modern applications, ideal for developers with experience in Python or R. Haskell is a language that provides a lot of security to modern implementations of AI due to its great flexibility and ability to handle errors, the use of lamba expressions, type classes, pattern matching make it very attractive for research, teaching and industrial applications.

The use of these programming languages has played an important role in the development of artificial intelligence. Understanding the nature of the problems to be solved and choosing the appropriate programming language are part of the understanding necessary to program artificial intelligence, this can make the difference in the effectiveness of the solution that could be obtained. Thanks to the result of the good solutions that have been developed by different researchers, associations, universities, companies and people who were attracted to AI programming, they have allowed transformation in each of the different sectors of society. Therefore, the good use of these programming languages, always with ethics and responsibility, will allow AI to continue growing positively and be a powerful tool to face the different problems that may arise and become a better world.

REFERENCES

Atha, H. (2022). Best Programming Language for AI Development. *moveoapps*. https://www.moveoapps.com/blog/best-programming-languages-ai-development/

Chatterjee, S. (2020). Top CC machine learning libraries for data science. *hackernoon*. https://hackernoon.com/top-cc-machine-learning-libraries-for-data-science-nl183wo1

Frankenfield, J. (2023). AI. *investopedia*. https://www.investopedia.com/terms/a/artificial-intelligence-ai.asp

History-Computer. (2023). Ferranti Mark 1 Computer Guide. *history-computer*. https://history-computer.com/ferranti-mark-1-computer-guide/

Medina-Quintero, J. M., Abrego-Almazán, D., & Ortiz-Rodríguez, F. (2018). Use and usefulness of the information systems measurement. a quality approach at the mexican northeastern region. *Cuadernos Americanos*, *31*(56), 7–30. doi:10.11144/Javeriana.cao.31-56.ubwm

Mendoza, M. L. (2020). *Tipos de lenguajes de proframacion*. OpenWebinar. openwebinars.net/blog/tipos-de-lenguajes-de-programacion/

Ortiz-Rodríguez, F., Palma, R., & Villazón-Terrazas, B. (2006). Semantic based P2P System for local e-Government. In Proceedings of Informatik 2006. GI-Edition-Lecture Notes in Informatics (LNI).

Quintero, J. M. M., Echeverría, O. R., & Rodríguez, F. O. (2022). Trust and information quality for the customer satisfaction and loyalty in e-Banking with the use of the mobile phone. *Contaduría y Administración*, *67*(1), 283–304.

Villazón-Terrazas, B., Ortiz-Rodríguez, F., Tiwari, S. M., & Shandilya, S. K. (2020). Knowledge graphs and semantic web. *Communications in Computer and Information Science*, *1232*, 1–225. doi:10.1007/978-3-030-65384-2

Chapter 11
Understanding Sensory Marketing and Women Consumers' Behavior

Anabel Sofia Villegas-Garza
Tamaulipas Autonomous University, Mexico

Melchor Medina-Quintero
Tamaulipas Autonomous University, Mexico

Fernando Ortiz-Rodriguez
https://orcid.org/0000-0003-2084-3462
Tamaulipas Autonomous University, Mexico

ABSTRACT

Sensory marketing has been evolving in tandem with consumer preferences, adapting new techniques to enhance the consumer experience. However, there is a need for gender-based research in sensory marketing, particularly about women. This study aims to analyze the impact of stimuli received through the five senses on consumer satisfaction and subsequent purchase intention among women. For this purpose, 208 questionnaires were distributed to women in Tamaulipas, Mexico, and structural equation modeling using SmartPLS 4 was employed for analysis. The study found that the sense of sight has the greatest influence on consumer satisfaction, while the senses of smell and hearing do not significantly impact this variable. Additionally, the study identified that consumer satisfaction is a significant factor influencing women's purchase intention.

DOI: 10.4018/979-8-3693-1119-6.ch011

Copyright © 2024, IGI Global. Copying or distributing in print or electronic forms without written permission of IGI Global is prohibited.

INTRODUCTION

Modern-day advances in sensory marketing call for consumer experiences, focusing on specific targets, giving an extra to allow consumers to make new ways of making purchases (Manchado et al., 2023). In the same way, over time, competition has increased among companies in the sector of different sectors such as commerce, mainly due to the increase in products and marketing tools that have been used in recent years. In past decades, companies gave greater relevance to aspects such as product quality, price, and service in the purchasing process for the design of their marketing strategies (Fernández et al., 2020). However, in recent years it has been identified that factors such as perception and emotions are key for consumers to remember a brand, so they should be considered when designing the marketing plan of organizations (Randhir et al., 2016).

Consequently, the use of new marketing tools to attract potential customers and the use of new sales channels that include and maintain the same sales experience have been arising (Reina & Jimenez, 2020). As a result, sensory marketing has become relevant for brands, because it stimulates the five senses of the consumer through experience (Santos et al., 2023; Zha et al., 2022). In this regard, the influence of sensory marketing on consumer behavior has been addressed in Mexico by the research of Ortegón-Cortázar and Gómez (2016), who identified the dominance of the sense of vision over persuasion and that smell presents a greater relationship with the level of information recall. As for the state of Tamaulipas (Mexico), González et al. (2019), through their study in the southern commercial area of the entity identified that the senses of vision, smell, and touch are the main determinants in which consumers in the region support their purchase decision.

To summarize the research found a lack of understanding of the relationship between sensory marketing and women's satisfaction and its impact on purchase intention. While extensive research has been conducted on sensory marketing, it has largely been genderless. Therefore, this study aims to analyze the impact of sensory stimuli on consumer satisfaction and purchase intention among women.

After though literature review, SmartPLS v4 was used as statistical tool for structural equation modeling to develop the final instrument and the results. The expected contribution of the research is to improve the current framework and provide insights into women's behavior inside the store. The results will provide valuable information to retailers and researchers by defining women's sensory marketing and their relationship.

SENSORY MARKETING

Companies have been searching for new sources to create value for their customers to differentiate themselves from their competitors (Barrios, 2012; Wibisono & Syah, 2019). In the field of marketing, one of the elements that has been of greatest interest to organizations is the experiences offered to consumers, since it has been shown that it allows understanding of their behavior as Holbrook and Hirschman mentioned in 1982.

The generation of experiences in individuals within their purchasing process can have several positive effects on customers such as boosting purchase intention, generating commitment to the brand, or increasing the perception of the satisfaction of their expectations (Hulten et al., 2009; Randhir et al., 2016; Moreira et al., 2017). Also, through experience marketing as a sales strategy, consumers can be made to remember companies to a greater extent if their senses are effectively stimulated (Koszembar, 2019).

Besides, experience to have a relevant impact, it must be based on the generation of emotions and sensations (Alan et al., 2015; Wibisono & Syah, 2019; Zha et al., 2022). Experiences in marketing can be divided into two types: direct or indirect, the former related to the purchase and consumption of the product or service, and the latter to the messages and communication activities carried out by organizations (Rodas & Montoya, 2018).

An important aspect of experiences is that they are usually integrated by different types of relationships between different actors (customers, brand, environment, among others), so it involves a wide range of consumer responses, which is why it is considered multidimensional (Rodas & Montoya, 2018; Haase & Wiedmann 2020). Incidentally, as seen in Figure 1, Hultén et al. (2009) show a division of a sensory experience, to illustrate the relation between the store, the experience, and the customer.

Figure 1. Sensory marketing
Source: Hultén et al. (2009)

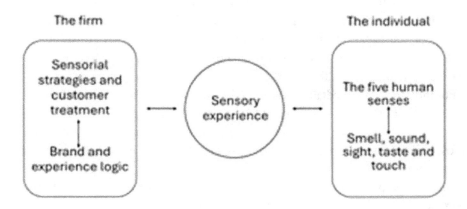

Sensory marketing requires two indispensable parts, the company and the customers. The customer section is made up of the five human senses (sight, touch, taste, hearing, and smell), while the company is made up of sensory strategies, and the treatment of the customer, which in turn is related to the brand and the logical experience. For this reason, it is concluded that sensory marketing analyzes the responses of customers' senses stimulated by the company (Rodas & Montoya, 2018; Wibisono & Syah, 2019). In this sense, sensory marketing can be defined as a holistic system that serves to communicate information regarding the company's brand, which considers not only the traditional channels of interaction with customers but also those methods that impact the five senses of the consumer allowing to establish a stronger and lasting emotional connection with them (Hultén et al., 2009; Hassan & Iqbal, 2016; Randhir et al., 2016; Rodas & Montoya, 2018).

This marketing archetype seeks to create a positive and pleasant experience for consumers before, during, and after the purchase decision (Hultén et al., 2009; Hassan & Iqbal, 2016; Randhir et al., 2016). It should be noted that to stimulate required specific factors, in addition, their use in the buying process differs among individuals and sectors (Barrios, 2012; Biswas et al., 2019; Carrizo et al., 2017; Haase & Wiedmann, 2020; Hepola et al., 2017).

According to Grimaldi et al. (2020) and Bobrie (2018), sight is the most used sense in the design of marketing strategies because, apart from making it easier to remember a brand, elements such as color or light intensity directly influence customers' emotions. Regarding the relationship of this sense with the consumer experience, it is considered the most dominant over the rest due to its high capacity for persuasion and memorization (Ortegón-Cortázar & Gómez, 2016). Similarly, it has been found that some visual elements of the product such as design, color, size, amount of text, packaging, and establishments such as decoration, presentation of furniture, appearance of employees, and aesthetics in general, contribute to the creation of value for consumers that encourages them to continue consuming goods or services in the same businesses (Sanchez & Iniesta, 2009; Alan et al., 2015; Haase & Wiedmann, 2020).

For their part, Hagtvedt and Brasel (2016) indicate that there is a correspondence between the frequency of sound and light, which influences customer behavior towards the product. Now, if there is an organization of the visual elements of the atmosphere, pleasure is produced, resulting in satisfaction and purchase reintention in customers who prefer hedonic purchases (Garaus, 2017).

Taste is the predominant sense in the food sector for the selection of food and beverages (Lund, 2015), and is strongly linked to smell, which stimulates the palate (Ortegón-Cortázar & Gómez, 2016). This sense presents differences according to the age of individuals, so that in childhood, it is generally stronger, while older people usually have less accuracy because their taste receptors decrease (Grimaldi et al., 2020). Thus, taste is considered to be the most intimate of the senses, since it requires direct contact for some time between the products and the customer (González et al., 2019). Incidentally, Haase and Wiedmann (2020) provided empirical evidence on the importance of the gustatory attributes of products (such as taste or if it looks appetizing), their influence on customer satisfaction, perception of the brand image, and the prices offered by companies.

Regarding hearing, according to González et al. (2019), the sounds presented in an establishment have the potential to generate positive or negative memories in consumers, because they generate feelings and emotions associated with their purchases. Similarly, according to Barrios (2012), it is an efficient way to contextualize customers about the products and services offered by the company. Biswas et al. (2019) identified that the volume of ambient music and background noise are capable factors of influence the level of sales in organizations. Similarly, it has been shown that when customers feel comfortable with the auditory environment during their purchases, a better perception of the quality of products and services is generated (Ortegón-Cortázar & Gómez, 2016), as well as the strengthening of commitment to the brand and buyer satisfaction (Haase & Wiedmann, 2020).

In the case of touch, it has been established that it increases customers' trust and feeling of ownership towards products, as well as better evaluations of goods (Ringler et al., 2019). It has also been identified that certain product attributes linked to this sense such as shape, comfort, and practicality, can generate in customers a positive assessment of their satisfaction or brand loyalty (Haase & Wiedmann, 2020). For Grimaldi et al. (2020), touch can have attraction and aversion effects, for example, customers are less likely to purchase certain products if someone else has touched them. Likewise, Gómez and Mejía (2012) point out that touch influences customer satisfaction because it allows them to get an idea of the quality of the product through aspects such as hardness, texture, weight, or temperature that for certain merchandise is relevant as in the case of electronics.

Regarding smell, Barrios (2012) mentions that those points of sale that offer their consumers pleasant smells in their facilities and products are more likely to receive a positive evaluation. Ortegón-Cortázar and Gómez (2016) point out that through the stimulation of aromas, it is possible to influence the behavior of customers unconsciously, boosting their purchase intention, without their attention being focused specifically on the smells.

The olfactory factors that stimulate the emotions of customers are divided in two: the first one is natural odors, which are characteristic of the products or found in the environment, and the second one is artificial odor, such as perfumes and fragrances (Barrios, 2012; Haase & Wiedmann, 2020). For sensory marketing, two characteristics of aromas are especially relevant: pleasure, which represents the pleasant experience of the smell, and congruence, which connects the smell with what it is intended to offer in terms of the company's products, facilities, and brand (González et al., 2019). Also, we can mention Trust (Quintero et al. 2020) and Usefulness (Quintero et al 2022).

Based on the previously cited literature that in sum describes how through the different dimensions of sensory marketing it is possible to influence customer satisfaction by providing them with certain experiences during their purchasing process the following research hypotheses are put forward:

H_1. A woman's satisfaction is positively correlated with her positive association with the sense of taste.

H_2. A woman's satisfaction is positively correlated with her positive association with the sense of sight.

H_3. A woman's satisfaction is positively correlated with her positive association with the sense of hearing.

H_4. A woman's satisfaction is positively correlated with her positive association with the sense of touch.

H_5. A woman's satisfaction is positively correlated with her positive association with the sense of smell.

Now, the study of the determinants of customer satisfaction is critical for companies, especially for those operating in highly competitive business environments, as it contributes among other aspects to motivating customer purchase intention (Wibisono & Syah, 2019). In this sense, satisfaction derives from the contrast that an individual makes about their expectations and reality, i.e., whether what they receive is less than, equal to, or greater than what they expected (Venter et al., 2018; Keni et al., 2019).

In this regard, a positive experience of the consumption of a certain product in which the expectations that the customer placed on it were met in a high percentage can increase their intention to purchase the same item in the future (Keni et al., 2019). Also, providing pleasant experiences to customers when they visit stores motivates them to make a future visit to the business (Suraj et al., 2021).

According to Venter et al. (2018), purchase intention refers to people's plan to purchase certain items, which involves the specific circumstances and timing of the purchase. This same author points out that when a brand meets the expectations of its customers based on the characteristics of its products and the experiences it offers them in their purchase, consumers are more likely to return to the store as Suraj et al. (2021).

Wibisono and Syah (2019), mention that when a company achieves high levels of customer satisfaction, it not only boosts their purchase intention but also increases their loyalty and encourages them to recommend the brand to third parties. Now, given that satisfaction depends on the experience for making decisions about the purchase of some product (Carrizo et al., 2017), in most cases, consumption is generated (Fernández et al., 2009). Similarly, Tu and Yang (2019) found that the quality and attractiveness with which products are presented promote customer satisfaction, in addition to influencing purchase intention. Carrizo et al. (2017) emphasize that one of the connections created by the experience is satisfaction, which is a predictor of customer behavior and purchase intention.

Thus, it is observed that when companies manage to meet their customers' expectations, they will have happy and satisfied consumers, thus encouraging their purchase intention (Alan et al. 2015; Aflaki & Popescu, 2014). Based on the literature review presented above, the following hypothesis of the existing relationship between satisfaction and purchase intention of women is established:

H_6. Women's satisfaction is a factor that influences their intention to purchase.

METHOD

To analyze whether the stimuli received through the five senses are satisfactory and lead customers to a purchase intention, the present research was conducted with a quantitative approach and explanatory scope. Likewise, it is a cross-sectional study because only the elements of sensory marketing, satisfaction, and purchase intention of the state of Tamaulipas (Mexico) women in a determined period were studied.

Correspondingly to the analysis of the relationship between the mentioned variables, the literature review was carried out, through which it was possible to operationalize them according to the following elements:

- Taste: consumption of products in the shop, delicious what is consumed, satisfaction with what I can consume.
- Sight: pleasant experience of the organization and tidiness of the shop, attractive arrangement, nice shop.
- Hearing: pleasant experience with the music and noises in the shop, adequate volume, attention to the music, enjoyment of the music.
- Touch: adequate room temperature in the shop, pleasant to touch the products.
- Smell: experience with the smell in the shop, pleasant smell, positive impression of the smell, liking the smell of cleanliness.
- Satisfaction: happiness when visiting the shop, good choice of shop, satisfaction with visiting the shop.
- Purchase intention: intention to purchase in the future, pleasant environment in the shop, products that I like.

A questionnaire was developed based on a review of the literature of Biswas et al. (2019), Carrizo et al. (2017), Fernández et al. (2009), Haase and Wiedmann (2020), Hepola et al. (2017), Alan et al. (2015) and Ringler et al. (2019), which were developed in English and applied in different social, political and economic contexts to the present in Tamaulipas, which is why the necessary adaptations were made for its application in the state.

The instrument designed on the one hand, collects socio-demographic data on the participants' sex, age, marital status, schooling, and income level. On the other hand, the questionnaire is also made up of 34 items measured on a 5-point Likert scale that measures the elements of the variables of sensory marketing (24 items), customer satisfaction (5 items), and purchase intention (5 items).

The empirical work was carried out in the main cities of Tamaulipas between October and November 2022, applying the instrument to both men and women over 18 years of age. The final sample consisted of 380 questionnaires, of which 208 were answered by women and 172 by men; however, for this study, only data from the first group were considered. All participants were informed that the information provided would be used anonymously and confidentially.

For the data analysis, in the first instance, the descriptive statistics of the study participants are presented, and in the second section, the inferential analysis is presented using the structural equation modeling technique. In this regard, when running the SmartPLS software, it was identified that some items did not meet the minimum load, so they were eliminated, these being Taste4, Taste5, Hearing2,

Touch4, and Smell5, for that purpose, the model was run again to improve it (Hair et al., 2019).

In this sense, with the 208 questionnaires and in conjunction with the SmartPLS parameters of a subsampling of 5000 subsamples, the confidence interval method used is Bias-Corrected and accelerated (BCa) Bootstrap, a one-tailed test type and the significance level of 0.05, the crosses of variables were obtained, as well as the correlation matrix, the factor loadings, t-statistic, the variance explained (R^2), the average variance extracted (AVE), the standardized path coefficients (β), the effect size (f^2), among others, to validate the values obtained and verify methodological aspects such as their consistency, heterogeneity and homogeneity, to contrast the proposed hypotheses.

Results

For descriptive statistics, in terms of the age of the respondents, the highest percentage was in the 20-29 age range with 31%. As a whole, those aged 39 and underrepresent 78%, those aged 40 to 49 7%, and those aged 50 and over 15%. Marital status, results show that 60.6% of the participants said they were single, while 25.5% said they were married, with both groups being the most frequent. On the other hand, the marital statuses of widowed and separated with 1.9% each were the least frequent among the respondents.

As for the level of education of the participants, 59.1% of them mentioned that they had higher education, while 40.4% indicated that they had a high school education. Finally, regarding the respondents' income, the range of $0 to $2400 (Mexican pesos) was the highest percentage with 40.4%, while the range of $9000 or less represents 71.2%, and the women who receive an income equal to or greater than $9001 represent 28.58%.

The inferential analysis of the data was carried out using SmartPLS 4 because, as mentioned by Hair et al. (2019), it is considered a suitable tool that allows, on one hand, to carry out a measurement model (psychometric properties of the scale used to measure the variables) and, on the other hand, to develop the structural equation modeling (to identify the strength and direction of the relationships between the variables analyzed).

Validation of the Measurement Model

To test the reliability of the items, the factor loadings of each item were examined under the methodological recommendations that indicate that the weight of the factor loading should be above 0.707 to be accepted as an explanatory element of a variable (Chin, 1998). In this sense, as can be seen in Table 1, it was identified that

19 items measure sensory marketing, 5 items measure customer satisfaction and 5 items measure purchase intention, showing acceptable values in their factor loadings between 0.814 and 0.961, being higher than the minimum recommended (0.707).

Concerning the internal consistency of the variables, this was measured through the Fornell and Larcker (1981) statistic, which is recommended to score above 0.707, and Cronbach's alpha, which is suggested to be greater than 0.700, a correct validation could be observed by exceeding the recommended values for both statistics (Table 1, Column 2).

Table 1. Item construct, individual item reliability, and internal consistency

Variable/ Item with factor loading	Internal consistency	Cronbach's alpha	AVE	R^2	rho_A
Taste	0.966	0.947	0.905	-	0.951
Taste1 (.943), Taste2 (.961), Taste3 (.949)					
Sight	0.806	0.940	0.806	-	0.940
Sight1 (.879), Sight2 (.921), Sight3 (.912), Sight4 (.860), Sight5 (.914)					
Hearing	0.720	0.871	0.720	-	0.883
Hearing1 (.855), Hearing3 (.841), Hearing4 (.834), Hearing5 (.863)					
Touch	0.774	0.854	0.774	-	0.855
Touch1 (.892), Touch2 (.910), Touch3 (.835)					
Smell	0.731	0.878	0.731	-	0.884
Smell1 (.857), Smell2 (.840), Smell3 (.908), Smell4 (.814)					
Satisfaction	0.870	0.963	0.870	0.572	0.963
Sat1 (.900), Sat2 (.935), Sat3 (.948), Sat4 (.939), Sat5 (.941)					
Purchase intention	0.961	0.949	0.832	0.723	0.950
Pi1 (.921), Pi2 (.928), Pi3 (.916), Pi4 (.886), Pi5 (.908)					

Regarding the convergent validation, it could be seen that the seven constructs presented values between 0.720 and 0.905 in the AVE statistic, which are higher than the methodologically recommended 0.500 (Fornell & Larcker, 1981). Likewise, to obtain the t-statistic values, a resampling was carried out with 5000 subsamples, so that based on the results presented in Table 1, it is established that four of the six hypotheses proposed have the necessary elements to be supported.

For the discriminant validation, it is specified that the different constructs obtained values between 0.855 and 0.963 for the Dijkstra - Henseler indicator (rho_A), which is recommended to be greater than 0.700, and this condition was fulfilled (Table 3). Similarly, the discriminant validation was also analyzed through the Fornell and Larcker (1981) criterion. In this respect, Table 2 shows that the square root of AVE between the variables and their measures were higher than the data located in the same column and row, thus fulfilling the condition of the inter-construct.

Table 2. Discriminant validity

	Taste	Purchase intention	Smell	Hearing	Satisfa-ction	Touch	Sight
Taste	0.951						
Purchase intention	0.420	0.912					
Smell	0.360	0.702	0.855				
Hearing	0.330	0.598	0.554	0.848			
Satisfaction	0.459	0.850	0.589	0.519	0.933		
Touch	0.394	0.748	0.680	0.630	0.645	0.880	
Sight	0.379	0.808	0.751	0.559	0.710	0.734	0.898

Validation of the Structural Model

Table 3 shows the evaluation of the model and the hypotheses established by the theoretical review. According to Chin (1998) the value of standardized path coefficient (β) should reach at least 0.200 and preferably be higher than 0.300, while R^2 to represent a substantial effect is suggested to be at a level of 0.670, up to a value of 0.330 such effect is considered moderate, and when its level is up to 0.190 it is weak. Also, for the significance criterion (t-statistic) it should be less than 0.05 (p<0.05) and for a one-tailed subsampling of 5000 (Hair et al., 2019): t (0.001; 4999) = 3.092, representing *** p<0.001; t (0.010; 4999) = 2.327, representing ** p<0.010, and t (0.050; 4999) = 1.645, representing * p<0.050.

Table 3. Inferential results with SmartPLS

Hypothesis	f²	β	T-statistic	P value	Results
H₁ Taste → Satisfaction	0.066	0.185 ***	3.361	0.000	Supported
H₂ Sight → Satisfaction	0.159	0.448 ***	4.685	0.000	Supported
H₃ Hearing → Satisfaction	0.010	0.086	1.274	0.101	Not supported
H₄ Touch → Satisfaction	0.027	0.177 *	2.017	0.022	Supported
H₅ Smell → Satisfaction	0.000	0.018	0.203	0.419	Not supported
H₆ Satisfaction → Purchase intenition	2.613	0.850 ***	34.75	0.000	Supported

Likewise, the f² index is used to identify whether the independent variable has a substantial impact on the dependent variable and its parameters based on Cohen (1988) are as follows: 0.020 represents a small effect, 0.150 corresponds to a moderate effect and 0.350 is a large effect. In this sense, according to the above methodological considerations, hypothesis 1 (H₁) is accepted with β=0.185 and a t-statistic of 3.361 (p<.001). Consuming food that is palatable to the consumer's palate in the shop produces general satisfaction and happiness at having chosen that place to shop.

H₂ was also accepted with β=0.448 and a t-statistic of 4.685 (p<.001), which indicates that the organization and order of the shop, the attractiveness of the arrangement inside the shop, and that the shop physically looks nice, are aspects that generate customer satisfaction among women when shopping. On the other hand, H₃ is rejected as it has a p-value equal to 0.101. This suggests that elements related to the sense of hearing, such as the experience with the type of music, the volume of the music, and the noise in the place where women shop, do not generate customer satisfaction.

In the case of H₄, it is accepted with β=0.177 and a t-statistic of 2.017 (p<0.001). This result indicates that the experience related to the sense of touch when shopping, such as the ambient temperature in the shop and the experience of the products that can be touched in the shop, are factors that influence the overall satisfaction of consumers.

H₅ was also rejected as it had a p-value of 0.419, which indicates that the experience with the smell in the shop, as well as the impression and taste of the store, do not produce satisfaction in women consumers in terms of the degree of happiness of visiting the shop or the perception of having visited that place.

About H₆, this is supported by β=0.850 and a t-statistic of 34.751 (p<0.001). Overall satisfaction and happiness of having chosen that place to shop has a significant relationship with the purchase intention of women, which translates into a future desire to continue consuming goods and services offered in the shop because they like it and, therefore, to make new visits to the establishment in the future.

The effects of the constructs of taste, sight, and touch in this study are consistent with the results of other research such as those of Sánchez and Iniesta (2009), Alan et al. (2015), González et al. (2019), Haase and Wiedmann (2020), who identified that these senses influence customer satisfaction, as the stimuli received in a sensory way help to increase their levels of confidence and perception of quality, regarding the products and services purchased.

Meanwhile, the non-significant effect of smell on the satisfaction of the identified consumers highlighted was mentioned by Barrios (2012) concerning the fact that women are generally more sensitive to smells, so if these are strong or irritating, they can generate dissatisfaction. In terms of hearing, the results suggest that the sound environment in which the participants make their purchases does not meet their expectations to generate satisfaction as indicated in the literature (Ortegón-Cortázar & Gómez, 2016; Biswas et al., 2019), and therefore, the achievement of this effect.

Finally, the relationship between consumer satisfaction with purchase intention is congruent with studies by Venter et al. (2018), Wibisono and Syah (2019), and Suraj et al. (2021), who identified that when customers perceive that the sensory environment in which they make their purchases is pleasant and satisfies as they expected, such feeling will promote the consumption of their products and services, thus the attitude oriented to make future visits to the same businesses.

CONCLUSION

In the current business context, the COVID-19 pandemic and rapid technological advancements have given rise to new business models and innovative marketing strategies. As such, it is essential to explore the effects of sensory marketing on consumer satisfaction and purchase intention, as exemplified in this study. Our findings indicate that sensory marketing elements, including taste, sight, hearing, touch, and smell, have a significant impact on women's satisfaction during shopping.

Notably, the sight was identified as the most influential sensory element that generates satisfaction among women. Additionally, the study highlights the importance of providing relevant information, such as store merchandising, to help women feel confident in their store selection. Given the current business environment, these findings emphasize the need to integrate sensory marketing elements into marketing strategies to enhance customer satisfaction, loyalty, and ultimately, organizational success.

Other findings from the present study have revealed that the sense of hearing and smell does not significantly contribute to customer satisfaction during store visits. These results suggest that consumers may not perceive the scent and noises in stores as pleasant, which could potentially damage the reputation of such stores and result in a decline in the number of customers who patronize them. Considering these findings, retailers need to assess the sensory elements within their establishments and make necessary adjustments to create a more enjoyable shopping experience for their customers. By doing so, they can not only increase customer satisfaction and purchase intention.

It has been discovered in the present study that customer satisfaction has a significant impact on the purchasing intentions of women. Specifically, when customers perceive that sensory elements within the establishment contribute to generating a pleasant experience during their visit, they are more likely to consider making purchases from such stores. This, in turn, leads to an increased likelihood of repeat purchases from the same business. These findings suggest that retailers should pay close attention to the sensory elements within their establishments to enhance the customer experience and boost customer loyalty.

According to the above, the strategic importance of sensory marketing for organizations operating is underscored by the aforementioned information, making it imperative to integrate this marketing approach into their commercial strategies. Sensory marketing, which utilizes the stimulation of various senses, has the potential to add value to consumers, ultimately fostering brand loyalty and repeat visits. As a result, it can provide businesses with a competitive edge in the marketplace.

It is important to note that this study only analyzed the sensory marketing elements that predict consumer satisfaction in Tamaulipas. However, other factors such as price, quality, and customer service also play a role in explaining this variable and may influence purchase intentions. Furthermore, as a cross-sectional study, the results are limited to the period analyzed.

Given the limitations of the current study and the business environment, it is recommended to continue research efforts similar to this study to further our understanding of consumer behavior, since the results cannot be generalized to the entire country. Considering this, future research could focus on investigating the differences in the effects of sensory marketing between men and women, as well as analyzing the impact of this marketing style on organizations in various sectors.

REFERENCES

Aflaki, S., & Popescu, I. (2014). Managing retention in service relationships. *Management Science*, *60*(2), 415–433. doi:10.1287/mnsc.2013.1775

Alan, A., Kabadayi, E., & Yilmaz, C. (2015). Cognitive and affective constituents of the consumption experience in retail service settings: Effects on store loyalty. *Service Business*, *10*(4), 715–735. doi:10.1007/s11628-015-0288-8

Barrios, M. (2012). Marketing de la experiencia: Principales conceptos y características. *Palermo Business Review, Buenos Aires*, 7, 67–89.

Biswas, D., Lund, K., & Szocs, C. (2019). Sounds like a healthy retail atmospheric strategy: Effects of ambient music and background noise on food sales. *Journal of the Academy of Marketing Science*, 47(1), 37–55. doi:10.1007/s11747-018-0583-8

Bobrie, F. (2018). Visual representations of goods and services through their brandings: The semiotic foundations of a language of brands. *Recherche et Applications en Marketing*, 33(3), 122–144. doi:10.1177/2051570718791784

Carrizo, A., Freitas, P., & Ferreira, V. (2017). Les effets des expériences de marque sur la qualité, la satisfaction et la fidélité: Une étude empirique dans le domaine des services multiples de télécommunications. *Innovar (Universidad Nacional de Colombia)*, 27(64), 23–38. doi:10.15446/innovar.v27n64.62366

Chin, W. (1998). *The partial least squares approach for structural equation modeling. Modern methods for business research*, 2, 295–336. Lawrence Erlbaum Associates Publishers.

Cohen, J. (1988). *Statistical Power Analysis for the Behavioral Sciences* (2nd ed.). Lawrence Erlbaum Associates, Publishers.

Fernández, C., Arribas, F., & Martín, C. (2020). Marketing sensorial en el sector de la moda femenina: El olor de las tiendas en Madrid. *Revista Academia & Negocios*, 7(1), 31–40. doi:10.29393/RAN6-1SMCF20001

Fernández, R., Ángeles, M., & Bonillo, I. (2009). La estética y la diversión como factores generadores de valor en la experiencia de consumo en servicios. *Innovar (Universidad Nacional de Colombia)*, 19(34), 7–24.

Fornell, C., & Larcker, D. (1981). Evaluating structural equation models with unobservable variables and measurement error. *JMR, Journal of Marketing Research*, 18(1), 39–50. doi:10.1177/002224378101800104

Garaus, M. (2017). Atmospheric harmony in the retail environment: Its influence on store satisfaction and re-patronage intention. *Journal of Consumer Behaviour*, 16(3), 265–278. doi:10.1002/cb.1626

Gómez, R., & Mejía, J. E. (2012). La gestión del Marketing que conecta con los sentidos. *Revista Escuela de Administración de Negocios*, 73(2), 168–183. doi:10.21158/01208160.n73.2012.592

González, N. H., Guzmán, J. C., Olguin, J. A., & Gamboa, F. (2019). La mercadotecnia sensorial en la zona comercial del sur de Tamaulipas, México. *Revista Observatorio de la Economía Latinoamericana* (octubre). EU Med. https://www.eumed.net/rev/oel/2019/10/mercadotecnia-sensorial-mexico.html

GrimaldiM. T.LadeiraR.LeocádioA. L.CoutinhoR. (2020). Experience marketing: a study of conceptual aspects. *Cuadernos EBAPE.BR, 18*(11), 781-793. http://dx.doi.org/ doi:10.1590/1679-395120190079x

Haase, J., & Wiedmann, K. (2020). The implicit sensory association test (ISAT): A measurement approach for sensory perception. *Journal of Business Research, 109*, 236–245. doi:10.1016/j.jbusres.2019.12.005

Hagtvedt, H., & Brasel, S. (2016). Cross-Modal Communication: Sound frequency Influences consumer responses to color Lightness. *JMR, Journal of Marketing Research, 53*(4), 551–562. doi:10.1509/jmr.14.0414

Hair, J. F., Risher, J. J., Sarstedt, M., & Ringle, C. M. (2019). When to use and how to report the results of PLS-SEM. *European Business Review, 31*(1), 2–24. doi:10.1108/EBR-11-2018-0203

Hassan, I., & Iqbal, J. (2016), Employing sensory marketing as a promotional advantage for Hepola creating brand differentiation and brand loyalty. *Pakistan Journal of Commerce & Social Sciences, 10*(3), 725-734. http://hdl.handle.net/10419/188276

Hepola, J., Karjaluoto, H., & Hintikka, A. (2017). The effect of sensory brand experience and involvement on brand equity directly and indirectly through consumer brand engagement. *Journal of Product and Brand Management, 26*(3), 282–293. doi:10.1108/JPBM-10-2016-1348

Holbrook, M. B., & Hirschman, E. C. (1982). The experiential aspects of consumption: Consumer fantasies, feelings and fun. *The Journal of Consumer Research, 9*(2), 132–140. doi:10.1086/208906

Hultén, B., Broweus, N., & Van-Dijk, M. (2009). What is Sensory Marketing? In *Sensory marketing* (pp. 1–23). Palgrave Macmillan. doi:10.1057/9780230237049_1

Keni, K., Aritonang, L., & Satria, A. (2019). Purchase intention, satisfaction, interest and previous purchase behaviour. *International Journal of Innovation, 5*(6), 1129–1140.

Koszembar, M. (2019). Sensory Marketing - Sensory Communication and its social perception. *Communication Today, 10*(2), 146–156.

Manchado, R., Mittal, S., & Bansal, S. (2023). Investigating the role of sensory marketing for studying the consumer response. *Lampyrid*, *13*, 97–106.

Medina-Quintero, J. M., Abrego-Almazán, D., & Ortiz-Rodríguez, F. (2018). Use and usefulness of the information systems measurement. a quality approach at the mexican northeastern region. *Cuadernos Americanos*, *31*(56), 7–30. doi:10.11144/Javeriana.cao.31-56.ubwm

Moreira, A., Fortes, N., & Santiago, R. (2017). Influence of sensory stimuli on brand experience, brand equity and purchase intention. *Journal of Business Economics and Management*, *18*(1), 68–83. doi:10.3846/16111699.2016.1252793

Ortegón-Cortázar, L., & Gómez, A. (2016). Gestión del marketing sensorial sobre la experiencia del consumidor. *Revista de Ciencias Sociales*, *22*(3), 67–83. doi:10.31876/rcs.v22i3.24869

Quintero, J. M. M., Echeverría, O. R., & Rodríguez, F. O. (2022). Trust and information quality for the customer satisfaction and loyalty in e-Banking with the use of the mobile phone. *Contaduría y Administración*, *67*(1), 283–304.

Randhir, R., Latasha, K., Tooraiven, P., & Monishan, B. (2016). Analyzing the impact of sensory marketing on consumers: A case study of KFC. *Journal of US-China Public Administration*, *13*(4), 278–292. doi:10.17265/1548-6591/2016.04.007

Reina, M., & Jimenez, D. (2020). Consumer experience and omnichannel behavior in various sales atmospheres. *Frontiers in Psychology*, *11*, 1972. doi:10.3389/fpsyg.2020.01972 PMID:32849155

Ringler, C., Sirianni, N., Gustafsson, A., & Peck, J. (2019). Look but don't touch! the impact of active interpersonal haptic blocking on compensatory touch and purchase behavior. *Journal of Retailing*, *95*(4), 186–203. doi:10.1016/j.jretai.2019.10.007

Rodas, J. A., & Montoya, L. A. (2018). Methodological proposal for the analysis and measurement of sensory marketing integrated to the consumer experience. *Dyna*, *85*(207), 54–59. doi:10.15446/dyna.v85n207.71937

Sánchez, R., & Iniesta, M. A. (2009). La estética y la diversión como factores generadores de valor en la experiencia de consumo en servicios. *Innovar (Universidad Nacional de Colombia)*, *19*(34), 7–24.

Santos, E., Barattucci, M., Oliveira, F., & Capela, V. (2023). The senses as experiences in wine tourism - A comparative statistical analysis between Abruzzo and Douro. *Heritage*, *6*(8), 5672–5688. doi:10.3390/heritage6080298

Suraj, S., Vasavada, M., & Sharma, M. (2021). Influence of sensory branding on consumer buying behavior: An empirical evidence with reference to coffee outlets of India. *International Journal of Management*, *12*(3), 654–668.

Tu, J., & Yang, C. (2019). Consumer needs for hand-touch product designs based on the experience economy. *Sustainability (Basel)*, *11*(7), 2064. doi:10.3390/su11072064

Venter, M., Chinomona, R., & Chuchu, T. (2018). The influence of store environment on brand attitude, brand experience and purchase intention. *South African Journal of Business Management*, *49*(1), 1–8. doi:10.4102/sajbm.v49i1.186

Wibisono, N., & Syah, E. (2019). The rol of experiential marketing towards satisfaction and re-intention to visit a tourist destination. *Journal of Tourism & Sports Management*, *1*(1), 1-14. Recovered: https://www.scitcentral.com/documents/f7fb700349e62d0cf290a203fedc95ac.pdf

Zha, D., Foroudi, P., Jin, Z., & Melewar, T. (2022). Making sense of sensory brand experience: Constructing an integrative framework for future research. *International Journal of Management Reviews*, *24*(1), 130–167. doi:10.1111/ijmr.12270

Compilation of References

Abdu, A.-K. (2018). A review of technology integration in ELT: From CALL to MALL. *Language Teaching and Educational Research*, *1*(1), 1–12.

Aflaki, S., & Popescu, I. (2014). Managing retention in service relationships. *Management Science*, *60*(2), 415–433. doi:10.1287/mnsc.2013.1775

Agbele, A. T., Oyelade, E. A., & Oluwatuyi, V. S. (2020). Assessment of students' performance in physics using two teaching techniques. *International Journal of Innovation and Scientific Research*, *7*(7), 55–59. doi:10.51244/IJRSI.2020.7702

Aguilar Luis, J. (2021). *Internet de las cosas, Un futuro hiperconectado: 5G*. Inteligencia Artificial, Big Data, Cloud, Blockchain, Ciberseguridad.

Akther, S., & Rahman, M. S. (2021). Investigating training effectiveness of public and private banks employees in this digital age: An empirical study. *International Journal of Manpower*, *42*(3), 542–568. doi:10.1108/IJM-04-2021-0240

Alama, E. M. (2008). *Capital intelectual y resultados empresariales en las empresas de servicios profesionales de españa*. EPrints. https://eprints.ucm.es/id/eprint/8709/1/T30356.pdf

Alan, A., Kabadayi, E., & Yilmaz, C. (2015). Cognitive and affective constituents of the consumption experience in retail service settings: Effects on store loyalty. *Service Business*, *10*(4), 715–735. doi:10.1007/s11628-015-0288-8

Alonso-Almeida, M. M., & Llach, J. (2013). Adoption and use of technology in small business environments. *Service Industries Journal*, *33*(15–16), 1456–1472. doi:10.1080/02642069.2011.634904

Amin, M. H., Mohamed, E. K. A., & Elragal, A. (2020). Corporate disclosure via social media: A data science approach. *Online Information Review*, *44*(1), 278–298. doi:10.1108/OIR-03-2019-0084

Anser, M. K., Yousaf, Z., Usman, M., & Yousaf, S. (2020). Towards strategic business performance of the hospitality sector: Nexus of ICT, e-marketing and organizational readiness. *Sustainability (Basel)*, *12*(4), 1346. doi:10.3390/su12041346

Compilation of References

Ardito, L., Dangelico, R. M., & Messeni Petruzzelli, A. (2021). The link between female representation in the boards of directors and corporate social responsibility: Evidence from B corps. *Corporate Social Responsibility and Environmental Management*, *28*(2), 704–720. doi:10.1002/csr.2082

Arends, F., Winnaar, L., & Mosimege, M. (2017). Teacher classroom practices and Mathematics performance in South African schools: A reflection on TIMSS 2011. *South African Journal of Education*, *37*(3), 1–11. Advance online publication. doi:10.15700/saje.v37n3a1362

Artaraz, M. (2002). *Teoria de las tres dimensiones de desarrollo sostenible*. Ecosistemas. https://www.aeet.org/ecosistemas/022/informe1.htm

Atha, H. (2022). Best Programming Language for AI Development. *moveoapps*. https://www.moveoapps.com/blog/best-programming-languages-ai-development/

Ayman, A., El-Helaly, M., & Shehata, N. (2019). Board diversity and earnings news dissemination on Twitter in the UK. *The Journal of Management and Governance*, *23*(3), 715–734. doi:10.1007/s10997-018-9441-9

Bai, B., Wang, J., & Chai, C. S. (2021). Understanding Hong Kong primary school English teachers' continuance intention to teach with ICT. *Computer Assisted Language Learning*, *34*(4), 528–551. doi:10.1080/09588221.2019.1627459

Bampton, R., & Maclagan, P. (2009). Does a 'care orientation' explain gender differences in ethical decision making? A critical analysis and fresh findings. *Business Ethics (Oxford, England)*, *18*(2), 179–191. doi:10.1111/j.1467-8608.2009.01556.x

Barrena-Martínez, J., López-Fernández, M., & Romero-Fernández, P. M. (2016). Efectos de las políticas de recursos humanos socialmente responsables en el capital intelectual. *Intangible Capital*, *12*(2), 549-590. https://upcommons.upc.edu/bitstream/handle/2117/87880/Jesus%20Barrena-Mart%C3%ADnez.pdf?sequence=1&isAllowed=y

Barrera, R. M., Martinez-Rodriguez, J. L., Tiwari, S., & Barrera, V. (2023). Political Marketing App Based on Citizens. In *G. P. Systems*. IGI Global. doi:10.4018/978-1-6684-6591-2.ch008

Barrios, M. (2012). Marketing de la experiencia: Principales conceptos y características. *Palermo Business Review, Buenos Aires*, *7*, 67–89.

Bartolomé-Pina, A., García-Ruiz, R., & Aguaded, I. (2018). Blended learning: overview and expectations. *REVISTA IBEROAMERICANA DE EDUCACION A DISTANCIA (REID)*, *21*(1), 33-56.

Bass, B. (1998). *Transformational leadership: Industrial, military, and educational impact*. Lawrence Erlbaum Associates.

Basuony, M. A. K., Mohamed, E. K. A., & Samaha, K. (2018). Board structure and corporate disclosure via social media: An empirical study in the UK. *Online Information Review*, *42*(5), 595–614. doi:10.1108/OIR-01-2017-0013

Batsoulis, A. N., Siatis, N. G., Kimbaris, A. C., Alissandrakis, E. K., Pappas, C. S., Tarantilis, P. A., & Polissiou, M. G. (2005). FT-Raman spectroscopic simultaneous determination of fructose and glucose in honey. *Journal of Agricultural and Food Chemistry*, *53*(2), 207–210. doi:10.1021/jf048793m

Becker, G. S. (1964). *Human capital: A theoretical and empirical analysis, with special reference to education*. University of Chicago Press.

Beji, R., Yousfi, O., Loukil, N., & Omri, A. (2020). Board diversity and Corporate Social Responsibility: Empirical evidence from France. *Journal of Business Ethics*, *173*(1), 133–155. doi:10.1007/s10551-020-04522-4

Bernardi, R. A., Bosco, S. M., & Vassill, K. M. (2006). Does female representation on boards of directors associate with Fortune's "100 best companies to work for" list? *Business & Society*, *45*(2), 235–248. doi:10.1177/0007650305283332

Bernardi, R., & Threadgill, V. (2010). Women directors and corporate social responsibility. *Electronic Journal of Business Ethics and Organizational Studies*, *15*(2), 15–21.

Best, M. L., & Maier, S. (2007). Gender, culture and ICT use in rural South India. *Gender, Technology and Development*, *11*(2), 137–155. doi:10.1177/097185240701100201

Beutel, A. M., & Marini, M. M. (1995). Gender and values. *American Sociological Review*, *60*(3), 436–448. doi:10.2307/2096423

Biswas, D., Lund, K., & Szocs, C. (2019). Sounds like a healthy retail atmospheric strategy: Effects of ambient music and background noise on food sales. *Journal of the Academy of Marketing Science*, *47*(1), 37–55. doi:10.1007/s11747-018-0583-8

Bobrie, F. (2018). Visual representations of goods and services through their brandings: The semiotic foundations of a language of brands. *Recherche et Applications en Marketing*, *33*(3), 122–144. doi:10.1177/2051570718791784

Bogdanov, S. (2007). Authenticity of honey and other bee products: state of the art. *Bulletin of university of agricultural sciences veterinary medicine cluj-napoca*, 1-8. USAMVLUJ. https://doi.org/http://www.usamvcluj.ro

Bogdanov, S. (2012). *Honey as nutrient and functional food, 100*. Proteins. https://doi.org/http://www.bee-hexagon.net/

Bogdanov, S., Jurendic, T., Sieber, R., & Gallmann, P. (2008). Honey for nutrition and health: A review. *Journal of the American College of Nutrition*, *27*(6), 677–689. doi:10.1080/07315724.2008.10719745 PMID:19155427

Bogdanov, S., Lüllmann, C., Martin, P., von der Ohe, W., Russmann, H., Vorwohl, G., Oddo, L. P., Sabatini, A.-G., Marcazzan, G. L., Piro, R., Flamini, C., Morlot, M., Lhéritier, J., Borneck, R., Marioleas, P., Tsigouri, A., Kerkvliet, J., Ortiz, A., Ivanov, T., & Vit, P. (2015). Honey quality and international regulatory standards: Review by the International Honey Commission. *Bee World*, *80*(2), 61–69. doi:10.1080/0005772X.1999.11099428

Compilation of References

Canu, M. E. (2017). *Economia Circular y Sostenibilidad.*

Carrizo, A., Freitas, P., & Ferreira, V. (2017). Les effets des expériences de marque sur la qualité, la satisfaction et la fidélité: Une étude empirique dans le domaine des services multiples de télécommunications. *Innovar (Universidad Nacional de Colombia), 27*(64), 23–38. doi:10.15446/innovar.v27n64.62366

Castillo, J. A. (2019). Fiber optics: what it is, what it's used for, and how it works. *Professional Review*. https://www.profesionalreview.com/2019/02/15/fibra-optica-que-es/

Chatterjee, S. (2020). Top CC machine learning libraries for data science. *hackernoon.* https://hackernoon.com/top-cc-machine-learning-libraries-for-data-science-nl183wo1

Chauhan, A. G., & Rai, S. (2020). Abridging Gender Gap in Intellectual Property. *Prestige International Journal of Management and Research, 8*, 8–11.

Cheng, C., & Piccoli, G. (2002). Web-based training in the hospitality industry: A conceptual definition, taxonomy, and preliminary investigation. *International Journal of Hospitality Information Technology, 2*(2), 19–33. doi:10.3727/153373402803617737

Chin, W. (1998). *The partial least squares approach for structural equation modeling. Modern methods for business research, 2, 295–336.* Lawrence Erlbaum Associates Publishers.

Chisango, G., Marongwe, N., Mtsi, N., & Matyedi, T. E. (2020). Teachers' perceptions of adopting information and communication technologies in teaching and learning at rural secondary schools in Eastern Cape, South Africa. *Africa Education Review, 17*(2), 1–19. doi:10.1080/18146627.2018.1491317

Chodorow, N. (1978). Mothering, object-relations, and the female oedipal configuration. *Feminist Studies, 4*(1), 137–158. doi:10.2307/3177630

Cinar, S. B., Eksi, A., & Coskun, I. (2014). Carbon isotope ratio (13C/12C) of pine honey and detection of HFCS adulteration. *Food Chemistry, 157*, 10–13. doi:10.1016/j.foodchem.2014.02.006 PMID:24679745

Cohen, J. (1988). *Statistical Power Analysis for the Behavioral Sciences* (2nd ed.). Lawrence Erlbaum Associates, Publishers.

Collins, C., Buhalis, D., & Peters, M. (2003). Enhancing SMTEs' business performance through the Internet and e-learning platforms. *Education + Training, 45*(8/9), 483–494. doi:10.1108/00400910310508874

ConsultoresN. (2021). *Principales.* IDC Online/ https://idconline.mx/laboral/2012/10/04/principales-teorias-de-la-motivacion

Contaduría Pública. (2020). *Responsabilidad.* Contaduria Publica. https://contaduriapublica.org.mx/2020/04/01/responsabilidad-laboral-del-capital-intelectual-en-las-organizaciones/

Cook, A., & Glass, C. (2018). Women on corporate boards: Do they advance corporate social responsibility? *Human Relations*, *71*(7), 897–924. doi:10.1177/0018726717729207

Cordeiro, J. J., Profumo, G., & Tutore, I. (2020). Board gender diversity and corporate environmental performance: The moderating role of family and dual-class majority ownership structures. *Business Strategy and the Environment*, *29*(3), 1127–1144. doi:10.1002/bse.2421

Corning. (n.d.). Mercados. *Tecnologías de comunicaciones ópticas: Un flujo de datos sin contratiempos. Corning Optical Communications*. https://www.corning.com/cala/es/markets/Optical-Communications-Market.html

Coursen, D. (1975). Vandalism Prevention. Office of Justice Programs.

Creswell, J. W. (2014). Research design. In Qualitative, quantitative, and mixed methods approaches (International student ed.). SAGE.

Cristobal-Fransi, E., Daries, N., Martin-Fuentes, E., & Montegut-Salla, Y. (2020). Industrial heritage 2.0: Internet presence and development of the electronic commerce of industrial tourism. *Sustainability (Basel)*, *12*(15), 5965. doi:10.3390/su12155965

Croson, R., & Gneezy, U. (2009). Gender differences in preferences. *Journal of Economic Literature*, *47*(2), 448–474. doi:10.1257/jel.47.2.448

Cruz, C., Justo, R., Larraza-Kintana, M., & Garcés-Galdeano, L. (2019). When do women make a better table? Examining the influence of women directors on family firm's corporate social performance. *Entrepreneurship Theory and Practice*, *43*(2), 282–301. doi:10.1177/1042258718796080

Cumming, D., Leung, T. Y., & Rui, O. (2015). Gender diversity and securities fraud. *Academy of Management Journal*, *58*(5), 1572–1593. doi:10.5465/amj.2013.0750

Da Costa, C. (2022). La economia circular, como eje de desarrollo de los países latinoamericanos. *Revista de Economia Política*, 11.

Dadanlar, H. H., & Abebe, M. A. (2020). Female CEO leadership and the likelihood of corporate diversity misconduct: Evidence from S&P 500 firms. *Journal of Business Research*, *118*, 398–405. doi:10.1016/j.jbusres.2020.07.011

Davis, F. D., Bagozzi, R. P., & Warshaw, P. R. (1989). User acceptance of computer technology: A comparison of two theoretical models. *Management Science*, *35*(8), 982–1003. doi:10.1287/mnsc.35.8.982

Dawson, L. M. (1997). Ethical differences between men and women in the sales profession. *Journal of Business Ethics*, *16*(11), 1143–1152. doi:10.1023/A:1005721916646

Daya, A., & Laher, S. (2020). Exploring the influence of educators' access to and attitudes towards educational technology on the use of educational technology in Johannesburg schools. *Africa Education Review*, *17*(1), 159–180. doi:10.1080/18146627.2018.1490154

Compilation of References

De la Fuente, Á., Ciccone, A., & Doménech, R. (2004). *La rentabilidad privada y social de la educación: un panorama y resultados para la UE*. Fundación Caixa Galicia, Centro de Investigación Económica y Financiera.

De Vera, J. L., Andrada, M. D., Bello, A., & De Vera, M. G. (2021). Teachers' competencies in educational technology integration on instructional methodologies in the new normal. *Lukad: An Online Journal of Pedagogy, 1*(1), 61–80.

Dearden, L., Reed, H., & Van Reenen, J. (2006). The impact of training on productivity and wages: Evidence from British panel data*. *Oxford Bulletin of Economics and Statistics, 68*(4), 397–421. doi:10.1111/j.1468-0084.2006.00170.x

Department of Education. (2004, September 2). White Paper on e-Education: Transforming Learning and Teaching through Information and Communication Technologies (ICTs). *Government Gazette* (26734), pp. 3 - 46.

Díaz Coutiño, R. (2015). *Desarrollo Sustentable, una oportunidad para la vida*. Mc Graw Hill.

Diggs, J., Mikolajczyk, S., Naismith, L., Reed, M., & Smith, R. (2021). *Flood Management in Texas: Planning for the Future*. Texas A&M.

Dik Rodriguez, D. & Niola Plaza, B. (2016). *Análisis y Diseño de la Migración de la Red Actual de Cobre, en la Ruta 13 de la Central Norte de CNT en la Ciudad de Guayaquil*. Red de Fibra Óptica.

Dixon, K. (2019). Access, capital, and the digital divide in a rural South African Primary School. In Stories from Inequity to Justice in Literacy Education: Confronting Digital Divides (pp. 15-33). Routledge.

Doff, P. A. (2015). *Integrated instruction in ELT*. Cambridge University Press.

Duan, J., & Liu, D. (2012). Influence of kinematic variables on apex offset in polishing process of fiber optic connectors. *Precision Engineering, 36*(2), 281–287. doi:10.1016/j.precisioneng.2011.10.009

Duffus-Miranda, D., & Briley, D. (2021). Turista digital: Variables que definen su comportamiento de compra. *Investigaciones Turísticas, 21*(21), 1–21. doi:10.14198/INTURI2021.21.1

Eagly, A. H., Johannesen-Schmidt, M. C., & Van Engen, M. L. (2003). Transformational, transactional, and laissez-faire leadership styles: A meta-analysis comparing women and men. *Psychological Bulletin, 129*(4), 569–591. doi:10.1037/0033-2909.129.4.569

Eagly, A. H., & Johnson, B. T. (1990). Gender and leadership style: A meta-analysis. *Psychological Bulletin, 108*(2), 233–256. doi:10.1037/0033-2909.108.2.233

EEA. (2023). *European Enviroment Agency*. EEA. https://www.eea.europa.eu/en

El-Bialee, N., & Sorour, M. (2011). Effect of adulteration on honey properties. *International Journal of Applied Science and Technology, 1*(6). https://doi.org/www.ijastnet.com

Ellermeijer, T., & Tran, T. B. (2019). Technology in teaching physics: Benefits, challenges, and solutions. In *Upgrading Physics Education to Meet the Needs of Society* (pp. 35–67). Springer. doi:10.1007/978-3-319-96163-7_3

Ely, R. J. (1995). The power in demography: Women's social constructions of gender identity at work. *Academy of Management Journal*, *38*(3), 589–634. doi:10.2307/256740

EMF. (2015). Obtenido de Towards the circular economy - Economic and business rationale for an accelerated transition. *Circular economy overview*. https://www.ellenmacarthurfoundation.org/circular-economy/overview/concept>

Escobar, A. M. (2021). *42 Factores*. Webly.com. https://adrianamartinezescobar.weebly.com/42-factores-de-la-productividad.html

Fakhlaei, R., Selamat, J., Khatib, A., Razis, A. F. A., Sukor, R., Ahmad, S., & Babadi, A. A. (2020). The Toxic Impact of Honey Adulteration: A Review. *Foods*, *9*(11), 1538. doi:10.3390/foods9111538 PMID:33114468

Farías, M. L. (2016). *La compensación por competencias y sus efectos sobre la motivación humana. VIII Congreso Internacional de Investigación y Práctica Profesional en Psicología XXIII Jornadas de Investigación XII Encuentro de Investigadores en Psicología del MERCOSUR*. Facultad de Psicología - Universidad de Buenos Aires, Buenos Aires, 2016. https://www.aacademica.org/000-044/356.pdf

Farjon, D., Smits, A., & Voogt, J. (2019). Technology integration of pre-service teachers explained by attitudes and beliefs, competency, access, and experience. *Computers & Education*, *130*, 81–93. doi:10.1016/j.compedu.2018.11.010

Faustino, C., & Pinheiro, L. (2021). Analytical Rheology of Honey: A State-of-the-Art Review. *Foods*, *10*(8), 1709. doi:10.3390/foods10081709 PMID:34441487

Feng, X., Groh, A., & Wang, Y. (2020). Board diversity and CSR. *Global Finance Journal*, *100578*(October), 100578. doi:10.1016/j.gfj.2020.100578

Fernández, C., Arribas, F., & Martín, C. (2020). Marketing sensorial en el sector de la moda femenina: El olor de las tiendas en Madrid. *Revista Academia & Negocios*, *7*(1), 31–40. doi:10.29393/RAN6-1SMCF20001

Fernández, R., Ángeles, M., & Bonillo, I. (2009). La estética y la diversión como factores generadores de valor en la experiencia de consumo en servicios. *Innovar (Universidad Nacional de Colombia)*, *19*(34), 7–24.

Fornell, C., & Larcker, D. (1981). Evaluating structural equation models with unobservable variables and measurement error. *JMR, Journal of Marketing Research*, *18*(1), 39–50. doi:10.1177/002224378101800104

Frankenfield, J. (2023). AI. *investopedia*. https://www.investopedia.com/terms/a/artificial-intelligence-ai.asp

Compilation of References

Galindo, M. y. (2015). Productividad en serie de estudios económicos. *México ¿Cómo vamos?*, 2.

Galloway, G. (2004). *USA: flood management–Mississippi River*. WMO/GWP Associated Programme on Flood Management.

Ganesh, U. L., & Rampur, V. V. (2016). Semi-automatic drain for sewage water treatment of floating materials. *International Journal of Research in Engineering and Technology*, *5*(7), 1–4.

Garaus, M. (2017). Atmospheric harmony in the retail environment: Its influence on store satisfaction and re-patronage intention. *Journal of Consumer Behaviour*, *16*(3), 265–278. doi:10.1002/cb.1626

Garbin-Praničević, D., & Mandić, A. (2020). ICTs in the hospitality industry. *Tourism (Zagreb)*, *68*(2), 221–234. doi:10.37741/t.68.2.9

Garcia Parra, M., Simo, P., & Sallan, J. M. (2006). *Redalyc.org*. Obtenido de https://www.redalyc.org/pdf/549/54920301.pdf

García, R., Aguaded, I., & Bartolomé, A. (2018). The blended learning revolution in distance education. *Revista Iberoamericana de Educación a Distancia, 21*(1).

Geographic, R. N. (2023). Economica circular que es y por que benefica al medio ambiente. *National Geographic*. https://www.nationalgeographicla.com/medio-ambiente/2022/05/economia-circular-que-es-y-por-que-beneficia-al-medio-ambiente

Gómez, R., & Mejía, J. E. (2012). La gestión del Marketing que conecta con los sentidos. *Revista Escuela de Administración de Negocios*, *73*(2), 168–183. doi:10.21158/01208160.n73.2012.592

González, N. H., Guzmán, J. C., Olguin, J. A., & Gamboa, F. (2019). La mercadotecnia sensorial en la zona comercial del sur de Tamaulipas, México. *Revista Observatorio de la Economía Latinoamericana* (octubre). EU Med. https://www.eumed.net/rev/oel/2019/10/mercadotecnia-sensorial-mexico.html

Goosen, L., & Van Heerden, D. (2017). Beyond the Horizon of Learning Programming with Educational Technologies. In U. I. Ogbonnaya, & S. Simelane-Mnisi (Ed.), *Proceedings of the South Africa International Conference on Educational Technologies* (pp. 78 - 90). Pretoria: African Academic Research Forum.

GrimaldiM. T.LadeiraR.LeocádioA. L.CoutinhoR. (2020). Experience marketing: a study of conceptual aspects. *Cuadernos EBAPE.BR, 18*(11), 781-793. http://dx.doi.org/ doi:10.1590/1679-395120190079x

Guido, R. M. (2013). Attitude and motivation towards learning physics. [IJERT]. *International Journal of Engineering Research & Technology (Ahmedabad)*, *2*(11), 2087–2093.

Gui, M., Parma, A., & Comi, S. (2018). Does public investment in ICTs improve learning performance? Evidence from Italy. *Policy and Internet*, *10*(2), 141–163. doi:10.1002/poi3.170

Guler, A., Kocaokutgen, H., Garipoglu, A. V., Onder, H., Ekinci, D., & Biyik, S. (2014). Detection of adulterated honey produced by honeybee (Apis mellifera L.) colonies fed with different levels of commercial industrial sugar (C(3) and C(4) plants) syrups by the carbon isotope ratio analysis. *Food Chemistry*, *155*, 155–160. doi:10.1016/j.foodchem.2014.01.033 PMID:24594168

Guzman-Sepulveda, J. R., Guzman-Cabrera, R., & Castillo-Guzman, A. A. (2021). Optical Sensing Using Fiber-Optic Multimode Interference Devices: A Review of Nonconventional Sensing Schemes. *Sensors (Basel)*, *21*(5), 1862. doi:10.3390/s21051862 PMID:33800041

Haase, J., & Wiedmann, K. (2020). The implicit sensory association test (ISAT): A measurement approach for sensory perception. *Journal of Business Research*, *109*, 236–245. doi:10.1016/j.jbusres.2019.12.005

Hagtvedt, H., & Brasel, S. (2016). Cross-Modal Communication: Sound frequency Influences consumer responses to color Lightness. *JMR, Journal of Marketing Research*, *53*(4), 551–562. doi:10.1509/jmr.14.0414

Hair, J. F., Risher, J. J., Sarstedt, M., & Ringle, C. M. (2019). When to use and how to report the results of PLS-SEM. *European Business Review*, *31*(1), 2–24. doi:10.1108/EBR-11-2018-0203

Hambrick, D. C., & Mason, P. A. (1984). Upper echelons: The organization as a reflection of its top managers. *Academy of Management Review*, *9*(2), 193–206. doi:10.2307/258434

Hannoon, A., Abdalla, Y. A., Musleh Al-Sartawi, A. M. A., & Khalid, A. A. (2021). Board of directors composition and social media financial disclosure: the case of the United Arab Emirates. In *The big data-driven digital economy: Artificial and computational intelligence* (pp. 229–241). Springer. doi:10.1007/978-3-030-73057-4_18

Hassan, I., & Iqbal, J. (2016), Employing sensory marketing as a promotional advantage for Hepola creating brand differentiation and brand loyalty. *Pakistan Journal of Commerce & Social Sciences*, *10*(3), 725-734. http://hdl.handle.net/10419/188276

Hazarika, M., & Chakraborty, J. (2019). Women in Local E-Governance. *Proceedings of the 12th International Conference on Theory and Practice of Electronic Governance*, (pp. 457–460). ACM. 10.1145/3326365.3326425

Hecht, E. (2017). *Optics*. Pearson.

Hennessy, S., D'Angelo, S., McIntyre, N., Koomar, S., Kreimeia, A., Cao, L., Brugha, M., & Zubairi, A. (2022). Technology use for teacher professional development in low-and middle-income countries: A systematic review. *Computers and Education Open*, *3*, 100080. doi:10.1016/j.caeo.2022.100080

Hepola, J., Karjaluoto, H., & Hintikka, A. (2017). The effect of sensory brand experience and involvement on brand equity directly and indirectly through consumer brand engagement. *Journal of Product and Brand Management*, *26*(3), 282–293. doi:10.1108/JPBM-10-2016-1348

Herzon, I., & Helenius, J. (2008). Agricultural drainage ditches, their biological importance and functioning. *Biological Conservation*, *141*(5), 1171–1183. doi:10.1016/j.biocon.2008.03.005

Compilation of References

Hilbert, M. (2011). Digital gender divide or technologically empowered women in developing countries? A typical case of lies, damned lies, and statistics. *Women's Studies International Forum*, *34*(6), 479–489. doi:10.1016/j.wsif.2011.07.001

History-Computer. (2023). Ferranti Mark 1 Computer Guide. *history-computer*. https://history-computer.com/ferranti-mark-1-computer-guide/

Holbrook, M. B., & Hirschman, E. C. (1982). The experiential aspects of consumption: Consumer fantasies, feelings and fun. *The Journal of Consumer Research*, *9*(2), 132–140. doi:10.1086/208906

Hultén, B., Broweus, N., & Van-Dijk, M. (2009). What is Sensory Marketing? In *Sensory marketing* (pp. 1–23). Palgrave Macmillan. doi:10.1057/9780230237049_1

Hunsperger, R. G., & Meyer-Arendt, J. R. J. A. O. (1992). *Integrated optics: theory and technology*. Harvard Press. https://doi.org/https://ui.adsabs.harvard.edu/abs/1992ApOpt.31Q.298H

INEGI. (2014). *Productividad total*. INEGI. http://internet.contenidos.inegi.org.mx/contenidos/productos//prod_serv/contenidos/espanol/bvinegi/productos/nueva_estruc/702825068103.pdf

INEGI. (2020). *Encuesta sobre el Impacto Económico Generado por COVID-19 en las Empresas*. INEGI. https://www.inegi.org.mx/programas/ecovidie/

Isa, N. M., Irawati, N., Rosol, A. H. A., Rahman, H. A., Ismail, W. I. W., Yusoff, M. H. M., & Naim, N. F. (2017). Silica Microfiber Sensor for the Detection of Honey Adulteration. *Advanced Science Letters*, *23*(6), 5532–5535. doi:10.1166/asl.2017.7415

Jaafar, M. B., Othman, M. B., Yaacob, M., Talip, B. A., Ilyas, M. A., Ngajikin, N. H., & Fauzi, N. A. M. (2020). A Review on Honey Adulteration and the Available Detection Approaches. *International Journal of Integrated Engineering*, *12*(2), 125–131. https://doi.org/https://doi.org/10.30880/ijie.2020.12.02.015. doi:10.30880/ijie.2020.12.02.015

Jaworski, C., Ravichandran, S., Karpinski, A. C., & Singh, S. (2018). The effects of training satisfaction, employee benefits, and incentives on part-time employees' commitment. *International Journal of Hospitality Management*, *74*, 1–12. https://www.educarex.es/pub/cont/com/0004/documentos/Programa_Operativo_Fondo_Social_Extremadura_2014_2020-1.pdf. doi:10.1016/j.ijhm.2018.02.011

Jita, T., & Munje, P. N. (2020). Teaching science through information and communication technologies: 'enablers' and 'constraints'. *The Independent Journal of Teaching and Learning*, *15*(2), 107-120.

Johnson, A. M., Jacovina, M. E., Russell, D. G., & Soto, C. M. (2016). Challenges and solutions when using technologies in the classroom. In *Adaptive Educational Technologies for Literacy Instruction* (pp. 13–32). Taylor and Francis. doi:10.4324/9781315647500-2

Junta de Extremadura. (2017). *Plan turístico de Extremadura 2017-2020*. Turismo Extremadure. https://www.turismoextremadura.com/viajar/shared/documentacion/publicaciones/PlanTuristicoExtremadura2017_2020.pdf

Junta de Extremadura. (2023). *Programa Operativo en el marco del objetivo de inversión en crecimiento y empleo*. Junta de Extremadura. https://www.juntaex.es/documents/77055/1158713/Programme_2014ES05SFOP016_9_1_es.pdf/fcc13324-df36-896d-4e6f-b455fec55e33?t=1676359990908

Kasa, M., Kho, J., Yong, D., Hussain, K., & Lau, P. (2020). Competently skilled human capital through education for the hospitality and tourism industry. *Worldwide Hospitality and Tourism Themes*, *12*(2), 175–184. doi:10.1108/WHATT-12-2019-0081

Kelan, E. K. (2007). Tools and toys: Communicating gendered positions towards technology. *Information Communication and Society*, *10*(3), 358–383. doi:10.1080/13691180701409960

Keni, K., Aritonang, L., & Satria, A. (2019). Purchase intention, satisfaction, interest and previous purchase behaviour. *International Journal of Innovation*, *5*(6), 1129–1140.

Kirchherr, J., Reike, D., & Hekkert, M. (2017). Conceptualizing the circular economy: An analysis of 114 definitions. *Elsevier, Resources, Conservation & Recycling, 127*, 221-232. doi:10.1016/j.resconrec.2017.09.005

Koszembar, M. (2019). Sensory Marketing - Sensory Communication and its social perception. *Communication Today*, *10*(2), 146–156.

Kowszyk, Y., Vanclay, F., & Maher, R. (2022). Conflict management in the extractive industries: A comparison of four mining projects in Latin America. *Elsevier. The Extractive Industries and Society*, 2–9. doi:10.1016/j.exis.2022.101161

Krishnan, H. A., & Park, D. (2005). A few good women—On top management teams. *Journal of Business Research*, *58*(12), 1712–1720. doi:10.1016/j.jbusres.2004.09.003

Krohn, D. A., Méndez, A., & MacDougall, T. (2014). *Fiber Optic Sensors: Fundamentals and Applications*. SPIE Press. doi:10.1117/3.1002910

Kuo, T. H., Ho, L. A., Lin, C., & Lai, K. K. (2010). Employee empowerment in a technology advanced work environment. *Industrial Management & Data Systems*, *110*(1), 24–42. doi:10.1108/02635571011008380

Kwami, J. D. (2015). Gender, entrepreneurship, and informal markets in Africa: Understanding how Ghanaian women traders self-organize with digital tools. In J. D. Kwami (Ed.), *Comparative Case Studies on Entrepreneurship in Developed and Developing Countries*. IGI Global. doi:10.4018/978-1-4666-7533-9.ch002

Lambarry, F., Cardoso, E. O., & Cortés, J. (2022). *Economía Circular. Indicadores de gestión empresarial*. Fontamara.

Laroche, M., Mérette, M., Ruggeri, G. C., Laroche, M., Mérette, M., & Ruggeri, G. C. (1999). On the concept and dimension of human capital in a knowledge-based. *Canadian Public Policy*, *25*(1), 87–100. https://econpapers.repec.org/RePEc:cpp:issued:v:25:y:1999:i:1:p:87-100. doi:10.2307/3551403

Compilation of References

Lee, B. H., Kim, Y. H., Park, K. S., Eom, J. B., Kim, M. J., Rho, B. S., & Choi, H. Y. (2012). Interferometric fiber optic sensors. *Sensors, 12*(3), 2467-2486.

Leiner, B. M., Cerf, V. G., Clark, D. D., Kahn, R. E., Kleinrock, L., Lynch, D. C., & Wolff, S. (1999). *Una breve historia de Internet.* HistInt. http://www. ati. es/DOCS/internet/histint/histint1. html

Li, J., Zhang, Y., Chen, S., Jiang, W., Wen, S., & Hu, Y. (2018). Demographic diversity on boards and employer/employee relationship. *Employee Relations, 40*(2), 298–312. doi:10.1108/ER-07-2016-0133

Liu, C. (2021). CEO gender and employee relations: Evidence from labor lawsuits. *Journal of Banking & Finance, 128,* 106136. doi:10.1016/j.jbankfin.2021.106136

Luis., J. A. (2021). *Internet de las cosas, Un futuro hiperconectado: 5G, Inteligencia Artificial, Big Data, Cloud, Blockchain, Ciberseguridad.*

Machado De-Melo, A. A., Almeida-Muradian, L. B., Sancho, M. T., & Pascual-Maté, A. (2017). Composition and properties of Apis mellifera honey: A review. *Journal of Apicultural Research, 57*(1), 5–37. doi:10.1080/00218839.2017.1338444

Mack, E. A., Marie-Pierre, L., & Redican, K. (2017). Entrepreneurs' use of internet and social media applications. *Telecommunications Policy, 41*(2), 120–139. doi:10.1016/j.telpol.2016.12.001

Madrigal, B. E. (2009). Capital humano e intelectual: su evaluación. *Observatorio Laboral Revista Venezolana, 2*(3). https://www.redalyc.org/pdf/2190/219016838004.pdf

Maestre Góngora, G. P., Colmenares Quintero, R. F., & Stansfield, K. (2020). Mapping concept and challenges for smart technologies: A systematic study approach. *Iberian Journal of Information Systems and Technologies, 32*(8), 28–40.

Malacara, D., & Harris, O. (1970). Interferometric measurement of angles. *Applied Optics, 9*(7), 1630–1633. doi:10.1364/AO.9.001630 PMID:20076433

Mallin, C. A., & Michelon, G. (2011). Board reputation attributes and corporate social performance: An empirical investigation of the US Best Corporate Citizens. *Accounting and Business Research, 41*(2), 119–144. doi:10.1080/00014788.2011.550740

Manchado, R., Mittal, S., & Bansal, S. (2023). Investigating the role of sensory marketing for studying the consumer response. *Lampyrid, 13,* 97–106.

Mankiw, G. (2021). *Principles of Economics* (9th ed.). Cengage.

Mantha, M., Urban, J. R., Mark, W. A., Chernyshev, A., & Kubachka, K. M. (2018). Direct Comparison of Cavity Ring Down Spectrometry and Isotope Ratio Mass Spectrometry for Detection of Sugar Adulteration in Honey Samples. *Journal of AOAC International, 101*(6), 1857–1863. doi:10.5740/jaoacint.17-0491 PMID:29618406

Maureen, H. (1998). *Sustainable community indicators trainer's workshop.* Sustainable Measures. http://www.sustainablemeasures.com/indicators/WhatIs.html

Ma, W., Grafton, R. Q., & Renwick, A. (2020). Smartphone use and income growth in rural China: Empirical results and policy implications. *Electronic Commerce Research*, *20*(4), 713–736. doi:10.1007/s10660-018-9323-x

Medina-Quintero, J. M., Abrego-Almazán, D., & Ortiz-Rodríguez, F. (2018). Use and usefulness of the information systems measurement. a quality approach at the mexican northeastern region. *Cuadernos Americanos*, *31*(56), 7–30. doi:10.11144/Javeriana.cao.31-56.ubwm

Medina-Quintero, J. M., Ortiz-Rodriguez, F., Tiwari, S., & Saenz, F. I. (2023). Trust in Electronic Banking With the Use of Cell Phones for User Satisfaction. In *Global Perspectives on the Strategic Role of Marketing Information Systems* (pp. 87–106). IGI Global. doi:10.4018/978-1-6684-6591-2.ch006

Medina-Quintero, J. M., Sahagun, M. A., Alfaro, J., & Ortiz-Rodriguez, F. (Eds.). (2023). *Global Perspectives on the Strategic Role of Marketing Information Systems*. IGI Global. https://www.igi-global.com/book/global-perspectives-strategic-role-marketing/302625 doi:10.4018/978-1-6684-6591-2

Mendoza, M. L. (2020). *Tipos de lenguajes de proframacion.* OpenWebinar. openwebinars.net/blog/tipos-de-lenguajes-de-programacion/

Merriam-Webster. (2022). Vandalism. *Merriam Webster Dictionary*. https://www.merriam-webster.com/dictionary/vandalism

Michos, K., & Hernández-Leo, D. (2020). CIDA: A collective inquiry framework to study and support teachers as designers in technological environments. *Computers & Education*, *143*, 103679. *Advance online publication.* doi:10.1016/j.compedu.2019.103679

Mikeska, J. N., Holtzman, S., McCaffrey, D. F., Liu, S., & Shattuck, T. (2019). Using classroom observations to evaluate science teaching: Implications of lesson sampling for measuring science teaching effectiveness across lesson types. *Science Education*, *10*(3), 123–144. doi:10.1002/sce.21482

Mlachila, M., & Moeletsi, T. (2019). Struggling to Make the Grade: A Review of the Causes and Consequences of the Weak Outcomes of South Africa's Education System. *International Monetary Fund (IMF). Working Papers*, *19*(47). https://www.elibrary.imf.org/openurl?genre=articlel&issn=1018-5941&volume=2019&issue=047&artnum=A001

Mlambo-Ngcuka, P. (2019). Minimum Wage & Fair Wage Practices. *Legal Momentum*, 25-28. https://www.legalmomentum.org/sites/default/files/wwbor/wv-toolkit-nys-25-28.pdf

Mohammed, W. S., Mehta, A., & Johnson, E. G. (2004). Wavelength Tunable Fiber Lens Based on Multimode Interference. *Journal of Lightwave Technology*, *22*(2), 469–477. doi:10.1109/JLT.2004.824379

Compilation of References

Mohammed, W. S., Smith, P. W., & Gu, X. (2006). All-fiber multimode interference bandpass filter. *Optics Letters*, *31*(17), 2547–2549. doi:10.1364/OL.31.002547 PMID:16902614

Moreira, A., Fortes, N., & Santiago, R. (2017). Influence of sensory stimuli on brand experience, brand equity and purchase intention. *Journal of Business Economics and Management*, *18*(1), 68–83. doi:10.3846/16111699.2016.1252793

Msila, V. (2015). Teacher readiness and information and communications technology (ICT) use in classrooms: A South African case study. *Creative Education*, *6*(18), 1973–1981. doi:10.4236/ce.2015.618202

Mulauzi, F., & Albright, K. S. (2009). Information and Communication Technologies (ICTs) and development information for professional women in Zambia. *International Journal of Technology Management*, *45*(1/2), 177–195. doi:10.1504/IJTM.2009.021527

Nadeem, M., Bahadar, S., Gull, A. A., & Iqbal, U. (2020). Are women eco-friendly? Board gender diversity and environmental innovation. *Business Strategy and the Environment*, *29*(8), 3146–3161. doi:10.1002/bse.2563

Naredo, J. M. (Marzo de 2002). *Instrumentos para paliar la insostenibilidad de los sistema urbanos, Ciudades para un futuro más sostenible"*. Habitat. http://habitat.aq.upm.es/boletin/n24/ajnar.html#fntext-1

National Conference of State Legislature. (2019). *Flood Mitigation*. National Conference of State Legislature. https://www.ncsl.org/research/environment-and-natural-resources/flood-mitigation.aspx#resources

Ndihokubwayo, K., Uwamahoro, J., Ndayambaje, I., & Ralph, M. (2020). Light phenomena conceptual assessment: An inventory tool for teachers. *Physics Education*, *55*(3), 035009. doi:10.1088/1361-6552/ab6f20

Nel, G., Scholtz, H., & Engelbrecht, W. (2020). Relationship between online corporate governance and transparency disclosures and board composition: Evidence from JSE listed companies. *Journal of African Business*. doi:10.1080/15228916.2020.1838831

Ngao, A. I., Sang, G., & Kihwele, J. E. (2022). Understanding teacher educators' perceptions and practices about ICT integration in teacher education program. *Education Sciences*, *12*(8), 549. doi:10.3390/educsci12080549

Ngao, A., Sang, G., Tondeur, J., Kihwele, J. E., & Chunga, J. O. (2023, June). Transforming Initial Teacher Education Program with Mobile Technologies. A synthesis of qualitative evidences. *Digital Education Review*, (43), 18–36. doi:10.1344/der.2023.43.18-34

Ngeze, L. V. (2017). ICT integration in teaching and learning in secondary schools in Tanzania: Readiness and way forward. *International Journal of Information and Education Technology (IJIET)*, *7*(6), 424–427. doi:10.18178/ijiet.2017.7.6.905

Nicolò, G., Sannino, G., & De Iorio, S. (2021). Gender diversity and online intellectual capital disclosure: Evidence from Italian-listed firms. *Journal of Public Affairs*, *2706*. doi:10.1002/pa.2706

Nord, J. H., Riggio, M. T., & Paliszkiewicz, J. (2017). Social and economic development through Information and Communications Technologies: Italy. *Journal of Computer Information Systems*, *57*(3), 278–285. doi:10.1080/08874417.2016.1213621

Novo-Corti, I., Varela-Candamio, L., & García-Álvarez, M. T. (2014). Breaking the walls of social exclusion of women rural by means of ICTs: The case of 'digital divides' in Galician. *Computers in Human Behavior*, *30*, 497–507. doi:10.1016/j.chb.2013.06.017

Oblitas, J., Sangay, M., Rojas, E., & Castro, W. (2019). EconomíaCircular en residuos de aparatos eléctricos y electrónicos. *Revista de Ciencias Sociales*, 195–205.

Okamoto, K. (2021). *Fundamentals of optical waveguides*. Elsevier.

Okoshi, T. (2012). *Optical fibers*. Elsevier.

Oroian, M., Ropciuc, S., & Paduret, S. (2018). Honey Adulteration Detection Using Raman Spectroscopy. *Food Analytical Methods*, *11*(4), 959–968. doi:10.1007/s12161-017-1072-2

Ortegón-Cortázar, L., & Gómez, A. (2016). Gestión del marketing sensorial sobre la experiencia del consumidor. *Revista de Ciencias Sociales*, *22*(3), 67–83. doi:10.31876/rcs.v22i3.24869

Ortiz-Rodríguez, F., Palma, R., & Villazón-Terrazas, B. (2006). Semantic based P2P System for local e-Government. In Proceedings of Informatik 2006. GI-Edition- Lecture Notes in Informatics (LNI).

Ortiz-Rodriguez, F., Tiwari, S., Amara, F. Z., & Sahagun, M. A. (2023). E-Government Success: An End-User Perspective. In Global Perspectives on the Strategic Role of Marketing Information Systems (pp. 168-186). IGI Global.

Ortiz-Rodriguez, F., Medina-Quintero, J. M., Tiwari, S., & Villanueva, V. (2022). EGODO ontology: sharing, retrieving, and exchanging legal documentation across e-government. In *Futuristic Trends for Sustainable Development and Sustainable Ecosystems* (pp. 261–276). IGI Global. doi:10.4018/978-1-6684-4225-8.ch016

Parkin, M. (2018). *Economía*. Pearson.

Paschotta, R. (2008). V number. In *Encyclopedia of Laser Physics and Technology* (Vol. 1). Wiley-VCH.

Peña, H. C., & Villón, S. G. (2017). Motivación Laboral. Elemento Fundamental en el Éxito Organizacional. *Revista Scientific*, *3*(7), 177-192. http://www.indteca.com/ojs/index.php/Revista_Scientific/article/view/181

Pratto, F., Stallworth, L. M., & Sidanius, J. (1997). The gender gap: Differences in political attitudes and social dominance orientation. *British Journal of Social Psychology*, *36*(1), 49–68. doi:10.1111/j.2044-8309.1997.tb01118.x

Priego, C. (2003). *La institucionalidad ambiental nacional e internacional. Conceptos básicos sobre medio ambiente y desarrollo sustentable*. INET, GTZ.

Compilation of References

Quintero, J. M. M., Echeverría, O. R., & Rodríguez, F. O. (2022). Trust and information quality for the customer satisfaction and loyalty in e-Banking with the use of the mobile phone. *Contaduría y Administración*, *67*(1), 283–304.

Rabah, J. (2015). Benefits and Challenges of Information and Communication Technologies (ICT) Integration in Québec English Schools. [TOJET]. *The Turkish Online Journal of Educational Technology*, *14*(2), 24–31.

Ramaila, S. (2021). Technology Integration in Natural Sciences Teaching and Learning in South African Township Schools. [Lisboa, Portugal: inScience Press.]. *Education and New Developments*, 102–105. doi:10.36315/2021end022

Ramaila, S. (2022). Promoting Self-Regulated Learning in Natural Sciences Teaching Through Technology Integration. *Education and New Developments*, *359-363*, 359–363. doi:10.36315/2022v1end081

Ramaila, S., & Molwele, A. J. (2022). The Role of Technology Integration in the Development of 21st Century Skills and Competencies in Life Sciences Teaching and Learning. *International Journal of Higher Education*, *11*(5), 9–17. doi:10.5430/ijhe.v11n5p9

Ramnarain, U., & Moosa, S. (2017). The use of simulations in correcting electricity misconceptions of grade 10 South African physical sciences learners. *International Journal of Innovation in Science and Mathematics Education*, *25*(5), 1–20.

Rana, K. (2018). *ICT in rural primary schools in Nepal: context and teachers' experiences.* New Zealand: [Unpublished doctoral dissertation, University of Canterbury].

Randhir, R., Latasha, K., Tooraiven, P., & Monishan, B. (2016). Analyzing the impact of sensory marketing on consumers: A case study of KFC. *Journal of US-China Public Administration*, *13*(4), 278–292. doi:10.17265/1548-6591/2016.04.007

Rao, Y. J., & Jackson, D. A. (2000). Principles of fiber-optic interferometry. In *Optical Fiber Sensor Technology: Fundamentals* (pp. 167–191). Springer US. doi:10.1007/978-1-4757-6081-1_5

Reina, M., & Jimenez, D. (2020). Consumer experience and omnichannel behavior in various sales atmospheres. *Frontiers in Psychology*, *11*, 1972. doi:10.3389/fpsyg.2020.01972 PMID:32849155

Reynosa, V. H. (2021). *Libro digital 2010.* Reysona. http://reynosaenelbicentenario.blogspot.com/

Ringler, C., Sirianni, N., Gustafsson, A., & Peck, J. (2019). Look but don't touch! the impact of active interpersonal haptic blocking on compensatory touch and purchase behavior. *Journal of Retailing*, *95*(4), 186–203. doi:10.1016/j.jretai.2019.10.007

Rochelau, D. (2016, March 2). *Polished connector geometries, APC.* Fiber Optic Center. https://focenter.com/es/geometr%C3%ADas-de-conector-pulido-apc-parte-1/

Rodas, J. A., & Montoya, L. A. (2018). Methodological proposal for the analysis and measurement of sensory marketing integrated to the consumer experience. *Dyna*, *85*(207), 54–59. doi:10.15446/dyna.v85n207.71937

Rodríguez, Y. (2009). *Fibra óptica*. El Cid Editor.

Sáenz Laín, C., & Gómez Ferreras, C. (2000). *Mieles españolas. Características e identificación mediante el análisis del polen*.

Sánchez, A. J., Melián, A., & Hormiga, E. (2007). El concepto de capital intelectual y sus dimensiones. *Investigaciones Europeas de Dirección y Economía de la Empresa*, *13*(2), 97–111. https://www.redalyc.org/articulo.oa?id=274120280005

Santos, E., Barattucci, M., Oliveira, F., & Capela, V. (2023). The senses as experiences in wine tourism - A comparative statistical analysis between Abruzzo and Douro. *Heritage*, *6*(8), 5672–5688. doi:10.3390/heritage6080298

Sarur, M. S. (2013). La importancia del capital intelectual en las Organizaciones. *Ciencia Administrativa*, *1*, 39-45. https://www.uv.mx/iiesca/files/2014/01/05CA201301.pdf

Schultz, T. W. (1961). Investment in Human Capital. *The American Economic Review*, *51*(1), 1–17.

Schultz, T. W. (1993). The economic importance of human capital in modernization. *Education Economics*, *1*(1), 13–19. doi:10.1080/09645299300000003

Sepulveda, S., Castro, A., & Rojas, P. (1998). *Metodología para estimar el nivel de desarrollo sostenible en espacios territoriales*. IICA.

Sharafizad, J. (2016). Women business owners' adoption of information and communication technology. *Journal of Systems and Information Technology*, *18*(4), 331–345. doi:10.1108/JSIT-07-2016-0048

Singh, S., Sharma, R., & Kaur, R. (2020). Teacher competencies for the integration of ICT in post graduate science stream teachers. *Studies in Indian Place Names, 40*(60), 2775-2788.

Snyder, A. W., & Love, J. D. (1976). Goos-Hanchen shift. *Applied Optics*, *15*(1), 236–238. doi:10.1364/AO.15.000236 PMID:20155209

Soares, S., Amaral, J. S., Oliveira, M., & Mafra, I. (2017). A Comprehensive Review on the Main Honey Authentication Issues: Production and Origin. *Comprehensive Reviews in Food Science and Food Safety*, *16*(5), 1072–1100. doi:10.1111/1541-4337.12278 PMID:33371614

Soldano, L. B., & Pennings, E. C. M. (1995). Optical multi-mode interference devices based on self-imaging: Principles and applications. *Journal of Lightwave Technology*, *13*(4), 615–627. doi:10.1109/50.372474

Spangenberg, E. D., & De Freitas, G. (2019). Mathematics teachers' levels of technological pedagogical content knowledge and information and communication technology integration barriers. *Pythagoras*, *40*(1), 1–13.

Compilation of References

Spanish Ministry of Education and Professional Training. (2022). *Educabase. Series históricas de estudiantes universitarios desde el curso 1985-1986*. Estadisticas. http://estadisticas.mecd.gob.es/EducaJaxiPx/Tabla.htm?path=/Universitaria/Alumnado/EEU_2022/Serie/GradoCiclo//l0/&file=HIS_Egr_GradCiclo_Rama_CA.px

Spekkers, M. H., Ten Veldhuis, J. A. E., & Clemens, F. H. L. R. (2011). *Collecting data for quantitative research on pluvial flooding*. In Proceedings of the 12th International Conference on Urban Drainage, Porto Alegre, Brazil (*Vol. 1116*, p. 461466). Academic Press.

Suraj, S., Vasavada, M., & Sharma, M. (2021). Influence of sensory branding on consumer buying behavior: An empirical evidence with reference to coffee outlets of India. *International Journal of Management, 12*(3), 654–668.

Tachie, S. A. (2019). Challenges and opportunities regarding usage of computers in the teaching and learning of Mathematics. *South African Journal of Education, 39*(S2), 1–10. doi:10.15700/saje.v39ns2a1690

Talha, M., Imran, M., Ahmad, M. H., Ahmad, R. S., Khan, M. K., Rahim, M. A., & Afzal, M. F. (2023). Honey Composition, Therapeutic Potential and Authentication through Novel Technologies: An Overview. https://doi.org/ doi:10.5772/intechopen.110007

Teijeiro, M. M., García, M. T., & Mariz, R. M. (2010). *La gestión del capital humano en el marco de la teoría del capital intelectual*. Una guía de indicadores. https://dialnet.unirioja.es/servlet/articulo?codigo=3405054

Thorlabs. (1999-2022). *Multimode Fiber Tutorial*. Thorlabs, Inc. https://www.thorlabs.com/newgrouppage9.cfm?objectgroup_id=10417

Tinoco, C. E., & Soler, S. M. (2011). Aspectos generales del concepto "capital humano". *Criterio Libre, 9* (14), 203-226. https://dialnet.unirioja.es/servlet/articulo?codigo=3697483

Tiwari, S., Ortiz-Rodríguez, F., Mishra, S., Vakaj, E., & Kotecha, K. (2023). *Artificial Intelligence: Towards Sustainable Intelligence*. First International Conference, AI4S 2023, Pune, India. . Springer Cham10.1007/978-3-031-47997-7

Tran, T. Q. (2020). Identifying female leadership and performance in small and medium-sized enterprises in a transition economy: The case study of Vietnam. *Asian Economic and Financial Review, 10*(2), 132–145. doi:10.18488/journal.aefr.2020.102.132.145

Tu, J., & Yang, C. (2019). Consumer needs for hand-touch product designs based on the experience economy. *Sustainability (Basel), 11*(7), 2064. doi:10.3390/su11072064

Ucko, D. A. (2013). *Basics for chemistry*. Elsevier. doi:10.1016/C2013-0-11632-7

Ugwuanyi, C. S., & Okeke, C. I. (2020). Enhancing University Students' Achievement in Physics Using Computer-Assisted Instruction. *International Journal of Higher Education, 9*(5), 115–124. doi:10.5430/ijhe.v9n5p115

Ukpere, C. L., Slabbert, A. D., & Ukpere, W. I. (2014). The relevance of modern technology usage on the business ventures of Kenyan women entrepreneurs. *Mediterranean Journal of Social Sciences*, *5*(10). doi:10.5901/mjss.2014.v5n10p58

Umugiraneza, O., Bansilal, S., & North, D. (2018). Exploring teachers' use of technology in teaching and learning mathematics in KwaZulu-Natal schools. *Pythagoras*, *39*(1), 1–13. doi:10.4102/pythagoras.v39i1.342

Uyar, A., Kilic, M., Koseoglu, M. A., Kuzey, C., & Karaman, A. S. (2020). The link among board characteristics, corporate social responsibility performance, and financial performance: Evidence from the hospitality and tourism industry. *Tourism Management Perspectives*, *35*(7), 100714. doi:10.1016/j.tmp.2020.100714

Valencia, M. (2005). El capital humano, otro activo de su empresa. *Entramado*, *1*(2). https://www.redalyc.org/pdf/2654/265420471004.pdf

Vandeyar, T. (2015). Policy intermediaries and the reform of e-Education in South Africa. *British Journal of Educational Technology*, *46*(2), 344–359. doi:10.1111/bjet.12130

Varank, I. (2007). Effectiveness of quantitative skills, qualitative skills, and gender in determining computer skills and attitudes: A causal analysis. *The Clearing House: A Journal of Educational Strategies, Issues and Ideas*, *81*(2), 71–80. doi:10.3200/TCHS.81.2.71-80

Velaz Rivas, J. I. (1996). *Motivos y Motivación en la Empresa*. Madrid España: Diaz de los Santos.

Venkatesh, V., Morris, M. G., & Ackerman, P. L. (2000). A longitudinal field investigation of gender differences in individual technology adoption decision-making processes. *Organizational Behavior and Human Decision Processes*, *83*(1), 33–60. doi:10.1006/obhd.2000.2896

Venkat, H., & Mathews, C. (2019). Improving multiplicative reasoning in a context of low performance. *ZDM Mathematics Education*, *51*(1), 95–108. doi:10.1007/s11858-018-0969-6

Venter, M., Chinomona, R., & Chuchu, T. (2018). The influence of store environment on brand attitude, brand experience and purchase intention. *South African Journal of Business Management*, *49*(1), 1–8. doi:10.4102/sajbm.v49i1.186

Veronica, B. (2021). *Oportunidades tecnológicas de la industria 4.0 en el sector empresarial de economía circular*.

Villazón-Terrazas, B., Ortiz-Rodríguez, F., Tiwari, S. M., & Shandilya, S. K. (2020). Knowledge graphs and semantic web. *Communications in Computer and Information Science*, *1232*, 1–225. doi:10.1007/978-3-030-65384-2

Walker, H. A., Ilari, B. C., McMahon, A. M., & Fennell, M. L. (1996). Gender, interaction, and leadership. *Social Psychology Quarterly*, *59*(3), 255–272. doi:10.2307/2787022

Waller, P., & Yitayew, M. (2015). *Irrigation and drainage engineering*. Springer.

Compilation of References

Wang, J. M., Xue, X. F., Du, X. J., Cheng, N., Chen, L. Z., Zhao, J., Zheng, J., & Cao, W. (2014). Identification of Acacia Honey Adulteration with Rape Honey Using Liquid Chromatography-Electrochemical Detection and Chemometrics. *Food Analytical Methods*, *7*(10), 2003–2012. doi:10.1007/s12161-014-9833-7

Wang, Q., Farrell, G., & Yan, W. (2008). Investigation on Single-Mode–Multimode–Single-Mode Fiber Structure. *Journal of Lightwave Technology*, *26*(5), 512–519. doi:10.1109/JLT.2007.915205

White, J., & Doner, L. W. (1980). *Honey composition and properties (Vol. 335)*.

Wibisono, N., & Syah, E. (2019). The rol of experiential marketing towards satisfaction and re-intention to visit a tourist destination. *Journal of Tourism & Sports Management*, *1*(1), 1-14. Recovered: https://www.scitcentral.com/documents/f7fb700349e62d0cf290a203fedc95ac.pdf

Williams, R. J. (2003). Women on corporate boards of directors and their influence on corporate philanthropy. *Journal of Business Ethics*, *42*(1), 1–10. doi:10.1023/A:1021626024014

Wood, B. K., & Blevins, B. K. (2019). Substituting the practical teaching of physics with simulations for the assessment of practical skills: An experimental study. *Physics Education*, *54*(3), 035004. doi:10.1088/1361-6552/ab0192

Wu, Q., Qu, Y., Liu, J., Yuan, J., Wan, S.-P., Wu, T., He, X.-D., Liu, B., Liu, D., Ma, Y., Semenova, Y., Wang, P., Xin, X., & Farrell, G. (2021). Singlemode-Multimode-Singlemode Fiber Structures for Sensing Applications—A Review. *IEEE Sensors Journal*, *21*(11), 12734–12751. doi:10.1109/JSEN.2020.3039912

Xie, J., Nozawa, W., & Managi, S. (2020). The role of women on boards in corporate environmental strategy and financial performance: A global outlook. *Corporate Social Responsibility and Environmental Management*, *27*(5), 2044–2059. doi:10.1002/csr.1945

Yammarino, F. J., & Bass, B. M. (1990). Long-term forecasting of transformational leadership and its effects among naval officers: Some preliminary findings. In K. E. Clark & M. R. Clark (Eds.), *Measures of leadership* (pp. 151–169). Center for Creative Leadership.

Yeo, B., & Grant, D. (2019). Exploring the effects of ICTs, workforce, and gender on capacity utilization. *Information Technology for Development*, *25*(1), 122–150. doi:10.1080/02681102.2017.1383876

Yin, S., Ruffin, P. B., & Francis, T. (2017). *Fiber optic sensors*. CRC press. doi:10.1201/9781420053661

Young, H. D., Freedman, R. A., Sears, F. W., Flores, V. A. F., Ford, A. L., & Zemansky, M. W. (2009). *Física universitaria 02*. Addison-Wesley ; Pearson Educación.

Zha, D., Foroudi, P., Jin, Z., & Melewar, T. (2022). Making sense of sensory brand experience: Constructing an integrative framework for future research. *International Journal of Management Reviews*, *24*(1), 130–167. doi:10.1111/ijmr.12270

Zhang, G. Y., & Abdulla, W. (2022). On honey authentication and adulterant detection techniques. *Food Control*, *138*, 108992. doi:10.1016/j.foodcont.2022.108992

Zhang, J. J., & Lee, S.-Y. T. (2007). A time series analysis of international ICT spillover. *Journal of Global Information Management*, *15*(4), 1–19. doi:10.4018/jgim.2007100104

Zhu, X., Schülzgen, A., Li, H., Li, L., Han, L., Moloney, J. V., & Peyghambarian, N. (2008). Detailed investigation of self-imaging in largecore multimode optical fibers for application in fiber lasers and amplifiers. *Optics Express*, *16*(21), 16632–16645. doi:10.1364/OE.16.016632

Related References

To continue our tradition of advancing academic research, we have compiled a list of recommended IGI Global readings. These references will provide additional information and guidance to further enrich your knowledge and assist you with your own research and future publications.

Aburezeq, I. M., & Dweikat, F. F. (2017). Cloud Applications in Language Teaching: Examining Pre-Service Teachers' Expertise, Perceptions and Integration. *International Journal of Distance Education Technologies*, *15*(4), 39–60. doi:10.4018/IJDET.2017100103

Acharjya, B., & Das, S. (2022). Adoption of E-Learning During the COVID-19 Pandemic: The Moderating Role of Age and Gender. *International Journal of Web-Based Learning and Teaching Technologies*, *17*(2), 1–14. https://doi.org/10.4018/IJWLTT.20220301.oa4

Adams, J. L., & Thomas, S. K. (2022). Non-Linear Curriculum Experiences for Student Learning and Work Design: What Is the Maximum Potential of a Chat Bot? In S. Ramlall, T. Cross, & M. Love (Eds.), *Handbook of Research on Future of Work and Education: Implications for Curriculum Delivery and Work Design* (pp. 299–306). IGI Global. https://doi.org/10.4018/978-1-7998-8275-6.ch018

Adera, B. (2017). Supporting Language and Literacy Development for English Language Learners. In J. Keengwe (Ed.), *Handbook of Research on Promoting Cross-Cultural Competence and Social Justice in Teacher Education* (pp. 339–354). Hershey, PA: IGI Global. doi:10.4018/978-1-5225-0897-7.ch018

Ahamer, G. (2017). Quality Assurance for a Developmental "Global Studies" (GS) Curriculum. In I. Management Association (Ed.), Educational Leadership and Administration: Concepts, Methodologies, Tools, and Applications (pp. 438-477). Hershey, PA: IGI Global. https://doi.org/ doi:10.4018/978-1-5225-1624-8.ch023

Ahamer, G. (2017). Quality Assurance for a Developmental "Global Studies" (GS) Curriculum. In I. Management Association (Ed.), Educational Leadership and Administration: Concepts, Methodologies, Tools, and Applications (pp. 438-477). Hershey, PA: IGI Global. https://doi.org/ doi:10.4018/978-1-5225-1624-8.ch023

Akayoğlu, S., & Seferoğlu, G. (2019). An Analysis of Negotiation of Meaning Functions of Advanced EFL Learners in Second Life: Negotiation of Meaning in Second Life. In M. Kruk (Ed.), *Assessing the Effectiveness of Virtual Technologies in Foreign and Second Language Instruction* (pp. 61–85). IGI Global. https://doi.org/10.4018/978-1-5225-7286-2.ch003

Akella, N. R. (2022). Unravelling the Web of Qualitative Dissertation Writing!: A Student Reflects. In A. Zimmerman (Ed.), *Methodological Innovations in Research and Academic Writing* (pp. 260–282). IGI Global. https://doi.org/10.4018/978-1-7998-8283-1.ch014

Alegre de la Rosa, O. M., & Angulo, L. M. (2017). Social Inclusion and Intercultural Values in a School of Education. In S. Mukerji & P. Tripathi (Eds.), *Handbook of Research on Administration, Policy, and Leadership in Higher Education* (pp. 518–531). Hershey, PA: IGI Global. doi:10.4018/978-1-5225-0672-0.ch020

Alexander, C. (2019). Using Gamification Strategies to Cultivate and Measure Professional Educator Dispositions. *International Journal of Game-Based Learning*, 9(1), 15–29. https://doi.org/10.4018/IJGBL.2019010102

Anderson, K. M. (2017). Preparing Teachers in the Age of Equity and Inclusion. In I. Management Association (Ed.), Medical Education and Ethics: Concepts, Methodologies, Tools, and Applications (pp. 1532-1554). Hershey, PA: IGI Global. doi:10.4018/978-1-5225-0978-3.ch069

Awdziej, M. (2017). Case Study as a Teaching Method in Marketing. In D. Latusek (Ed.), *Case Studies as a Teaching Tool in Management Education* (pp. 244–263). Hershey, PA: IGI Global. doi:10.4018/978-1-5225-0770-3.ch013

Bakos, J. (2019). Sociolinguistic Factors Influencing English Language Learning. In N. Erdogan & M. Wei (Eds.), *Applied Linguistics for Teachers of Culturally and Linguistically Diverse Learners* (pp. 403–424). IGI Global. https://doi.org/10.4018/978-1-5225-8467-4.ch017

Related References

Banas, J. R., & York, C. S. (2017). Pre-Service Teachers' Motivation to Use Technology and the Impact of Authentic Learning Exercises. In L. Tomei (Ed.), *Exploring the New Era of Technology-Infused Education* (pp. 121–140). Hershey, PA: IGI Global. doi:10.4018/978-1-5225-1709-2.ch008

Barton, T. P. (2021). Empowering Educator Allyship by Exploring Racial Trauma and the Disengagement of Black Students. In C. Reneau & M. Villarreal (Eds.), *Handbook of Research on Leading Higher Education Transformation With Social Justice, Equity, and Inclusion* (pp. 186–197). IGI Global. https://doi.org/10.4018/978-1-7998-7152-1.ch013

Benhima, M. (2021). Moroccan English Department Student Attitudes Towards the Use of Distance Education During COVID-19: Moulay Ismail University as a Case Study. *International Journal of Information and Communication Technology Education*, 17(3), 105–122. https://doi.org/10.4018/IJICTE.20210701.oa7

Beycioglu, K., & Wildy, H. (2017). Principal Preparation: The Case of Novice Principals in Turkey. In I. Management Association (Ed.), Educational Leadership and Administration: Concepts, Methodologies, Tools, and Applications (pp. 1152-1169). Hershey, PA: IGI Global. https://doi.org/ doi:10.4018/978-1-5225-1624-8.ch054

Bharwani, S., & Musunuri, D. (2018). Reflection as a Process From Theory to Practice. In M. Khosrow-Pour, D.B.A. (Ed.), Encyclopedia of Information Science and Technology, Fourth Edition (pp. 1529-1539). Hershey, PA: IGI Global. doi:10.4018/978-1-5225-2255-3.ch132

Bhushan, A., Garza, K. B., Perumal, O., Das, S. K., Feola, D. J., Farrell, D., & Birnbaum, A. (2022). Lessons Learned From the COVID-19 Pandemic and the Implications for Pharmaceutical Graduate Education and Research. In C. Ford & K. Garza (Eds.), *Handbook of Research on Updating and Innovating Health Professions Education: Post-Pandemic Perspectives* (pp. 324–345). IGI Global. https://doi.org/10.4018/978-1-7998-7623-6.ch014

Bintz, W., Ciecierski, L. M., & Royan, E. (2021). Using Picture Books With Instructional Strategies to Address New Challenges and Teach Literacy Skills in a Digital World. In L. Haas & J. Tussey (Eds.), *Connecting Disciplinary Literacy and Digital Storytelling in K-12 Education* (pp. 38–58). IGI Global. https://doi.org/10.4018/978-1-7998-5770-9.ch003

Bohjanen, S. L., Cameron-Standerford, A., & Meidl, T. D. (2018). Capacity Building Pedagogy for Diverse Learners. In J. Keengwe (Ed.), *Handbook of Research on Pedagogical Models for Next-Generation Teaching and Learning* (pp. 195–212). Hershey, PA: IGI Global. doi:10.4018/978-1-5225-3873-8.ch011

Brewer, J. C. (2018). Measuring Text Readability Using Reading Level. In M. Khosrow-Pour, D.B.A. (Ed.), Encyclopedia of Information Science and Technology, Fourth Edition (pp. 1499-1507). Hershey, PA: IGI Global. doi:10.4018/978-1-5225-2255-3.ch129

Brookbanks, B. C. (2022). Student Perspectives on Business Education in the USA: Current Attitudes and Necessary Changes in an Age of Disruption. In A. Zhuplev & R. Koepp (Eds.), *Global Trends, Dynamics, and Imperatives for Strategic Development in Business Education in an Age of Disruption* (pp. 214–231). IGI Global. doi:10.4018/978-1-7998-7548-2.ch011

Brown, L. V., Dari, T., & Spencer, N. (2019). Addressing the Impact of Trauma in High Poverty Elementary Schools: An Ecological Model for School Counseling. In K. Daniels & K. Billingsley (Eds.), *Creating Caring and Supportive Educational Environments for Meaningful Learning* (pp. 135–153). IGI Global. https://doi.org/10.4018/978-1-5225-5748-7.ch008

Brown, S. L. (2017). A Case Study of Strategic Leadership and Research in Practice: Principal Preparation Programs that Work – An Educational Administration Perspective of Best Practices for Master's Degree Programs for Principal Preparation. In V. Wang (Ed.), *Encyclopedia of Strategic Leadership and Management* (pp. 1226–1244). Hershey, PA: IGI Global. doi:10.4018/978-1-5225-1049-9.ch086

Brzozowski, M., & Ferster, I. (2017). Educational Management Leadership: High School Principal's Management Style and Parental Involvement in School Management in Israel. In V. Potocan, M. Ünğan, & Z. Nedelko (Eds.), *Handbook of Research on Managerial Solutions in Non-Profit Organizations* (pp. 55–74). Hershey, PA: IGI Global. doi:10.4018/978-1-5225-0731-4.ch003

Cahapay, M. B. (2020). Delphi Technique in the Development of Emerging Contents in High School Science Curriculum. *International Journal of Curriculum Development and Learning Measurement*, 1(2), 1–9. https://doi.org/10.4018/IJCDLM.2020070101

Camacho, L. F., & Leon Guerrero, A. E. (2022). Indigenous Student Experience in Higher Education: Implementation of Culturally Sensitive Support. In P. Pangelinan & T. McVey (Eds.), *Learning and Reconciliation Through Indigenous Education in Oceania* (pp. 254–266). IGI Global. https://doi.org/10.4018/978-1-7998-7736-3.ch016

Cannaday, J. (2017). The Masking Effect: Hidden Gifts and Disabilities of 2e Students. In P. Dickenson, P. Keough, & J. Courduff (Eds.), *Preparing Pre-Service Teachers for the Inclusive Classroom* (pp. 220–231). Hershey, PA: IGI Global. doi:10.4018/978-1-5225-1753-5.ch011

Related References

Cederquist, S., Fishman, B., & Teasley, S. D. (2022). What's Missing From the College Transcript?: How Employers Make Sense of Student Skills. In Y. Huang (Ed.), *Handbook of Research on Credential Innovations for Inclusive Pathways to Professions* (pp. 234–253). IGI Global. https://doi.org/10.4018/978-1-7998-3820-3.ch012

Cockrell, P., & Gibson, T. (2019). The Untold Stories of Black and Brown Student Experiences in Historically White Fraternities and Sororities. In P. Hoffman-Miller, M. James, & D. Hermond (Eds.), *African American Suburbanization and the Consequential Loss of Identity* (pp. 153–171). IGI Global. https://doi.org/10.4018/978-1-5225-7835-2.ch009

Cohen, M. (2022). Leveraging Content Creation to Boost Student Engagement. In T. Driscoll III, (Ed.), *Designing Effective Distance and Blended Learning Environments in K-12* (pp. 223–239). IGI Global. https://doi.org/10.4018/978-1-7998-6829-3.ch013

Contreras, E. C., & Contreras, I. I. (2018). Development of Communication Skills through Auditory Training Software in Special Education. In M. Khosrow-Pour, D.B.A. (Ed.), Encyclopedia of Information Science and Technology, Fourth Edition (pp. 2431-2441). Hershey, PA: IGI Global. doi:10.4018/978-1-5225-2255-3.ch212

Cooke, L., Schugar, J., Schugar, H., Penny, C., & Bruning, H. (2020). Can Everyone Code?: Preparing Teachers to Teach Computer Languages as a Literacy. In J. Mitchell & E. Vaughn (Eds.), *Participatory Literacy Practices for P-12 Classrooms in the Digital Age* (pp. 163–183). IGI Global. https://doi.org/10.4018/978-1-7998-0000-2.ch009

Cooley, D., & Whitten, E. (2017). Special Education Leadership and the Implementation of Response to Intervention. In F. Topor (Ed.), *Handbook of Research on Individualism and Identity in the Globalized Digital Age* (pp. 265–286). Hershey, PA: IGI Global. doi:10.4018/978-1-5225-0522-8.ch012

Cosner, S., Tozer, S., & Zavitkovsky, P. (2017). Enacting a Cycle of Inquiry Capstone Research Project in Doctoral-Level Leadership Preparation. In I. Management Association (Ed.), Educational Leadership and Administration: Concepts, Methodologies, Tools, and Applications (pp. 1460-1481). Hershey, PA: IGI Global. doi:10.4018/978-1-5225-1624-8.ch067

Crawford, C. M. (2018). Instructional Real World Community Engagement. In M. Khosrow-Pour, D.B.A. (Ed.), Encyclopedia of Information Science and Technology, Fourth Edition (pp. 1474-1486). Hershey, PA: IGI Global. doi:10.4018/978-1-5225-2255-3.ch127

Crosby-Cooper, T., & Pacis, D. (2017). Implementing Effective Student Support Teams. In P. Dickenson, P. Keough, & J. Courduff (Eds.), *Preparing Pre-Service Teachers for the Inclusive Classroom* (pp. 248–262). Hershey, PA: IGI Global. doi:10.4018/978-1-5225-1753-5.ch013

Curran, C. M., & Hawbaker, B. W. (2017). Cultivating Communities of Inclusive Practice: Professional Development for Educators – Research and Practice. In C. Curran & A. Petersen (Eds.), *Handbook of Research on Classroom Diversity and Inclusive Education Practice* (pp. 120–153). Hershey, PA: IGI Global. doi:10.4018/978-1-5225-2520-2.ch006

Dass, S., & Dabbagh, N. (2018). Faculty Adoption of 3D Avatar-Based Virtual World Learning Environments: An Exploratory Case Study. In I. Management Association (Ed.), Technology Adoption and Social Issues: Concepts, Methodologies, Tools, and Applications (pp. 1000-1033). Hershey, PA: IGI Global. https://doi.org/ doi:10.4018/978-1-5225-5201-7.ch045

Davison, A. M., & Scholl, K. G. (2017). Inclusive Recreation as Part of the IEP Process. In C. Curran & A. Petersen (Eds.), *Handbook of Research on Classroom Diversity and Inclusive Education Practice* (pp. 311–330). Hershey, PA: IGI Global. doi:10.4018/978-1-5225-2520-2.ch013

DeCoito, I. (2018). Addressing Digital Competencies, Curriculum Development, and Instructional Design in Science Teacher Education. In M. Khosrow-Pour, D.B.A. (Ed.), Encyclopedia of Information Science and Technology, Fourth Edition (pp. 1420-1431). Hershey, PA: IGI Global. https://doi.org/ doi:10.4018/978-1-5225-2255-3.ch122

DeCoito, I., & Richardson, T. (2017). Beyond Angry Birds™: Using Web-Based Tools to Engage Learners and Promote Inquiry in STEM Learning. In I. Levin & D. Tsybulsky (Eds.), *Digital Tools and Solutions for Inquiry-Based STEM Learning* (pp. 166–196). Hershey, PA: IGI Global. doi:10.4018/978-1-5225-2525-7.ch007

Delmas, P. M. (2017). Research-Based Leadership for Next-Generation Leaders. In R. Styron Jr & J. Styron (Eds.), *Comprehensive Problem-Solving and Skill Development for Next-Generation Leaders* (pp. 1–39). Hershey, PA: IGI Global. doi:10.4018/978-1-5225-1968-3.ch001

Demiray, U., & Ekren, G. (2018). Administrative-Related Evaluation for Distance Education Institutions in Turkey. In K. Buyuk, S. Kocdar, & A. Bozkurt (Eds.), *Administrative Leadership in Open and Distance Learning Programs* (pp. 263–288). Hershey, PA: IGI Global. doi:10.4018/978-1-5225-2645-2.ch011

Related References

Dickenson, P. (2017). What do we Know and Where Can We Grow?: Teachers Preparation for the Inclusive Classroom. In P. Dickenson, P. Keough, & J. Courduff (Eds.), *Preparing Pre-Service Teachers for the Inclusive Classroom* (pp. 1–22). Hershey, PA: IGI Global. doi:10.4018/978-1-5225-1753-5.ch001

Ding, Q., & Zhu, H. (2021). Flipping the Classroom in STEM Education. In J. Keengwe (Ed.), *Handbook of Research on Innovations in Non-Traditional Educational Practices* (pp. 155–173). IGI Global. https://doi.org/10.4018/978-1-7998-4360-3.ch008

Dixon, T., & Christison, M. (2021). Teaching English Grammar in a Hybrid Academic ESL Course: A Mixed Methods Study. In K. Kelch, P. Byun, S. Safavi, & S. Cervantes (Eds.), *CALL Theory Applications for Online TESOL Education* (pp. 229–251). IGI Global. https://doi.org/10.4018/978-1-7998-6609-1.ch010

Donne, V., & Hansen, M. (2017). Teachers' Use of Assistive Technologies in Education. In L. Tomei (Ed.), *Exploring the New Era of Technology-Infused Education* (pp. 86–101). Hershey, PA: IGI Global. doi:10.4018/978-1-5225-1709-2.ch006

Donne, V., & Hansen, M. A. (2018). Business and Technology Educators: Practices for Inclusion. In I. Management Association (Ed.), Business Education and Ethics: Concepts, Methodologies, Tools, and Applications (pp. 471-484). Hershey, PA: IGI Global. https://doi.org/ doi:10.4018/978-1-5225-3153-1.ch026

Dos Santos, L. M. (2022). Completing Student-Teaching Internships Online: Instructional Changes During the COVID-19 Pandemic. In M. Alaali (Ed.), *Assessing University Governance and Policies in Relation to the COVID-19 Pandemic* (pp. 106–127). IGI Global. https://doi.org/10.4018/978-1-7998-8279-4.ch007

Dreon, O., Shettel, J., & Bower, K. M. (2017). Preparing Next Generation Elementary Teachers for the Tools of Tomorrow. In M. Grassetti & S. Brookby (Eds.), *Advancing Next-Generation Teacher Education through Digital Tools and Applications* (pp. 143–159). Hershey, PA: IGI Global. doi:10.4018/978-1-5225-0965-3.ch008

Durak, H. Y., & Güyer, T. (2018). Design and Development of an Instructional Program for Teaching Programming Processes to Gifted Students Using Scratch. In J. Cannaday (Ed.), *Curriculum Development for Gifted Education Programs* (pp. 61–99). Hershey, PA: IGI Global. doi:10.4018/978-1-5225-3041-1.ch004

Egorkina, E., Ivanov, M., & Valyavskiy, A. Y. (2018). Students' Research Competence Formation of the Quality of Open and Distance Learning. In V. Mkrttchian & L. Belyanina (Eds.), *Handbook of Research on Students' Research Competence in Modern Educational Contexts* (pp. 364–384). Hershey, PA: IGI Global. doi:10.4018/978-1-5225-3485-3.ch019

Ekren, G., Karataş, S., & Demiray, U. (2017). Understanding of Leadership in Distance Education Management. In I. Management Association (Ed.), *Educational Leadership and Administration: Concepts, Methodologies, Tools, and Applications* (pp. 34-50). Hershey, PA: IGI Global. https://doi.org/ doi:10.4018/978-1-5225-1624-8.ch003

Elmore, W. M., Young, J. K., Harris, S., & Mason, D. (2017). The Relationship between Individual Student Attributes and Online Course Completion. In K. Shelton & K. Pedersen (Eds.), *Handbook of Research on Building, Growing, and Sustaining Quality E-Learning Programs* (pp. 151–173). Hershey, PA: IGI Global. doi:10.4018/978-1-5225-0877-9.ch008

Ercegovac, I. R., Alfirević, N., & Koludrović, M. (2017). School Principals' Communication and Co-Operation Assessment: The Croatian Experience. In I. Management Association (Ed.), Educational Leadership and Administration: Concepts, Methodologies, Tools, and Applications (pp. 1568-1589). Hershey, PA: IGI Global. https://doi.org/ doi:10.4018/978-1-5225-1624-8.ch072

Everhart, D., & Seymour, D. M. (2017). Challenges and Opportunities in the Currency of Higher Education. In K. Rasmussen, P. Northrup, & R. Colson (Eds.), *Handbook of Research on Competency-Based Education in University Settings* (pp. 41–65). Hershey, PA: IGI Global. doi:10.4018/978-1-5225-0932-5.ch003

Farmer, L. S. (2017). Managing Portable Technologies for Special Education. In V. Wang (Ed.), *Encyclopedia of Strategic Leadership and Management* (pp. 977–987). Hershey, PA: IGI Global. doi:10.4018/978-1-5225-1049-9.ch068

Farmer, L. S. (2018). Optimizing OERs for Optimal ICT Literacy in Higher Education. In J. Keengwe (Ed.), *Handbook of Research on Mobile Technology, Constructivism, and Meaningful Learning* (pp. 366–390). Hershey, PA: IGI Global. doi:10.4018/978-1-5225-3949-0.ch020

Ferguson, B. T. (2019). Supporting Affective Development of Children With Disabilities Through Moral Dilemmas. In S. Ikuta (Ed.), *Handmade Teaching Materials for Students With Disabilities* (pp. 253–275). IGI Global. doi:10.4018/978-1-5225-6240-5.ch011

Fındık, L. Y. (2017). Self-Assessment of Principals Based on Leadership in Complexity. In I. Management Association (Ed.), Educational Leadership and Administration: Concepts, Methodologies, Tools, and Applications (pp. 978-991). Hershey, PA: IGI Global. https://doi.org/ doi:10.4018/978-1-5225-1624-8.ch047

Related References

Flor, A. G., & Gonzalez-Flor, B. (2018). Dysfunctional Digital Demeanors: Tales From (and Policy Implications of) eLearning's Dark Side. In I. Management Association (Ed.), The Dark Web: Breakthroughs in Research and Practice (pp. 37-50). Hershey, PA: IGI Global. https://doi.org/ doi:10.4018/978-1-5225-3163-0.ch003

Floyd, K. K., & Shambaugh, N. (2017). Instructional Design for Simulations in Special Education Virtual Learning Spaces. In T. Kidd & L. Morris Jr., (Eds.), *Handbook of Research on Instructional Systems and Educational Technology* (pp. 202–215). Hershey, PA: IGI Global. doi:10.4018/978-1-5225-2399-4.ch018

Freeland, S. F. (2020). Community Schools: Improving Academic Achievement Through Meaningful Engagement. In R. Kronick (Ed.), *Emerging Perspectives on Community Schools and the Engaged University* (pp. 132–144). IGI Global. https://doi.org/10.4018/978-1-7998-0280-8.ch008

Ghanbarzadeh, R., & Ghapanchi, A. H. (2019). Applied Areas of Three Dimensional Virtual Worlds in Learning and Teaching: A Review of Higher Education. In I. Management Association (Ed.), *Virtual Reality in Education: Breakthroughs in Research and Practice* (pp. 172-192). IGI Global. https://doi.org/10.4018/978-1-5225-8179-6.ch008

Giovannini, J. M. (2017). Technology Integration in Preservice Teacher Education Programs: Research-based Recommendations. In M. Grassetti & S. Brookby (Eds.), *Advancing Next-Generation Teacher Education through Digital Tools and Applications* (pp. 82–102). Hershey, PA: IGI Global. doi:10.4018/978-1-5225-0965-3.ch005

Good, S., & Clarke, V. B. (2017). An Integral Analysis of One Urban School System's Efforts to Support Student-Centered Teaching. In J. Keengwe & G. Onchwari (Eds.), *Handbook of Research on Learner-Centered Pedagogy in Teacher Education and Professional Development* (pp. 45–68). Hershey, PA: IGI Global. doi:10.4018/978-1-5225-0892-2.ch003

Guetzoian, E. (2022). Gamification Strategies for Higher Education Student Worker Training. In C. Lane (Ed.), *Handbook of Research on Acquiring 21st Century Literacy Skills Through Game-Based Learning* (pp. 164–179). IGI Global. https://doi.org/10.4018/978-1-7998-7271-9.ch009

Hamidi, F., Owuor, P. M., Hynie, M., Baljko, M., & McGrath, S. (2017). Potentials of Digital Assistive Technology and Special Education in Kenya. In C. Ayo & V. Mbarika (Eds.), *Sustainable ICT Adoption and Integration for Socio-Economic Development* (pp. 125–151). Hershey, PA: IGI Global. doi:10.4018/978-1-5225-2565-3.ch006

Hamim, T., Benabbou, F., & Sael, N. (2022). Student Profile Modeling Using Boosting Algorithms. *International Journal of Web-Based Learning and Teaching Technologies*, *17*(5), 1–13. https://doi.org/10.4018/IJWLTT.20220901.oa4

Henderson, L. K. (2017). Meltdown at Fukushima: Global Catastrophic Events, Visual Literacy, and Art Education. In R. Shin (Ed.), *Convergence of Contemporary Art, Visual Culture, and Global Civic Engagement* (pp. 80–99). Hershey, PA: IGI Global. doi:10.4018/978-1-5225-1665-1.ch005

Hudgins, T., & Holland, J. L. (2018). Digital Badges: Tracking Knowledge Acquisition Within an Innovation Framework. In I. Management Association (Ed.), Wearable Technologies: Concepts, Methodologies, Tools, and Applications (pp. 1118-1132). Hershey, PA: IGI Global. https://doi.org/ doi:10.4018/978-1-5225-5484-4.ch051

Hwang, R., Lin, H., Sun, J. C., & Wu, J. (2019). Improving Learning Achievement in Science Education for Elementary School Students via Blended Learning. *International Journal of Online Pedagogy and Course Design*, *9*(2), 44–62. https://doi.org/10.4018/IJOPCD.2019040104

Jančec, L., & Vodopivec, J. L. (2019). The Implicit Pedagogy and the Hidden Curriculum in Postmodern Education. In J. Vodopivec, L. Jančec, & T. Štemberger (Eds.), *Implicit Pedagogy for Optimized Learning in Contemporary Education* (pp. 41–59). IGI Global. https://doi.org/10.4018/978-1-5225-5799-9.ch003

Janus, M., & Siddiqua, A. (2018). Challenges for Children With Special Health Needs at the Time of Transition to School. In I. Management Association (Ed.), Autism Spectrum Disorders: Breakthroughs in Research and Practice (pp. 339-371). Hershey, PA: IGI Global. doi:10.4018/978-1-5225-3827-1.ch018

Jesus, R. A. (2018). Screencasts and Learning Styles. In M. Khosrow-Pour, D.B.A. (Ed.), Encyclopedia of Information Science and Technology, Fourth Edition (pp. 1548-1558). Hershey, PA: IGI Global. doi:10.4018/978-1-5225-2255-3.ch134

John, G., Francis, N., & Santhakumar, A. B. (2022). Student Engagement: Past, Present, and Future. In S. Ramlall, T. Cross, & M. Love (Eds.), *Handbook of Research on Future of Work and Education: Implications for Curriculum Delivery and Work Design* (pp. 329–341). IGI Global. https://doi.org/10.4018/978-1-7998-8275-6.ch020

Karpinski, A. C., D'Agostino, J. V., Williams, A. K., Highland, S. A., & Mellott, J. A. (2018). The Relationship Between Online Formative Assessment and State Test Scores Using Multilevel Modeling. In M. Khosrow-Pour, D.B.A. (Ed.), Encyclopedia of Information Science and Technology, Fourth Edition (pp. 5183-5192). Hershey, PA: IGI Global. doi:10.4018/978-1-5225-2255-3.ch450

Related References

Kats, Y. (2017). Educational Leadership and Integrated Support for Students with Autism Spectrum Disorders. In I. Management Association (Ed.), Educational Leadership and Administration: Concepts, Methodologies, Tools, and Applications (pp. 101-114). Hershey, PA: IGI Global. https://doi.org/ doi:10.4018/978-1-5225-1624-8.ch007

Kaya, G., & Altun, A. (2018). Educational Ontology Development. In M. Khosrow-Pour, D.B.A. (Ed.), Encyclopedia of Information Science and Technology, Fourth Edition (pp. 1441-1450). Hershey, PA: IGI Global. doi:10.4018/978-1-5225-2255-3.ch124

Keough, P. D., & Pacis, D. (2017). Best Practices Implementing Special Education Curriculum and Common Core State Standards using UDL. In P. Dickenson, P. Keough, & J. Courduff (Eds.), *Preparing Pre-Service Teachers for the Inclusive Classroom* (pp. 107–123). Hershey, PA: IGI Global. doi:10.4018/978-1-5225-1753-5.ch006

Kilburn, M., Henckell, M., & Starrett, D. (2018). Factors Contributing to the Effectiveness of Online Students and Instructors. In M. Khosrow-Pour, D.B.A. (Ed.), Encyclopedia of Information Science and Technology, Fourth Edition (pp. 1451-1462). Hershey, PA: IGI Global. doi:10.4018/978-1-5225-2255-3.ch125

Koban Koç, D. (2021). Gender and Language: A Sociolinguistic Analysis of Second Language Writing. In E. Hancı-Azizoglu & N. Kavaklı (Eds.), *Futuristic and Linguistic Perspectives on Teaching Writing to Second Language Students* (pp. 161–177). IGI Global. https://doi.org/10.4018/978-1-7998-6508-7.ch010

Konecny, L. T. (2017). Hybrid, Online, and Flipped Classrooms in Health Science: Enhanced Learning Environments. In I. Management Association (Ed.), Flipped Instruction: Breakthroughs in Research and Practice (pp. 355-370). Hershey, PA: IGI Global. https://doi.org/ doi:10.4018/978-1-5225-1803-7.ch020

Kupietz, K. D. (2021). Gaming and Simulation in Public Education: Teaching Others to Help Themselves and Their Neighbors. In N. Drumhiller, T. Wilkin, & K. Srba (Eds.), *Simulation and Game-Based Learning in Emergency and Disaster Management* (pp. 41–62). IGI Global. https://doi.org/10.4018/978-1-7998-4087-9.ch003

Kwee, C. T. (2022). Assessing the International Student Enrolment Strategies in Australian Universities: A Case Study During the COVID-19 Pandemic. In M. Alaali (Ed.), *Assessing University Governance and Policies in Relation to the COVID-19 Pandemic* (pp. 162–188). IGI Global. https://doi.org/10.4018/978-1-7998-8279-4.ch010

Lauricella, S., & McArthur, F. A. (2022). Taking a Student-Centred Approach to Alternative Digital Credentials: Multiple Pathways Toward the Acquisition of Microcredentials. In D. Piedra (Ed.), *Innovations in the Design and Application of Alternative Digital Credentials* (pp. 57–69). IGI Global. https://doi.org/10.4018/978-1-7998-7697-7.ch003

Llamas, M. F. (2019). Intercultural Awareness in Teaching English for Early Childhood: A Film-Based Approach. In E. Domínguez Romero, J. Bobkina, & S. Stefanova (Eds.), *Teaching Literature and Language Through Multimodal Texts* (pp. 54–68). IGI Global. https://doi.org/10.4018/978-1-5225-5796-8.ch004

Lokhtina, I., & Kkese, E. T. (2022). Reflecting and Adapting to an Academic Workplace Before and After the Lockdown in Greek-Speaking Cyprus: Opportunities and Challenges. In A. Zhuplev & R. Koepp (Eds.), *Global Trends, Dynamics, and Imperatives for Strategic Development in Business Education in an Age of Disruption* (pp. 126–148). IGI Global. https://doi.org/10.4018/978-1-7998-7548-2.ch007

Lovell, K. L. (2017). Development and Evaluation of Neuroscience Computer-Based Modules for Medical Students: Instructional Design Principles and Effectiveness. In J. Stefaniak (Ed.), *Advancing Medical Education Through Strategic Instructional Design* (pp. 262–276). Hershey, PA: IGI Global. doi:10.4018/978-1-5225-2098-6.ch013

Maher, D. (2019). The Use of Course Management Systems in Pre-Service Teacher Education. In J. Keengwe (Ed.), *Handbook of Research on Blended Learning Pedagogies and Professional Development in Higher Education* (pp. 196–213). IGI Global. https://doi.org/10.4018/978-1-5225-5557-5.ch011

Makewa, L. N. (2019). Teacher Technology Competence Base. In L. Makewa, B. Ngussa, & J. Kuboja (Eds.), *Technology-Supported Teaching and Research Methods for Educators* (pp. 247–267). IGI Global. https://doi.org/10.4018/978-1-5225-5915-3.ch014

Mallett, C. A. (2022). School Resource (Police) Officers in Schools: Impact on Campus Safety, Student Discipline, and Learning. In G. Crews (Ed.), *Impact of School Shootings on Classroom Culture, Curriculum, and Learning* (pp. 53–70). IGI Global. https://doi.org/10.4018/978-1-7998-5200-1.ch004

Related References

Marinho, J. E., Freitas, I. R., Leão, I. B., Pacheco, L. O., Gonçalves, M. P., Castro, M. J., Silva, P. D., & Moreira, R. J. (2022). Project-Based Learning Application in Higher Education: Student Experiences and Perspectives. In A. Alves & N. van Hattum-Janssen (Eds.), *Training Engineering Students for Modern Technological Advancement* (pp. 146–164). IGI Global. https://doi.org/10.4018/978-1-7998-8816-1.ch007

McCleskey, J. A., & Melton, R. M. (2022). Rolling With the Flow: Online Faculty and Student Presence in a Post-COVID-19 World. In S. Ramlall, T. Cross, & M. Love (Eds.), *Handbook of Research on Future of Work and Education: Implications for Curriculum Delivery and Work Design* (pp. 307–328). IGI Global. https://doi.org/10.4018/978-1-7998-8275-6.ch019

McCormack, V. F., Stauffer, M., Fishley, K., Hohenbrink, J., Mascazine, J. R., & Zigler, T. (2018). Designing a Dual Licensure Path for Middle Childhood and Special Education Teacher Candidates. In D. Polly, M. Putman, T. Petty, & A. Good (Eds.), *Innovative Practices in Teacher Preparation and Graduate-Level Teacher Education Programs* (pp. 21–36). Hershey, PA: IGI Global. doi:10.4018/978-1-5225-3068-8.ch002

McDaniel, R. (2017). Strategic Leadership in Instructional Design: Applying the Principles of Instructional Design through the Lens of Strategic Leadership to Distance Education. In V. Wang (Ed.), *Encyclopedia of Strategic Leadership and Management* (pp. 1570–1584). Hershey, PA: IGI Global. doi:10.4018/978-1-5225-1049-9.ch109

McKinney, R. E., Halli-Tierney, A. D., Gold, A. E., Allen, R. S., & Carroll, D. G. (2022). Interprofessional Education: Using Standardized Cases in Face-to-Face and Remote Learning Settings. In C. Ford & K. Garza (Eds.), *Handbook of Research on Updating and Innovating Health Professions Education: Post-Pandemic Perspectives* (pp. 24–42). IGI Global. https://doi.org/10.4018/978-1-7998-7623-6.ch002

Meintjes, H. H. (2021). Learner Views of a Facebook Page as a Supportive Digital Pedagogical Tool at a Public South African School in a Grade 12 Business Studies Class. *International Journal of Smart Education and Urban Society*, *12*(2), 32–45. https://doi.org/10.4018/IJSEUS.2021040104

Melero-García, F. (2022). Training Bilingual Interpreters in Healthcare Settings: Student Perceptions of Online Learning. In J. LeLoup & P. Swanson (Eds.), *Handbook of Research on Effective Online Language Teaching in a Disruptive Environment* (pp. 288–310). IGI Global. https://doi.org/10.4018/978-1-7998-7720-2.ch015

Meletiadou, E. (2022). The Use of Peer Assessment as an Inclusive Learning Strategy in Higher Education Institutions: Enhancing Student Writing Skills and Motivation. In E. Meletiadou (Ed.), *Handbook of Research on Policies and Practices for Assessing Inclusive Teaching and Learning* (pp. 1–26). IGI Global. https://doi.org/10.4018/978-1-7998-8579-5.ch001

Memon, R. N., Ahmad, R., & Salim, S. S. (2018). Critical Issues in Requirements Engineering Education. In I. Management Association (Ed.), Computer Systems and Software Engineering: Concepts, Methodologies, Tools, and Applications (pp. 1953-1976). Hershey, PA: IGI Global. doi:10.4018/978-1-5225-3923-0.ch081

Mendenhall, R. (2017). Western Governors University: CBE Innovator and National Model. In K. Rasmussen, P. Northrup, & R. Colson (Eds.), *Handbook of Research on Competency-Based Education in University Settings* (pp. 379–400). Hershey, PA: IGI Global. doi:10.4018/978-1-5225-0932-5.ch019

Mense, E. G., Griggs, D. M., & Shanks, J. N. (2018). School Leaders in a Time of Accountability and Data Use: Preparing Our Future School Leaders in Leadership Preparation Programs. In E. Mense & M. Crain-Dorough (Eds.), *Data Leadership for K-12 Schools in a Time of Accountability* (pp. 235–259). Hershey, PA: IGI Global. doi:10.4018/978-1-5225-3188-3.ch012

Mense, E. G., Griggs, D. M., & Shanks, J. N. (2018). School Leaders in a Time of Accountability and Data Use: Preparing Our Future School Leaders in Leadership Preparation Programs. In E. Mense & M. Crain-Dorough (Eds.), *Data Leadership for K-12 Schools in a Time of Accountability* (pp. 235–259). Hershey, PA: IGI Global. doi:10.4018/978-1-5225-3188-3.ch012

Mestry, R., & Naicker, S. R. (2017). Exploring Distributive Leadership in South African Public Primary Schools in the Soweto Region. In I. Management Association (Ed.), Educational Leadership and Administration: Concepts, Methodologies, Tools, and Applications (pp. 1041-1064). Hershey, PA: IGI Global. doi:10.4018/978-1-5225-1624-8.ch050

Monaghan, C. H., & Boboc, M. (2017). (Re)Defining Leadership in Higher Education in the U.S. In V. Wang (Ed.), *Encyclopedia of Strategic Leadership and Management* (pp. 567–579). Hershey, PA: IGI Global. doi:10.4018/978-1-5225-1049-9.ch040

Morall, M. B. (2021). Reimagining Mobile Phones: Multiple Literacies and Digital Media Compositions. In C. Moran (Eds.), *Affordances and Constraints of Mobile Phone Use in English Language Arts Classrooms* (pp. 41-53). IGI Global. https://doi.org/10.4018/978-1-7998-5805-8.ch003

Related References

Mthethwa, V. (2022). Student Governance and the Academic Minefield During COVID-19 Lockdown in South Africa. In M. Alaali (Ed.), *Assessing University Governance and Policies in Relation to the COVID-19 Pandemic* (pp. 255–276). IGI Global. https://doi.org/10.4018/978-1-7998-8279-4.ch015

Muthee, J. M., & Murungi, C. G. (2018). Relationship Among Intelligence, Achievement Motivation, Type of School, and Academic Performance of Kenyan Urban Primary School Pupils. In M. Khosrow-Pour, D.B.A. (Ed.), Encyclopedia of Information Science and Technology, Fourth Edition (pp. 1540-1547). Hershey, PA: IGI Global. https://doi.org/ doi:10.4018/978-1-5225-2255-3.ch133

Naranjo, J. (2018). Meeting the Need for Inclusive Educators Online: Teacher Education in Inclusive Special Education and Dual-Certification. In D. Polly, M. Putman, T. Petty, & A. Good (Eds.), *Innovative Practices in Teacher Preparation and Graduate-Level Teacher Education Programs* (pp. 106–122). Hershey, PA: IGI Global. doi:10.4018/978-1-5225-3068-8.ch007

Nkabinde, Z. P. (2017). Multiculturalism in Special Education: Perspectives of Minority Children in Urban Schools. In J. Keengwe (Ed.), *Handbook of Research on Promoting Cross-Cultural Competence and Social Justice in Teacher Education* (pp. 382–397). Hershey, PA: IGI Global. doi:10.4018/978-1-5225-0897-7.ch020

Nkabinde, Z. P. (2018). Online Instruction: Is the Quality the Same as Face-to-Face Instruction? In J. Keengwe (Ed.), *Handbook of Research on Digital Content, Mobile Learning, and Technology Integration Models in Teacher Education* (pp. 300–314). Hershey, PA: IGI Global. doi:10.4018/978-1-5225-2953-8.ch016

Nugroho, A., & Albusaidi, S. S. (2022). Internationalization of Higher Education: The Methodological Critiques on the Research Related to Study Overseas and International Experience. In H. Magd & S. Kunjumuhammed (Eds.), *Global Perspectives on Quality Assurance and Accreditation in Higher Education Institutions* (pp. 75–89). IGI Global. https://doi.org/10.4018/978-1-7998-8085-1.ch005

Nulty, Z., & West, S. G. (2022). Student Engagement and Supporting Students With Accommodations. In P. Bull & G. Patterson (Eds.), *Redefining Teacher Education and Teacher Preparation Programs in the Post-COVID-19 Era* (pp. 99–116). IGI Global. https://doi.org/10.4018/978-1-7998-8298-5.ch006

O'Connor, J. R. Jr, & Jackson, K. N. (2017). The Use of iPad® Devices and "Apps" for ASD Students in Special Education and Speech Therapy. In Y. Kats (Ed.), *Supporting the Education of Children with Autism Spectrum Disorders* (pp. 267–283). Hershey, PA: IGI Global. doi:10.4018/978-1-5225-0816-8.ch014

Okolie, U. C., & Yasin, A. M. (2017). TVET in Developing Nations and Human Development. In U. Okolie & A. Yasin (Eds.), *Technical Education and Vocational Training in Developing Nations* (pp. 1–25). Hershey, PA: IGI Global. doi:10.4018/978-1-5225-1811-2.ch001

Pack, A., & Barrett, A. (2021). A Review of Virtual Reality and English for Academic Purposes: Understanding Where to Start. *International Journal of Computer-Assisted Language Learning and Teaching*, *11*(1), 72–80. https://doi.org/10.4018/IJCALLT.2021010105

Pashollari, E. (2019). Building Sustainability Through Environmental Education: Education for Sustainable Development. In L. Wilson, & C. Stevenson (Eds.), *Building Sustainability Through Environmental Education* (pp. 72-88). IGI Global. https://doi.org/10.4018/978-1-5225-7727-0.ch004

Paulson, E. N. (2017). Adapting and Advocating for an Online EdD Program in Changing Times and "Sacred" Cultures. In I. Management Association (Ed.), Educational Leadership and Administration: Concepts, Methodologies, Tools, and Applications (pp. 1849-1876). Hershey, PA: IGI Global. https://doi.org/doi:10.4018/978-1-5225-1624-8.ch085

Petersen, A. J., Elser, C. F., Al Nassir, M. N., Stakey, J., & Everson, K. (2017). The Year of Teaching Inclusively: Building an Elementary Classroom for All Students. In C. Curran & A. Petersen (Eds.), *Handbook of Research on Classroom Diversity and Inclusive Education Practice* (pp. 332–348). Hershey, PA: IGI Global. doi:10.4018/978-1-5225-2520-2.ch014

Pfannenstiel, K. H., & Sanders, J. (2017). Characteristics and Instructional Strategies for Students With Mathematical Difficulties: In the Inclusive Classroom. In C. Curran & A. Petersen (Eds.), *Handbook of Research on Classroom Diversity and Inclusive Education Practice* (pp. 250–281). Hershey, PA: IGI Global. doi:10.4018/978-1-5225-2520-2.ch011

Phan, A. N. (2022). Quality Assurance of Higher Education From the Glonacal Agency Heuristic: An Example From Vietnam. In H. Magd & S. Kunjumuhammed (Eds.), *Global Perspectives on Quality Assurance and Accreditation in Higher Education Institutions* (pp. 136–155). IGI Global. https://doi.org/10.4018/978-1-7998-8085-1.ch008

Related References

Preast, J. L., Bowman, N., & Rose, C. A. (2017). Creating Inclusive Classroom Communities Through Social and Emotional Learning to Reduce Social Marginalization Among Students. In C. Curran & A. Petersen (Eds.), *Handbook of Research on Classroom Diversity and Inclusive Education Practice* (pp. 183–200). Hershey, PA: IGI Global. doi:10.4018/978-1-5225-2520-2.ch008

Randolph, K. M., & Brady, M. P. (2018). Evolution of Covert Coaching as an Evidence-Based Practice in Professional Development and Preparation of Teachers. In V. Bryan, A. Musgrove, & J. Powers (Eds.), *Handbook of Research on Human Development in the Digital Age* (pp. 281–299). Hershey, PA: IGI Global. doi:10.4018/978-1-5225-2838-8.ch013

Rell, A. B., Puig, R. A., Roll, F., Valles, V., Espinoza, M., & Duque, A. L. (2017). Addressing Cultural Diversity and Global Competence: The Dual Language Framework. In L. Leavitt, S. Wisdom, & K. Leavitt (Eds.), *Cultural Awareness and Competency Development in Higher Education* (pp. 111–131). Hershey, PA: IGI Global. doi:10.4018/978-1-5225-2145-7.ch007

Richards, M., & Guzman, I. R. (2020). Academic Assessment of Critical Thinking in Distance Education Information Technology Programs. In I. Management Association (Ed.), *Learning and Performance Assessment: Concepts, Methodologies, Tools, and Applications* (pp. 1-19). IGI Global. https://doi.org/10.4018/978-1-7998-0420-8.ch001

Riel, J., Lawless, K. A., & Brown, S. W. (2017). Defining and Designing Responsive Online Professional Development (ROPD): A Framework to Support Curriculum Implementation. In T. Kidd & L. Morris Jr., (Eds.), *Handbook of Research on Instructional Systems and Educational Technology* (pp. 104–115). Hershey, PA: IGI Global. doi:10.4018/978-1-5225-2399-4.ch010

Roberts, C. (2017). Advancing Women Leaders in Academe: Creating a Culture of Inclusion. In S. Mukerji & P. Tripathi (Eds.), *Handbook of Research on Administration, Policy, and Leadership in Higher Education* (pp. 256–273). Hershey, PA: IGI Global. doi:10.4018/978-1-5225-0672-0.ch012

Rodgers, W. J., Kennedy, M. J., Alves, K. D., & Romig, J. E. (2017). A Multimedia Tool for Teacher Education and Professional Development. In C. Martin & D. Polly (Eds.), *Handbook of Research on Teacher Education and Professional Development* (pp. 285–296). Hershey, PA: IGI Global. doi:10.4018/978-1-5225-1067-3.ch015

Romanowski, M. H. (2017). Qatar's Educational Reform: Critical Issues Facing Principals. In I. Management Association (Ed.), Educational Leadership and Administration: Concepts, Methodologies, Tools, and Applications (pp. 1758-1773). Hershey, PA: IGI Global. https://doi.org/ doi:10.4018/978-1-5225-1624-8.ch080

Ruffin, T. R., Hawkins, D. P., & Lee, D. I. (2018). Increasing Student Engagement and Participation Through Course Methodology. In M. Khosrow-Pour, D.B.A. (Ed.), Encyclopedia of Information Science and Technology, Fourth Edition (pp. 1463-1473). Hershey, PA: IGI Global. doi:10.4018/978-1-5225-2255-3.ch126

Sabina, L. L., Curry, K. A., Harris, E. L., Krumm, B. L., & Vencill, V. (2017). Assessing the Performance of a Cohort-Based Model Using Domestic and International Practices. In I. Management Association (Ed.), Educational Leadership and Administration: Concepts, Methodologies, Tools, and Applications(pp. 913-929). Hershey, PA: IGI Global. https://doi.org/ doi:10.4018/978-1-5225-1624-8.ch044

Samkian, A., Pascarella, J., & Slayton, J. (2022). Towards an Anti-Racist, Culturally Responsive, and LGBTQ+ Inclusive Education: Developing Critically-Conscious Educational Leaders. In E. Cain-Sanschagrin, R. Filback, & J. Crawford (Eds.), *Cases on Academic Program Redesign for Greater Racial and Social Justice* (pp. 150–175). IGI Global. https://doi.org/10.4018/978-1-7998-8463-7.ch007

Santamaría, A. P., Webber, M., & Santamaría, L. J. (2017). Effective School Leadership for Māori Achievement: Building Capacity through Indigenous, National, and International Cross-Cultural Collaboration. In I. Management Association (Ed.), Educational Leadership and Administration: Concepts, Methodologies, Tools, and Applications (pp. 1547-1567). Hershey, PA: IGI Global. https://doi.org/ doi:10.4018/978-1-5225-1624-8.ch071

Santamaría, L. J. (2017). Culturally Responsive Educational Leadership in Cross-Cultural International Contexts. In I. Management Association (Ed.), Educational Leadership and Administration: Concepts, Methodologies, Tools, and Applications (pp. 1380-1400). Hershey, PA: IGI Global. https://doi.org/ doi:10.4018/978-1-5225-1624-8.ch064

Segredo, M. R., Cistone, P. J., & Reio, T. G. (2017). Relationships Between Emotional Intelligence, Leadership Style, and School Culture. *International Journal of Adult Vocational Education and Technology*, 8(3), 25–43. doi:10.4018/IJAVET.2017070103

Shalev, N. (2017). Empathy and Leadership From the Organizational Perspective. In Z. Nedelko & M. Brzozowski (Eds.), *Exploring the Influence of Personal Values and Cultures in the Workplace* (pp. 348–363). Hershey, PA: IGI Global. doi:10.4018/978-1-5225-2480-9.ch018

Related References

Siamak, M., Fathi, S., & Isfandyari-Moghaddam, A. (2018). Assessment and Measurement of Education Programs of Information Literacy. In R. Bhardwaj (Ed.), *Digitizing the Modern Library and the Transition From Print to Electronic* (pp. 164–192). Hershey, PA: IGI Global. doi:10.4018/978-1-5225-2119-8.ch007

Siu, K. W., & García, G. J. (2017). Disruptive Technologies and Education: Is There Any Disruption After All? In I. Management Association (Ed.), Educational Leadership and Administration: Concepts, Methodologies, Tools, and Applications (pp. 757-778). Hershey, PA: IGI Global. https://doi.org/ doi:10.4018/978-1-5225-1624-8.ch037

Slagter van Tryon, P. J. (2017). The Nurse Educator's Role in Designing Instruction and Instructional Strategies for Academic and Clinical Settings. In J. Stefaniak (Ed.), *Advancing Medical Education Through Strategic Instructional Design* (pp. 133–149). Hershey, PA: IGI Global. doi:10.4018/978-1-5225-2098-6.ch006

Slattery, C. A. (2018). Literacy Intervention and the Differentiated Plan of Instruction. In *Developing Effective Literacy Intervention Strategies: Emerging Research and Opportunities* (pp. 41–62). Hershey, PA: IGI Global. doi:10.4018/978-1-5225-5007-5.ch003

Smith, A. R. (2017). Ensuring Quality: The Faculty Role in Online Higher Education. In K. Shelton & K. Pedersen (Eds.), *Handbook of Research on Building, Growing, and Sustaining Quality E-Learning Programs* (pp. 210–231). Hershey, PA: IGI Global. doi:10.4018/978-1-5225-0877-9.ch011

Souders, T. M. (2017). Understanding Your Learner: Conducting a Learner Analysis. In J. Stefaniak (Ed.), *Advancing Medical Education Through Strategic Instructional Design* (pp. 1–29). Hershey, PA: IGI Global. doi:10.4018/978-1-5225-2098-6.ch001

Spring, K. J., Graham, C. R., & Ikahihifo, T. B. (2018). Learner Engagement in Blended Learning. In M. Khosrow-Pour, D.B.A. (Ed.), Encyclopedia of Information Science and Technology, Fourth Edition (pp. 1487-1498). Hershey, PA: IGI Global. doi:10.4018/978-1-5225-2255-3.ch128

Storey, V. A., Anthony, A. K., & Wahid, P. (2017). Gender-Based Leadership Barriers: Advancement of Female Faculty to Leadership Positions in Higher Education. In V. Wang (Ed.), *Encyclopedia of Strategic Leadership and Management* (pp. 244–258). Hershey, PA: IGI Global. doi:10.4018/978-1-5225-1049-9.ch018

Stottlemyer, D. (2018). Develop a Teaching Model Plan for a Differentiated Learning Approach. In *Differentiated Instructional Design for Multicultural Environments: Emerging Research and Opportunities* (pp. 106–130). Hershey, PA: IGI Global. doi:10.4018/978-1-5225-5106-5.ch005

Stottlemyer, D. (2018). Developing a Multicultural Environment. In *Differentiated Instructional Design for Multicultural Environments: Emerging Research and Opportunities* (pp. 1–27). Hershey, PA: IGI Global. doi:10.4018/978-1-5225-5106-5.ch001

Swagerty, T. (2022). Digital Access to Culturally Relevant Curricula: The Impact on the Native and Indigenous Student. In E. Reeves & C. McIntyre (Eds.), *Multidisciplinary Perspectives on Diversity and Equity in a Virtual World* (pp. 99–113). IGI Global. https://doi.org/10.4018/978-1-7998-8028-8.ch006

Swami, B. N., Gobona, T., & Tsimako, J. J. (2017). Academic Leadership: A Case Study of the University of Botswana. In N. Baporikar (Ed.), *Innovation and Shifting Perspectives in Management Education* (pp. 1–32). Hershey, PA: IGI Global. doi:10.4018/978-1-5225-1019-2.ch001

Swanson, K. W., & Collins, G. (2018). Designing Engaging Instruction for the Adult Learners. In M. Khosrow-Pour, D.B.A. (Ed.), Encyclopedia of Information Science and Technology, Fourth Edition (pp. 1432-1440). Hershey, PA: IGI Global. doi:10.4018/978-1-5225-2255-3.ch123

Swartz, B. A., Lynch, J. M., & Lynch, S. D. (2018). Embedding Elementary Teacher Education Coursework in Local Classrooms: Examples in Mathematics and Special Education. In D. Polly, M. Putman, T. Petty, & A. Good (Eds.), *Innovative Practices in Teacher Preparation and Graduate-Level Teacher Education Programs* (pp. 262–292). Hershey, PA: IGI Global. doi:10.4018/978-1-5225-3068-8.ch015

Taliadorou, N., & Pashiardis, P. (2017). Emotional Intelligence and Political Skill Really Matter in Educational Leadership. In I. Management Association (Ed.), Educational Leadership and Administration: Concepts, Methodologies, Tools, and Applications (pp. 1274-1303). Hershey, PA: IGI Global. https://doi.org/doi:10.4018/978-1-5225-1624-8.ch060

Tandoh, K. A., & Ebe-Arthur, J. E. (2018). Effective Educational Leadership in the Digital Age: An Examination of Professional Qualities and Best Practices. In J. Keengwe (Ed.), *Handbook of Research on Digital Content, Mobile Learning, and Technology Integration Models in Teacher Education* (pp. 244–265). Hershey, PA: IGI Global. doi:10.4018/978-1-5225-2953-8.ch013

Tobin, M. T. (2018). Multimodal Literacy. In M. Khosrow-Pour, D.B.A. (Ed.), Encyclopedia of Information Science and Technology, Fourth Edition (pp. 1508-1516). Hershey, PA: IGI Global. doi:10.4018/978-1-5225-2255-3.ch130

Related References

Torres, K. M., Arrastia-Chisholm, M. C., & Tackett, S. (2019). A Phenomenological Study of Pre-Service Teachers' Perceptions of Completing ESOL Field Placements. *International Journal of Teacher Education and Professional Development*, 2(2), 85–101. https://doi.org/10.4018/IJTEPD.2019070106

Torres, M. C., Salamanca, Y. N., Cely, J. P., & Aguilar, J. L. (2020). All We Need is a Boost! Using Multimodal Tools and the Translanguaging Strategy: Strengthening Speaking in the EFL Classroom. *International Journal of Computer-Assisted Language Learning and Teaching*, 10(3), 28–47. doi:10.4018/IJCALLT.2020070103

Torres, M. L., & Ramos, V. J. (2018). Music Therapy: A Pedagogical Alternative for ASD and ID Students in Regular Classrooms. In P. Epler (Ed.), *Instructional Strategies in General Education and Putting the Individuals With Disabilities Act (IDEA) Into Practice* (pp. 222–244). Hershey, PA: IGI Global. doi:10.4018/978-1-5225-3111-1.ch008

Toulassi, B. (2017). Educational Administration and Leadership in Francophone Africa: 5 Dynamics to Change Education. In S. Mukerji & P. Tripathi (Eds.), *Handbook of Research on Administration, Policy, and Leadership in Higher Education* (pp. 20–45). Hershey, PA: IGI Global. doi:10.4018/978-1-5225-0672-0.ch002

Umair, S., & Sharif, M. M. (2018). Predicting Students Grades Using Artificial Neural Networks and Support Vector Machine. In M. Khosrow-Pour, D.B.A. (Ed.), Encyclopedia of Information Science and Technology, Fourth Edition (pp. 5169-5182). Hershey, PA: IGI Global. doi:10.4018/978-1-5225-2255-3.ch449

Vettraino, L., Castello, V., Guspini, M., & Guglielman, E. (2018). Self-Awareness and Motivation Contrasting ESL and NEET Using the SAVE System. In M. Khosrow-Pour, D.B.A. (Ed.), Encyclopedia of Information Science and Technology, Fourth Edition (pp. 1559-1568). Hershey, PA: IGI Global. doi:10.4018/978-1-5225-2255-3.ch135

Wiemelt, J. (2017). Critical Bilingual Leadership for Emergent Bilingual Students. In I. Management Association (Ed.), Educational Leadership and Administration: Concepts, Methodologies, Tools, and Applications (pp. 1606-1631). Hershey, PA: IGI Global. doi:10.4018/978-1-5225-1624-8.ch074

Wolf, F., Seyfarth, F. C., & Pflaum, E. (2018). Scalable Capacity-Building for Geographically Dispersed Learners: Designing the MOOC "Sustainable Energy in Small Island Developing States (SIDS)". In U. Pandey & V. Indrakanti (Eds.), *Open and Distance Learning Initiatives for Sustainable Development* (pp. 58–83). Hershey, PA: IGI Global. doi:10.4018/978-1-5225-2621-6.ch003

Woodley, X. M., Mucundanyi, G., & Lockard, M. (2017). Designing Counter-Narratives: Constructing Culturally Responsive Curriculum Online. *International Journal of Online Pedagogy and Course Design*, 7(1), 43–56. doi:10.4018/IJOPCD.2017010104

Yell, M. L., & Christle, C. A. (2017). The Foundation of Inclusion in Federal Legislation and Litigation. In C. Curran & A. Petersen (Eds.), *Handbook of Research on Classroom Diversity and Inclusive Education Practice* (pp. 27–52). Hershey, PA: IGI Global. doi:10.4018/978-1-5225-2520-2.ch002

Zinner, L. (2019). Fostering Academic Citizenship With a Shared Leadership Approach. In C. Zhu & M. Zayim-Kurtay (Eds.), *University Governance and Academic Leadership in the EU and China* (pp. 99–117). IGI Global. https://doi.org/10.4018/978-1-5225-7441-5.ch007

About the Contributors

Gina Maestre-Góngora is an Associate Professor in Universidad de Antioquia at Medellin, Colombia. With experience in Information Technology Management and Digital Transformation. She received a Ph.D. degree in systems engineering and computer science, a master's degree in engineering, and a bachelor's degree in systems engineering. Currently is a Senior Researcher at the Ministry of Science, Technology, and Innovation of Colombia. Her research interests include smart cities, information technology management, data governance, enterprise architecture, and IT project management.

Fernando Ortiz-Rodriguez is a Full Professor and Head of the Artificial Intelligence and Innovation Lab at Tamaulipas Autonomous University. He was the Executive Director at the International Institute of Studies (IIES). He created the First Business School in Tamaulipas, Mexico. He worked as the Information Technology Manager at Emerson Electric, where he developed more than 40 pieces of software, some of them used globally in Emerson and achieved technology convergence by implementing the first efforts on IoT and Industry 4.0. Fernando is a member of National Systems Researchers (SNI) Level 1 of the National Council of Science and Technology (CONACYT) and INDEX IT Advisor

Philippe Aniorte Director INDICATIC AIP Panamá since 2022. Full-Professor at Université de Pau et de Pays de L'Adour - UPPA (Francia) since 2006. He is entitled to supervise research since 2004 when he defended his HDR "Habilitation à diriger des recherches" (specific French grade, is a post-doctoral degree) at UPPA untitled "Towards heterogeneous distributed Systems: A Model Driven Engineering (MDE) component-based approach". His Ph.D. Thesis was defended in 1990 at Université Paul Sabatier (UPS) - Toulouse (France).

About the Contributors

Oscar Baldovino Pantaleón earned his PhD degree from the Autonomous National University of Mexico (UNAM). Between 2006-2009 he joined the group of Professor Rubén Ramos García as a postdoctoral associate at the National Institute of Astrophysics, Optics, and Electronics (INAOE), Puebla, Mexico. He has conducted projects and training programs as a Visiting Research Scientist at the Liquid Crystal Institute at Kent State University, Ohio, and the University of California at Riverside. In 2009, Dr. Baldovino joined the Autonomous University of Tamaulipas as an associate researcher at the Department of Electronics Engineering. His current research interest focuses on the synthesis and characterization of organic and organometallic compounds, and the linear- and nonlinear-optical properties, and their sensor and biosensor applications.

René Domínguez-Cruz is a full professor in the Electrical and Electronic Department at the Autonomous University of Tamaulipas, UAT (Tamaulipas, México). He has a bachelor's degree in physics by Universidad Veracruzana. He received his MS degree in Optics and his Ph.D. degree in Optics from the National Institute of Astrophysics, Optics and Electronics (INAOE) in 1998 and 2002, respectively. His research interest includes micro-structured and special optical fibers applied as sensors of physical parameters.

Yakira Fernández-Torres. Lecturer in the Department of Financial Economics and Accounting at the University of Extremadura, Spain. Her research interests include the study of gender diversity on the board of directors in the banking sector and its influence on business performance, which includes financial and Corporate Social Responsibility (CSR) performance.

Yadira Aracely Fuentes-Rubio is an associated professor in the Electronic Department at the Autonomous University of Tamaulipas, UAT (Tamaulipas, México). She received her MS degree and his Ph.D. degree in Electrical and Electronics from the UAT, in 2014 and 2022, respectively. Her research includes the development of fiber optic devices with applications to sensors and biosensors for the measurement of physical and biophysical parameters. She is a member of the Mexican National System of Researchers (SNI level C).

Clara Gallego-Sosa. Best academic record a Degree in Accounting and Finance, Degree in Business Administration and Management, and a Master's in Research in Social Sciences and Law. She is hired by the University of Extremadura through a predoctoral contract financed by the Ministry of Education and Vocational Training (Spain), where she is developing her Ph.D., about the relationship between gender diversity on the board of directors and environmental performance. Her research

About the Contributors

interests include the study of corporate governance and its influence on Corporate Social Responsibility (CSR). She has published in numerous high-impact journals.

Luis Antonio Garcia Garza received the M.Sc. in Electronic Engineering with a specialty in Instrumentation in 2012 and PhD in Electrical and Electronic Engineering passant in 2022, both at the Autonomous University of Tamaulipas (UAT), Mexico, he has been a full-time professor since 1995, coordinator of the computer systems engineering from 2002 to 2014 and has been Academic Secretary of the UAM Reynosa Rodhe UAT from 2015 to 2023.

Leila Goosen is a full professor in the Department of Science and Technology Education of the University of South Africa. Prof. Goosen was an Associate Professor in the School of Computing, and the module leader and head designer of the fully online signature module for the College for Science, Engineering and Technology, rolled out to over 92,000 registered students since the first semester of 2013. She also supervises ten Masters and Doctoral students, and has successfully completed supervision of 43 students at postgraduate level. Previously, she was a Deputy Director at the South African national Department of Education. In this capacity, she was required to develop ICT strategies for implementation. She also promoted, coordinated, managed, monitored and evaluated ICT policies and strategies, and drove the research agenda in this area. Before that, she had been a lecturer of Information Technology (IT) in the Department for Science, Mathematics and Technology Education in the Faculty of Education of the University of Pretoria. Her research interests have included cooperative work in IT, effective teaching and learning of programming and teacher professional development.

Milagros Gutiérrez-Fernández. Lecturer in the Department of Financial Economics and Accounting at the University of Extremadura, Spain. Her PhD dissertation was an analysis of the Spanish banking sector and its efficiency. Her research interests include the study of gender diversity on the board of directors in the banking sector and its influence on business performance, which includes financial and Corporate Social Responsibility (CSR) performance. She also has published in numerous high-impact journals.

Olegario Mendez Cabrera, Full-time Research Professor. Autonomous University of Tamaulipas. Reynosa-Rodhe Multidisciplinary Academic Unit. Reynosa, Tamaulipas, Mexico. Email: olmendez@docentes.uat.edu.mx.

Mayeli Anaís Pérez-Rosas has a bachelor's degree in Electronics Engineering by the Autonomous University of Tamaulipas (UAT, México). Her interests are mechatronics systems, applied engineering, and the evaluation of optical fiber devices as novel sensors.

María Catalina Ramírez Cajiao, Industrial,Engineering & Management PhD,Politecnico di Milano. Master's in Industrial Engineering,UniAndes.Bachelor's in Industrial Engineering,Pontificia Universidad Javeriana. Associate professor of Industrial Engineering Department at UniAndes.Vice-director of the Industrial Engineering Department. Scientific Director Green Business Transformation with Gobernación de Cundinamarca;Director of the project Fostering Water Saving Strategies on Rural Areas with Gobernación de Cundinamarca;Scientific Director of the project Technology to reduce inequality in Colombia - Colombian Technology Ministry.Planning Director Engineering School UniAndes;National Education Ministry consultant;Contraloría General de la República consultant; Microcredit programme director Corporación Minuto de Dios. IISEVicepresident Central and South America Institute Industrial and System Engineering;Director Engineers without Borders Colombia; Guest Editor EJEE European Journal Engineering Education;Board IEEE HAC IEEE Humanitarian Activities Committee;Board REEN Research Engineering Education Network ;Chair REES Research Engineering Education2017;Engineering Social Justice and Peace Chair2011.

Marcelino Sánchez-Rivero. Lecturer in the Department of Economics at the University of Extremadura, Spain. His research interests include the study of tourism destination competitiveness and sustainable tourism. He leads a project titled 'Analysis of the critical factors for tourism development in Extremadura'. He is a reviewer and she has published in numerous high-impact journals specialized in tourism as 'Journal of Sustainable Tourism', 'Tourism Economics' or 'Current Issues in Tourism'

Jimena Sánchez Saavedra, Doctorado en Ciencias Económicas Administrativas Maestría en Desarrollo de Recursos Humanos Full-time Research Professor. Autonomous University of Tamaulipas. Reynosa-Rodhe Multidisciplinary Academic Unit. Reynosa, Tamaulipas, Mexico. Email: jisanchez@docentes.uat.edu.mx..

Vicente Villanueva, Doctorado en Investigación Educativa, Maestría en Educación Superior, Licenciado en Computación Administrativa. Sistema Nacional de Investigadores SNI 1 (Conahcyt). 3 Certificaciones como Académico Certificado en Informática Administrativa (ANFECA), 3 Certificaciones CONOCER, Reconocimiento como Profesor: Extraordinario, Emérito y Mérito.

Index

A

Artificial Intelligence 8-9, 11, 184, 192-200

C

Code 137-138, 192, 196-198
Compensation 39-44, 53, 127-128

D

Digital Gap 169, 171, 174-177, 179, 181, 187, 190
Digital Gap Factors 169
Digital Inclusion 169-172, 174-177, 180, 187-188, 190-191
Digital Transformation 8, 63, 169-174, 179-180, 189-190

E

Economic Dispatch 77-79, 88-89

F

Fiber Optic Measuring fixture 120

G

gender diversity 14, 18-19, 33-34, 36-37, 173

H

honey adulteration 90-92, 114-118

human capital 2, 12-13, 32, 35-37, 43, 45-48, 172-173

I

ICT Constraints 75
ICT Enablers 75
ICT Integration 57, 59, 62, 64-65, 68, 73, 75
ICT Intensity 75
ICT Tools 59-60, 64-65, 75
ICT training 12-15, 17, 19-21, 23-31, 64
Information Communication Technologies (ICTs) 75
Intellectual Capital 18, 37, 39-48, 52-53

L

Linear programming 76, 78-79, 89

M

managers 12-13, 15-24, 26-31, 34, 40, 50-51, 61
Manufacturing 8-9, 120, 200
measurement 11, 45-48, 54, 108, 112-113, 120, 122-123, 125, 128-129, 131-136, 140-146, 148-149, 185-187, 201, 210, 216-218
multimode interference 116-117
Multi-region 79

P

Physical Sciences Teachers Integrating Information and Communication

Technologies 56, 59, 61
Productivity 13-15, 34, 39, 41-44, 50-51, 53, 60, 170, 180, 188
Programming 60-61, 71, 76-79, 89, 135-137, 170, 192-200

S

satisfaction 11-12, 15, 19-21, 25-26, 29-30, 35, 48-49, 54, 61, 72, 185, 201-204, 206-209, 211, 213-219
Sensory marketing 202-205, 207-209, 211, 214-215, 217-218
shopping intention 202
STEM 13, 15, 29-30, 56, 58, 61, 68, 169, 171-177, 179-181, 184, 187-190
STEM Education 13, 15, 29, 171, 173-174, 180, 188

T

Trash management 151

Publishing Tomorrow's Research Today

Uncover Current Insights and Future Trends in Education
with IGI Global's Cutting-Edge Recommended Books

Print Only, E-Book Only, or Print + E-Book.
Order direct through IGI Global's Online Bookstore at www.igi-global.com or through your preferred provider.

ISBN: 9781668493007
© 2023; 234 pp.
List Price: US$ 215

ISBN: 9798369300749
© 2024; 383 pp.
List Price: US$ 230

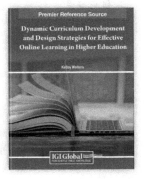

ISBN: 9781668486467
© 2023; 471 pp.
List Price: US$ 215

ISBN: 9781668465387
© 2024; 389 pp.
List Price: US$ 215

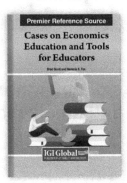

ISBN: 9781668475836
© 2024; 359 pp.
List Price: US$ 215

ISBN: 9781668444238
© 2023; 334 pp.
List Price: US$ 240

Do you want to stay current on the latest research trends, product announcements, news, and special offers?
Join IGI Global's mailing list to receive customized recommendations, exclusive discounts, and more.
Sign up at: www.igi-global.com/newsletters.

Scan the QR Code here to view more related titles in Education.

www.igi-global.com | Sign up at www.igi-global.com/newsletters | facebook.com/igiglobal | twitter.com/igiglobal | linkedin.com/igiglobal

Ensure Quality Research is Introduced to the Academic Community

Become a Reviewer for IGI Global Authored Book Projects

 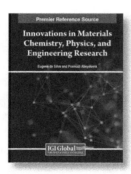 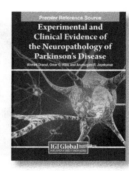 

The overall success of an authored book project is dependent on quality and timely manuscript evaluations.

Applications and Inquiries may be sent to:
development@igi-global.com

Applicants must have a doctorate (or equivalent degree) as well as publishing, research, and reviewing experience. Authored Book Evaluators are appointed for one-year terms and are expected to complete at least three evaluations per term. Upon successful completion of this term, evaluators can be considered for an additional term.

If you have a colleague that may be interested in this opportunity, we encourage you to share this information with them.

Publishing Tomorrow's Research Today
IGI Global's Open Access Journal Program

Including Nearly 200 Peer-Reviewed, Gold (Full) Open Access Journals across IGI Global's Three Academic Subject Areas: Business & Management; Scientific, Technical, and Medical (STM); and Education

Consider Submitting Your Manuscript to One of These Nearly 200 Open Access Journals for to Increase Their Discoverability & Citation Impact

Choosing IGI Global's Open Access Journal Program Can Greatly Increase the Reach of Your Research

Higher Usage
Open access papers are 2-3 times more likely to be read than non-open access papers.

Higher Download Rates
Open access papers benefit from 89% higher download rates than non-open access papers.

Higher Citation Rates
Open access papers are 47% more likely to be cited than non-open access papers.

Submitting an article to a journal offers an invaluable opportunity for you to share your work with the broader academic community, fostering knowledge dissemination and constructive feedback.

Submit an Article and Browse the IGI Global Call for Papers Pages

We can work with you to find the journal most well-suited for your next research manuscript.
For open access publishing support, contact: journaleditor@igi-global.com

Are You Ready to Publish Your Research?

IGI Global offers book authorship and editorship opportunities across three major subject areas, including Business, STM, and Education.

Benefits of Publishing with IGI Global:

- Free one-on-one editorial and promotional support.
- Expedited publishing timelines that can take your book from start to finish in less than one (1) year.
- Choose from a variety of formats, including Edited and Authored References, Handbooks of Research, Encyclopedias, and Research Insights.
- Utilize IGI Global's eEditorial Discovery® submission system in support of conducting the submission and double-blind peer review process.
- IGI Global maintains a strict adherence to ethical practices due in part to our full membership with the Committee on Publication Ethics (COPE).
- Indexing potential in prestigious indices such as Scopus®, Web of Science™, PsycINFO®, and ERIC – Education Resources Information Center.
- Ability to connect your ORCID iD to your IGI Global publications.
- Earn honorariums and royalties on your full book publications as well as complimentary content and exclusive discounts.

Join Your Colleagues from Prestigious Institutions, Including:
Australian National University, Massachusetts Institute of Technology, Johns Hopkins University, Tsinghua University, Harvard University, Columbia University in the City of New York

Learn More at: www.igi-global.com/publish
or by Contacting the Acquisitions Department at: acquisition@igi-global.com

Individual Article & Chapter Downloads
US$ 37.50/each

Easily Identify, Acquire, and Utilize Published Peer-Reviewed Findings in Support of Your Current Research

- Browse Over **170,000+ Articles & Chapters**
- **Accurate & Advanced** Search
- Affordably Acquire **International Research**
- **Instantly Access** Your Content
- Benefit from the **InfoSci® Platform Features**

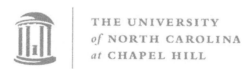

" *It really provides an excellent entry into the research literature of the field. It presents a manageable number of highly relevant sources on topics of interest to a wide range of researchers. The sources are scholarly, but also accessible to 'practitioners'.* "

- Ms. Lisa Stimatz, MLS, University of North Carolina at Chapel Hill, USA

Printed in the USA
CPSIA information can be obtained
at www.ICGtesting.com
LVHW081927041124
795688LV00041B/1308